LITERATURE FOR CHILDREN

Children's literature has recently produced a body of criticism with a highly distinctive voice. Accessible and relevant to a wide audience, this new interdisciplinary field is exciting and expanding. *Literature for Children: Contemporary criticism* consolidates our understanding of this area by reprinting some of the most important essays published in the field in the last five years, demonstrating the links between literary criticism, education, psychology, history and scientific theory. Essays address a range of issues from metafiction and postmodernism to fractal geometry, and examine texts ranging from picture books to *The Wizard of Oz* and the Australian classic *Midnite*. Also included are three new essays on folklore and science fiction, psychology, and cultural studies, and an examination of the theory of poetry in education.

Peter Hunt places each essay within its critical context, and his introduction explores the relationships between children's literature criticism and academia. He shows how the strategies adopted to establish a place both within the literary/critical hierarchy and outside it have produced a unique and lively critical form.

The book should prove indispensable to students and specialists working in a range of critical, cultural and theoretical disciplines, and also to those working with children and books.

Peter Hunt is a Senior Lecturer in the School of English at the University of Wales, Cardiff.

Also published by Routledge

CHILDREN'S LITERATURE
The development of criticism
Edited by Peter Hunt

LITERATURE FOR CHILDREN

Contemporary criticism

◆

edited by PETER HUNT

LONDON AND NEW YORK

First published 1992
by Routledge
11 New Fetter Lane, London EC4P 4EE
Simultaneously published
in the USA and Canada by
Routledge
29 West 35th Street, New York, NY 10001

Phototypeset in 10/12pt Palatino by
Intype, London
Printed in Great Britain by
Clays Ltd, St Ives plc

British Library Cataloguing in Publication Data
A catalogue record for this book is available from
the British Library.

Library of Congress Cataloging in Publication Data
applied for

ISBN 0-415-06825-6   0-415-06827-4 (Pbk)

Contents

Acknowledgements

We are grateful for permission given to reproduce the following:

Peter Hollindale, 'Ideology and the Children's Book', *Signal* 55 (January 1988): 3–22.

Geoff Moss, 'Metafiction, Illustration, and the Poetics of Children's Literature', *Children's Literature Association Quarterly* 15(2) (Summer 1990): 50–2.

Lissa Paul, 'Intimations of Imitations: Mimesis, Fractal Geometry and Children's Literature', *Signal* 59 (May 1989): 128–37.

Sarah Gilead, 'Magic Abjured: Closure in Children's Fantasy Fiction', *PMLA* 106(2) (March 1991): 277–93.

Rhonda Bunbury and Reinbert Tabbert, 'A Bicultural Study of Identification: Readers' Responses to the Ironic Treatment of a National Hero', *Children's Literature in Education* 20(1) (1989): 25–35.

Also extracts from Michael Benton, 'Poetry for Children: a Neglected Art', *Children's Literature in Education* 9(3) (1978): 111–26.

Contributors

Michael Benton, Senior Lecturer in Education at the University of Southampton, is co-author of twelve teaching anthologies of poetry and humanities books.

Rhonda Bunbury, currently President of the International Research Society for Children's Literature, lectures at Deakin University in Australia, and has worked extensively with Aboriginal communities in the Northern Territory.

Sarah Gilead is Senior Lecturer in English at the University of Haifa in Israel, and is working on a book on *Liminality and the Victorian Novel*.

Peter Hollindale is Senior Lecturer in English and Education at the University of York. Recent publications include the World's Classics edition of Barrie's *Peter Pan in Kensington Gardens* and *Peter and Wendy*. 'Ideology and the children's book' won the Children's Literature Association Literary Criticism Award for 1988.

Geoff Moss teaches English at a school near Reading, England.

Lissa Paul teaches children's literature at the University of New Brunswick, Canada.

C. W. Sullivan III, a Professor of English at East Carolina University, is the author of *Welsh Celtic Myth in Modern Fantasy* (Greenwood, 1989) and is editor of the *Children's Folklore Review*.

Reinbert Tabbert teaches English and children's literature in Germany.

Nicholas Tucker teaches psychology at the University of Sussex; among his many books is *The Child and the Book* (Cambridge, 1981).

Tony Watkins developed the first British MA in children's literature, which he teaches at the University of Reading.

Introduction

1

Children's literature is an amorphous, ambiguous creature; its relationship to its audience is difficult; its relationship to the rest of literature, problematic. As I suggested in the companion volume to this book, *Children's Literature: the development of criticism*, its critics have had to grapple with fundamental issues of classification and evaluation, to encompass a huge field and a large number of 'adjacent' disciplines, as well as communicating to a largely lay audience.

There is no doubt that these paradoxes have produced a body of criticism with an idiosyncratic range of reference and, very often, a distinctive voice. The essays and extracts reprinted here, and the new essays written specifically for this book, are intended to demonstrate this range, and to suggest the kinds of links increasingly made in the field. It may seem that texts as diverse as Sarah Gilead's contribution to *PMLA* on closure in children's fantasy fiction, or Lissa Paul's experimental discussion of fractal geometry, or Michael Benton's work on poetry and education have nothing in common except the occasional use of the term 'children's literature'. I would argue that they all share an awareness of working in a new field, where the ability to make links across disciplinary and cultural boundaries is vital, and a recognition of the interaction of audiences and texts is central.

Similarly, behind most of the writing collected here is an awareness of the shifting status of the study of children's literature in the context of a change in the value systems of literature. Increasingly, the ancient 'verities' of the western cultural tradition are being seen as the tastes of a powerful minority. K. M. Newton has pointed out in his *In Defence of Literary Interpretation* that the interpretation of texts is bound by the decision of the dominant culture: '[T]he interpreter coexists with the literary institution and is dependent on it, for it is the institutionalisation of literary criticism that guarantees it . . . its role in society as a legitimate activity which should be supported and funded' (Newton 1986: 222). Children's literature, although widely accepted institutionally, has tended to remain uncanonical and culturally marginalized. This has produced the paradox that writers in the field need to operate within the academic/educational world, and yet their subject is perhaps best seen as existing outside conventional value systems.

It is this highly creative tension that lies behind the recent developments in the criticism of children's literature, and this book hopes to demonstrate the richness that is derived from bringing together, for example, concepts of metafiction and the picture book, of translation, cultural difference, the evidence of real readers, of psychology and fantasy.

2

In many ways, an instructive parallel can be drawn between the emergence of children's literature and other 'new' literatures (national, ethnic, feminist, post-colonial) that are becoming part of the institutional/cultural critical map. Just as the literatures of colonized countries have had to fight against the dominant culture, so children's literature (as a concept) has had to fight against the academic hegemony of 'Eng. Lit.' to gain any recognition. As a body of texts, as well as a body of criticism, it does not fit into the dominant system's hierarchies or classifications, and consequently, like colonial or feminist literatures, it has presented an irritant to established thinking. Just as colonizing countries have adopted a paternalistic stance towards the 'natives' and a patronizing one to their writings, so, within what seems to be a single culture, the same attitude has been taken to children's books.

The conventional literary system is, after all, very like the traditional family: adult male literature dominates, women's literature is secondary (and grudgingly recognized) (Spender 1989), while children's literature is not only at the bottom of the heap, but (worse) it is very much the province of women. It was pointed out by the President of the Association for Library and Information Science Education in the USA in 1987 that in the field of children's and young adult literature, 92 per cent of the teaching faculty were women, and yet fewer than 10 per cent of those were full professors (Hearne 1991: 111). That women, for whatever reason, appear to work more in the lower-status areas of practice, rather than the higher-status ones of theory (at least in children's books, thus far) is, regrettably, reflected in the sexual imbalance of this book.

The choices of a 'new' literature (texts and criticism) are straightforward. It can either adapt itself to, or present itself as recognizably similar to canonical literatures; or it can attempt to engineer a change in mainstream attitudes; or it can wait until such a change occurs; or it can find a home in another discipline; or it can set itself up as a new, independent province, with its own laws and standards.

Children's literature has done all these things, and it has been helped by a change in attitudes to (if not concepts of) childhood, much in the way that attitudes to 'natives' have changed post-colonially (and perhaps with a similar ambivalence). It has also been helped, more directly, by changes in both the academic climate and structure. This has been bound up with a revolution in critical thinking, that has allowed the subject to be *thinkable*.

3

To a certain extent, the texts that comprise (in whatever definition) children's literature seem to be intractable to conventional evaluation. 'Three-dimensional', multi-media books such as Janet and Allan Ahlberg's innovative *The Jolly Postman* (Ahlberg 1986) do not match any of the conventional models; others, like John Burningham's *Granpa* (Burningham 1984), present complex problems of both textual and cultural decoding and their relationships with their audiences (Meek 1988: 22–4; Hunt 1991: 194–5). Forced to describe themselves in terms of established norms, children's books do not shape up very well: their narratives are often novellas rather than novels; their verse is doggerel rather than poetry; their drama is improvisation rather than mediated text. As with other popular forms of literature, genre can degenerate rapidly into formula.

A positive response to these problems has been suggested by Perry Nodelman in his 'Interpretation and the apparent sameness of children's novels':

Children's fiction thwarts would-be interpreters simply because so *few* children's novels move much beyond the formulaic or stereotypical . . .

Yet even those more complex children's novels seem to have more in common with works of popular fiction and with each other than do interpretable books for adults. A quick glance through any journal devoted to the criticism of children's literature reveals how frequently interpretations of quite different sorts of excellent children's books uncover the same or quite similar patterns and themes: not only is E.B. White's *Charlotte's Web* as much about acceptance of one's lot as are R.L. Stevenson's *Treasure Island* and Virginia Hamilton's *Arilla Sun Down*, but it brings its characters to that acceptance by similar means.

This apparent sameness of even important children's books demands one of two conclusions. We can accept the implications of the critical endeavour throughout history, and say that 'good' children's novels are not in fact good novels, because interpretation cannot show us how they are different from each other. Or we can accept what our instinct tells us – that some children's novels stand out, and are, indeed, especially worthy of critical attention, even though interpretation tells us that they are much like other children's novels. If we are wise enough to make the second choice, then we face another choice. We may conclude that the similarity of good children's books to each other makes children's fiction different from adult fiction – different enough that it requires its own interpretive approach. Or we may reach a quite different, and, to my mind, more sensible conclusion – that in fact, children's fiction is less significantly a special sort of fiction than a serious challenge to conventional ideas about interpretation and distinctness, that traditional means of interpretation are *always* misleading, and that the central cores critics uncover in complex adults novels do not actually explain what is special about those novels either. Perhaps Susan Sontag was right when she suggested that interpretation as conventionally practised 'violates' art [Sontag 1966: 10]. . . . If interpretation of these books does not give us any insight into what makes them unique, then perhaps the information that interpretation of more 'complex' novels provides is equally misleading. Perhaps the apparently unique themes and patterns we find in those more complex novels do not adequately explain their uniqueness either; perhaps we must search for other means of interpretation.

We must certainly do so if we wish to understand excellence in children's fiction, for traditional interpretation of children's novels can do little more than uncover the expected and the obvious. Until we develop a new approach, we will not understand how a children's novel can in fact be unique even though its characters, its story, its 'simple' language, and even its central core of patterns and ideas are not. (Nodelman 1985: 5, 6, 20)

Similarly, children's literature has a unique problem in the relationship between narrators and narratees which has only recently been addressed. Barbara Wall in *The Narrator's Voice, The Dilemma of Children's Fiction* (1991) quotes William Roscoe:

Many books ostensibly written for children, are spoiled because the author always has a side-glance at a wider audience. The possible verdict of an adult reader exercises a disturbing influence on his work, his subject no longer possesses his mind in its integrity, and he deserves to fail, as he almost inevitably does, not because a work must be written expressly for children in order to suit their wants, but because a man cannot without confusion undertake a work of art from two different points of view. (Roscoe 1855: 40)

The 'success' of, for example, A. A. Milne's children's books points up the difficulty. Wall continues, suggesting the conventional cultural corollary:

Roscoe's comment serves to remind us that criticism has rarely accorded stories for children the status of works of art . . . and suggests one reason why this should be so. Even without the 'side-glance at a wider audience' the single-mindedness needed to produce a work of art is likely to be compromised by the need to take into account the existence of a double audience. And for some writers [this] results in the highly self-conscious cultivation of two distinct and separate audiences. (Wall 1991: 20–1)

Children's literature is a maverick in two other ways: it is generally defined in terms of its audience, and the concept of that audience shifts with time and place; and it is written for a subservient audience, which has led to a good deal of definition by *use* (Crago 1974: 158) and, of course, that use is generally to serve the dominant culture.

Children's books, whatever they may have achieved, have been deeply influenced by the critical and cultural response to them, and have tended to define themselves away from their interactive, oral origins (ironically so, as this feature of literature is now becoming legitimized) and to attempt to conform to modes and patterns belonging to the adult-literary culture. As Rose pointed out, this has meant that the classic realist novel has been endorsed by children's book critics in the past, and she saw this as a covert form of indoctrination (Rose 1984: 1–2). I would say rather that it was a betrayal of a subversive form – far more subversive and able to look after itself than most critics (and publishers) would admit. Only recently has certain kinds of publishing for children been seen in metafictional terms (see the work of Geoff Moss in this volume), and metafictions as such been published.

It is with such problems as these in the background that children's literature criticism has evolved.

4

Initially, children's literature was rejected by the English Literature establishment except for a few borderline (and usually lesser) authors: Kipling is the classic case. Academic research was admissible into minor authors, as long as they were legitimized by time, and thus there has been work on, for example, Hofland, Edgeworth and Mrs Ewing (Hunt 1982). Then there were a few classics, such as *The Wind in the Willows* and *Alice in Wonderland*, which have been produced in scholarly editions and have been accorded the complete paraphernalia of literary respectability. One excellent indicator of the borders drawn is the fact that one can search in vain through criticism of an impressive list of major authors – Dickens, Hardy, Joyce, Woolf, Thackeray – without finding any mention of their work for children.

Children's books, then, were seen as marginal to literary studies, and were only studied either as historical footnotes or as bibliographical curiosities. The outstanding historical and bibliographical work in the field, Harvey Darton's *Children's Books in England* (Darton 1982) was specifically not concerned with matters of literary value.

Children's literature thus became a matter of, as it were, 'applied culture', and found a home in departments concerned with practice and which, even now, have a lowly status in the humanities – Education and Librarianship. Here, of course, they form only a small corner of those vast subjects; in librarianship, both the courses and the material that has emerged (with the honourable recent exception of the *International Review of Children's Literature and Librarianship*) have tended to be descriptive – an attempt to organize and classify, rather than to judge; the criticism produced (and the award-giving associated with it), has been based upon a resolutely untheoretical stance, often responding directly to the views of child-readers. Until very recently, such pragmatism, along with the 'erratic' (that is, real) reactions it monitors, has been subversive of – and rejected by – the mainstream critical tradition.

Writers in education, similarly, have been caught between conflicting interests: is the book used for acquiring reading skills, or purely for entertainment? Is there a necessary distinction between the canonical text, which is read functionally for examination purposes, and uncanonical texts which are given an 'absorbed' and hence 'literary' reading (Thompson 1987)? Many of the resultant publications have rested on educational, rather than literary, theory (see the work of Michael Benton in this volume). Literature has often been seen as an educational tool, and criticism as a tool to discriminate for practical purposes – hence the vast numbers of booklists, and 'activities' based on books. As before, there is nothing in this that is intrinsically lesser than any other activity, although it has led to a great deal of anti-intellectualism and 'soft' criticism (Hunt 1991: 21–6).

The reason that writing on education did not generate a strong tradition of individual response-criticism was because individual response was seen as anarchic as well as valuable, and was therefore used to generalize back again to pseudo-universals – aspiring to the 'Eng. Lit.' patterns. Naturally, without the force of the establishment behind it, this form of textual validation was unsuccessful in the face of the even more arbitrary (but authorized) tradition.

It has been argued that, far from being a bad thing, the adoption of children's literature by library schools and education departments was correct: the books could then reach their true audience without being 'misused' by the dominant literature departments. There is something in this, but to a large extent children's literature was ghettoized, and, as we have seen, its very fabric downgraded.

One of the many ironies in the progress of children's literature is that the reader-involved approaches that were developed 'in the ghetto' are now being legitimized in reader-response and poststructuralist and historicist discourse – just as the multicultural riches of post-colonial literatures are now being recognized on their own terms.

But children's literature – like post-colonial literature – had already made other inroads into academia. There are two international organizations: the Children's Literature Association and the International Research Society for Children's Literature. Both of these have international conferences and seminars; there are academic journals, including *Children's Literature*, published by Yale University Press; there are division meetings at the annual MLA convention; there are research collections, and huge libraries.

A sceptic might say that all of this is not necessarily admirable: perhaps as the literary lodes have become thinner, academics have turned to children's books as an unmined set of texts upon which to exercise the established critical techniques. While this is true to some extent, the tendency has been more than balanced by a recognition that children's literary studies cannot – both by the nature of their subject and the nature of their audience – afford to be too abstract or inward looking.

Samuel Pickering has put the case trenchantly in his 'The function of criticism in children's literature':

> Like art for art's sake, which spread at the end of the last century in reaction against the hegemony of science, so criticism for criticism's sake has become popular today. Instead of revealing significant matters beyond itself, this branch of criticism has become a form of decadent high church religion. Emphasis is placed on ceremony (artifice or play) rather than upon doctrine or substance. The play, like well-wrought ritual, is often at a high and cabalistic

level and is found in the clever but fantastic criticism of deconstruction.

Some few critics – those who, against all evidence, have wished themselves into belief and think criticism influences society – see this artifice as positive. If reasonable men, so the argument runs, have gotten the world into such trouble, then what is needed is criticism revolutionary in style and content. The trouble with this, of course, is that the style of deconstructionists is so ornate and consequently so obscure that their criticism becomes 'just personal'. In striving to be messianic, they have become cryptic, writing only for a small band of followers, and like the emperor striding confidently along without clothes, convinced by them and their inward monitions that their criticism is effecting changes in society.

If this then is the state of contemporary criticism at its cutting edge, what should critics of children's literature do? Since the age of the prophetic mode is over, we could begin with small things. Perhaps all that can be attempted is to make good literature more accessible to more people. Certainly this cannot be accomplished by imitating deconstructionists, and their methods should be avoided lest readers conclude that even criticism of children's literature has lost contact with the realities of human experience. Moreover, efforts to deconstruct books like *Horton Hatches the Egg*, *Charlotte's Web*, and *The Lion, the Witch, and the Wardrobe* would appear silly. To write obscurantist prose about the simple prose and poetry that is children's literature would be both perverse and indecorous. (Pickering 1982: 14–15)

This may seem perilously close to downgrading the subject matter, and many critics, including myself, would dispute the idea that children's literature is, or could be 'simple prose and poetry'. However, Pickering goes on to argue for the virtues of contextual or holistic criticism:

The simplicity of the books which he reads prevents the critic of children's literature from arguing, as is common nowadays, that fiction is about itself and the corollary that criticism is about itself. Because it is difficult for criticism of children's literature to be imprisoned by the text, such criticism can appear useful or at least in touch with ordinary life. And if criticism is ever to assume a significant role in society, it must provide insight into human experience and examine the problems which most concern society.

Too often in the past, critics of children's literature have interpreted attacks on their writings as distaste for the study of children's literature itself. We should disabuse ourselves of this comforting view. Not only is it self-serving, but it creates an unprofitable adversary relationship with other studies. Children's literature is part of a greater literary whole. To separate it from other studies denies roots and influence and considerably weakens the study. This is also true of various other present-day literary studies which claim to be separate intellectual entities. This splintering of literature into small, oftentimes arbitrary fragments of culture contributes to the diminution of both literature and criticism. Because many of society's concerns are reflected in children's literature more rapidly than in other literary studies, except in higher journalism, critics of children's literature are uniquely able to reach out from their studies and embrace other critical and social concerns. With the potential for, almost necessity of, drawing heavily upon other studies, good criticism of children's literature could in the future become a model for much literary study. (Pickering 1982: 15–16)

It is also fortunate that the growth of children's literature studies has coincided with the burgeoning of literary theory. Theory (along with other movements) is leading to the breakdown of the established literary canon and with it the dominance of literary studies in the humanities; the acceptance of reader response and deconstruction; a questioning of the power structures of western culture; the development of new readings of history and literature (such as feminist or post-colonial), and the acceptance of new readings and new literatures as equal but different. Aidan Chambers's axiom: '*Any comprehensively useful criticism of children's literature must incorporate a critical exploration of the questions raised by the problem of helping the children to read the literature*' (Chambers 1985: 123) is no longer a heresy.

Contemporary criticism of children's literature at its best is eclectic, using new techniques, rereading and remapping old territories, and exploring new ones. There have been recent realignments of the history of children's literature, as in Richards's *Imperialism and Juvenile Literature* (Richards 1989), and Reynolds's essentially feminist rereading of children's fiction from 1880 to 1910, *Girls Only?* (Reynolds 1990). The tone of Reynolds's discussion is, I think, significant. She points out that the 'manufacture of separate literatures for boys and girls' in the mid-nineteenth century

> rejected modifications to attitudes towards sexual difference (and particularly those surrounding the nature of femininity) which were being incorporated in adult fiction. Whereas through the dialectical nature of the relationship between literature and culture adult novels were accustoming the public to changes in the social meanings of masculinity and feminity, both boys' and girls' fiction can instead be seen as conservative examples of what Althusser has identified as literature's unique capacity to reveal (and rupture) dominant contemporary ideologies. (Reynolds 1990: 153–4)

Other writers have sketched out protocols for the future, in the case of Mitzi Myers, for example, contrasting the conservatism of some contemporary critics with possible developments:

> A New Historicism of children's literature would *integrate* text and socio-historic context, demonstrating on the one hand how extraliterary cultural formations shape literary discourse and on the other how literary practices are actions that make things happen – by shaping the psychic and moral consciousness of young readers but also by performing many more diverse kinds of cultural work, from satisfying authorial fantasies to legitimating or subverting dominant class and gender ideologies, from meditating social inequalities to propagandizing for causes, from popularizing new knowledges and discoveries to addressing live issues like slavery and the condition of the working class. It would want to know how and why a tale or poem came to say what it does, what the environing circumstances were (including the uses a particular sort of children's literature served for its author, its child and adult readers, and its culture), and what

kinds of cultural statements and questions the work was responding to. It would pay particular attention to the conceptual and symbolic fault lines denoting a text's time-, place-, gender-, and class-specific ideological mechanisms, being aware that the most seemingly artless and orthodox work may conceal an oppositional or contestatory subtext. It would examine too a book's material production, its publishing history, its audiences and their reading practices, its initial reception, and its critical history, including how it got inscribed in or deleted from the canon. It would need to do all these things and more to elucidate significant links between social and aesthetic forms, the particular cultural meanings codified in particular aesthetic expressions, for formal properties can't be sealed off from their social and historical matrix. Recognizing that human subjectivity itself, much less its literary expression, is culture-bound, it couldn't reify or essentialize The Child and Children's Literature (or even Literature) and What Children Like. If the Romantics . . . dictated the organicist and idealist terms in which subsequent critics have obligingly construed their poems, so too have Wordsworthian notions of child nature and nurture informed subsequent discussion of literature for the young; witness, for example, the Romantics' privileging of fairy tale over more realistic fiction, the context of which is only beginning to be explored critically, though we have long starred fantasy, glorified 'imagination', and relied on Romantic ideologies of childhood to structure our thinking about 'appropriate' literature. What a New Historical orientation could not make central to its program is what much historically-based study of children's literature still does: organize material within preconceived patterns implying an evolutionary view of historical progress. Linearly organized, always *toward*, most literary histories aren't analytic history, but teleology. (Myers 1988: 42)

Similarly, Perry Nodelman has demonstrated the kinds of critical link that need to be made, in discussing 'deconstruction' and the interpretation of fairy tales.

And if interpretations are merely new versions, it is only

because all versions are merely interpretations. We too often use our conviction of the authenticity of the Grimm versions as a weapon to attack the inadequacies of versions we like less; we say that the trouble with the Disney movie versions or with supermarket pop-up versions is their inauthenticity, their distance from oral sources. Bettelheim, for instance, insists that 'the true meaning and impact of a fairy tale can be appreciated, its enchantment can be experienced, only from the story in its original form' [Bettelheim 1976: 19] Once we realize that there *is* no original form, no form with priority, then we must learn to be more honest, and to attack versions we dislike on more legitimate grounds: our lack of agreement with the values they consciously or unconsciously espouse and express. Disney fails to the degree to which he successfully and authentically conveys contemporary mainstream North-American values, not the degree to which he varies from a presumed authentic original.

Our faith in the authenticity of such originals has yet wider implications. Derrida says, 'Man *calls himself* man only by drawing limits excluding his other . . .: the purity of nature, of animality, primitivism, childhood, madness, divinity' [Derrida 1976: 244]. Derrida suggests that this is a dangerously self-abusing privileging of the prior and more primitive by those who see themselves as coming after, and thus degenerated from, a state of innocence. Specialists in children's literature often view childhood as this sort of 'other'. Our common clichés about the ways in which children are close to nature or to God, about how their ignorance is really a saving innocence, disguise a profound distrust for the realities of life as we must view it as adults – and perhaps most significantly, a nostalgia for that which never was. For as Derrida shows, there never was an 'other' – never anything before writing, never a prior, truer mode of speaking or thinking except the ones we invent as a means of belittling our adult selves; and similarly, there surely never was a childhood, in the sense of something surer and safer and happier than the world we perceive as adults. In privileging childhood as this sort of 'other', we misrepresent and belittle what we are; more significantly, we belittle childhood and allow ourselves to ignore our actual knowledge of real children. For while all that we see as 'other' may appear to be privileged, it is so only at the expense of becoming inhuman, marginalized, actually insignificant. To express nostalgia for a childhood we no longer share is to deny the actual significance and humanity of children.

If children are different from adults, it's not because they are wiser, but merely because they are less experienced. Our obligation is not to deprive them of our knowledge in the faith that their ignorance represents a wonderful otherness, a priority, a closeness to truth and nature and even God. It is to allow them to know as much as possible about the only reality that actually matters – the world that they share with us. (Nodelman 1990: 147)

5

The emphasis of this book is upon theory rather than practice, upon general conclusions rather than specific readings. The essays collected here range in style from the formal academic and scholarly approach which treats children's literature as an equal part of literature in general (Gilead), to an exemplar of advanced, one might almost say lateral, critical thinking (Paul). Peter Hollindale's much-admired article on ideology places children's literature in its political context, while Bunbury and Tabbert's work on German children reading an Australian classic children's novel is characteristic of increasing internationalism and cross-cultural collaboration in children's book criticism. Geoff Moss's application of postmodernist concepts to both metafictions and the picture book demonstrates some of the links that can be made. Together with the three survey articles commissioned for this book, the aim is to present as comprehensive and characteristic a picture as possible of contemporary critical approaches and directions.

There are, however, three notable gaps in the critical literature. I have been unable to find a single essay that adequately explores the problems of discussing – or even defining – verse and poetry *for* children. Similarly, although a great deal of work has been done on mediating books to children in the classroom, there is a lack of any extensive theoretical discussion of the links between children's literature and education. In an attempt to partially remedy this, I have edited together a series of extracts, notably from the work of Michael Benton, which may provide a basis for further critical developments.

The third gap is the lack of any critical work on drama. Aidan Chambers in the introduction to his guide *Plays for Young People to Read and Perform* describes the situation succinctly.

Yet in the discussion about children's books that has gone on for two hundred years now, and with deepening professional and institutionalized seriousness over the last two decades, almost nothing has been written at any length about children's plays. Reviewing of them has been sketchy and erratic, to say the least; there have been few listings, and those that are available are intended for people wanting to choose a play for performance rather than for people with a literary interest in the form itself. Children's libraries, as far as I can discover, rarely include a section of plays. The published surveys of children's literature mostly do not even mention them. I share – just to take one example – the general admiration and affection for F. J. Harvey Darton's *Children's Books in England* [Darton 1982] but Darton says nothing about drama except to mention *Peter Pan*, remarking that 'for all its dramatic form' it set a fashion, stimulated new ideas and made people realize that 'plays meant specially for children were a necessity – in fact there eventually appeared a theatre specially for children'. Its plays, however, he could not discuss because, he wrote, 'they are not books, any more than toys are books'.

There are easily understood reasons for Darton adopting in the 1930s what now seems a peculiarly unthinking position. In a guide that attempts to stake out a place for children's plays as a form within the whole of children's literature, it is necessary to outline what those reasons are. . . .

Plays depend utterly on language for their origins and being: for their communication among those involved in their creation, from writer to actor; for their preservation and their communication to people outside and beyond the place and time of their beginnings. They tell stories;

15

that is, they are always narrative events dealing in the matter of *what happens, to whom and why*. All this in every way allies them with any kind of creation we usually accept as literary. And though plays present special critical problems, and possess features not shared by other literary forms, this is no less true of the other major forms: the novel and poetry. The important feature is that they are all primarily linguistic, narrative constructs; they are all part of the 'unique relationship between language and form' we call literature (the phrase is Hoggart's). That plays belong to literature seems to me self-evident. What Darton means by their not being 'books' is a sociological rather than a literary argument.

The other reasons for the universal lack of attention to children's plays are less philosophical. Pre-Elizabethan and Elizabethan plays written for the young have been lost or are not much read now. Most people do not even know they existed. Since Jacobean times and up to about 1960, though a considerable number were published and even more were written, very few proved themselves durable. No wonder Darton found little he wanted to say about the ones available in his day.

Since Darton's time, however, and especially from the 1950s, there has been a revitalized movement in children's theatre, just as there has been in British professional theatre. But the plays that resulted have been published mainly by educational firms intending them for reading in classrooms, for book-in-hand performances, and for productions as the annual 'school play'. This matters because children's-book commentators have a not altogether unconscious prejudice against educational publishers. (Chambers 1982: 5–6)

Within these limitations, then, this book aims to provide the broadest possible picture: to further the interaction of disparate disciplines and attitudes, and to continue the progress of children's literature criticism, of all kinds, towards greater rigour. As Geoffrey Williams put it,

Confining attention reductively to questions of enthusiasm and enjoyment does not elevate the field, it diminishes it. What is needed is not less but more adequate theory: accounts, for example, through the hard work of detailed analyses, of why some texts invite and sustain children's enthusiastic reading through their complexity, not despite it. . . . To attempt to find more reasoned theoretical ground to discuss books for children is not to betray the field . . . but genuinely to respect children, their reading capacities and the efforts of those who write and illustrate for them. (Williams 1986: 11)

1

Ideology

One of the most useful insights of modern criticism has been that no work, even the most apparently simple book for children, can be innocent of some ideological freight. As James Watson, a writer whose novels confront serious political issues, has observed: 'The dominant discourses of our time are rarely challenged, so much so that we are often in danger of forgetting that alternative discourses even exist' (Watson 1986: 70).

In children's literature, where there is a very obvious power relationship between writer and reader, and where writers and publishers are constrained and influenced by many pressure groups, this is a particularly emotive issue. As a result, work in this area has tended to be polemic (Dixon 1977; Leeson 1985), or to address specific issues such as censorship or covert racialism (Moore and MacCann 1986). Theoretical explorations are rather rarer, and as late as 1985 it was possible for *Children's Literature in Education* to publish an essay on political ideologies in literature for children that began by spelling out what might now seem to be obvious.

> Like other writers, authors of children's books are inescapably influenced by their views and assumptions when selecting what goes into the work (and what does not), when developing plot and character, determining the nature of conflicts and their resolutions, casting and depicting heroes and villains, evoking readers' emotional responses, eliciting readers' judgments, finding ways to illustrate their themes, and pointing morals. The books thus express their authors' personal ideologies (whether consciously or unconsciously, openly or indirectly). To publish books which express one's ideology is in essence to promulgate one's values. To promulgate one's values by sending a potentially influential book into public arenas already bristling with divergent, competing, and

18

sometimes violently opposed ideologies is a political act. Seen in this light, the author's views *are* the author's politics; and the books expressing these views, when made accessible to the public, become purveyors of these politics, and potentially persuasive. (Sutherland 1985: 143–4)

Between this and John Stephens's *Language and Ideology in Children's Fiction*, which treats of, for example, 'the linguistic constitution of fantasy and realism as discoursal modes' (Stephens 1992: 243) there is a considerable conceptual distance, which indicates how rapidly interest in this area has developed. Similarly, Peter Hollindale's article, reprinted below, first appeared in *Signal* in 1988 and has been successfully reissued as a separate pamphlet by the Thimble Press. Hollindale, who has had a distinguished career in the fields of both English literature and education, has been influential in establishing the complexity of the issues.

Ideology and the Children's Book
Peter Hollindale

IDEOLOGY.4. A systematic scheme of ideas, usu. relating to politics or society, or to the conduct of a class or group, and regarded as justifying actions, esp. one that is held implicitly or adopted as a whole and maintained regardless of the course of events.

Oxford English Dictionary

I will start with an assortment of disconnected statements.

It is a good thing for children to read fiction.

Children's own tastes are important.

Some novels for children are better than others.

It is a good thing to help children to enjoy better books than they did before.

A good children's book is not necessarily more difficult or less enjoyable than a bad children's book.

Children are individuals, and have different tastes.

Children of different ages tend to like different sorts of books.

Children of different ethnic and social backgrounds may differ in their tastes and needs.

19

Some books written for children are liked by adults.

Some books written for adults are liked by children.

Adults and children may like (or dislike) the same book for different reasons.

Children are influenced by what they read.

Adults are influenced by what they read.

A novel written for children may be a good novel even if children in general do not enjoy it.

A novel written for children may be a bad novel even if children in general do enjoy it.

Every story is potentially influential for all its readers.

A novel may be influential in ways that its author did not anticipate or intend.

All novels embody a set of values, whether intentionally or not.

A book may be well written yet embody values that in a particular society are widely deplored.

A book may be badly written yet embody values that in a particular society are widely approved.

A book may be undesirable for children because of the values it embodies.

The same book may mean different things to different children.

It is sensible to pay attention to children's judgement of books, whether or not most adults share them.

It is sensible to pay attention to adults' judgements of children's books, whether or not most children share them.

Some of these statements are clearly paired or linked, but they can be read separately in isolation. All of them seem to me to be truisms. It would surprise me if any serious commentator on children's reading were to quarrel seriously with any of them. He or she might wish to qualify them, to respond as to Dr F.R. Leavis's famous 'This is so, isn't it?' with his permitted answer. 'Yes, but . . .'. Even so, I would expect a very wide consensus.

However, if this series of statements is brought to bear on the controversy in recent years between so-called book people and so-called child people, it will be found I think that most of them drift naturally towards either one side or the other. In particular, there is likely to be a somewhat one-sided emphasis on remarks about adult judgements and their importance (book people); about children's judgements and their importance (child people); about differences of literary merit (book people) and about the influence on readers of a book's social and political values (child people).

If these two little exercises do indeed produce the results that I expect them to, much of the division between literary and social priorities which has arisen over the last fifteen years or so may come to seem exaggerated and sterile. We have differences of emphasis disguised as differences of principle. (This may have happened because the extremes of each alternative reflect a much larger public controversy about the chief purpose of education. People slip without realizing it from talking about children's books to talking about educational philosophy.) One result is particularly odd. By my own idiosyncratic but convinced reckoning, the statements which are left over, which seem not to bend towards the critical priorities of either side, are those which concern the individuality of children, and differences of taste or need between children and adults or between one child or group of children and another. It is a curious fact that these, the most obvious truisms of all, are also the most contentious statements. They are contentious because on the one hand they cast doubt on the supremacy of adult literary judgement, and on the other they suggest that we cannot generalize about children's interests.

It is very easy and tempting to simplify a debate until its nature becomes conveniently binary, and matters which are not associated by any kind of logical necessity, or even loosely connected, become coalesced in the same ideological system. Something of this sort has happened in the schism between child people and book people. In the evolution of debate, the child people have become associated not only with a prime concern with the child reader rather than the literary artefact but with the propagation through children's books of a 'progressive' ideology expressed through social values. The book people, on the other hand, have become linked with a broadly conservative and 'reactionary' ideological position. The result is a crude but damaging conjunction of attitudes on each side, not as it necessarily is but as it is perceived by the other. A concern for the literary quality of children's books as works of imagination has become linked in a caricatured manifesto with indifference to the child reader and with tolerance or approval of obsolete, or traditional, or 'reactionary' political values. A concern with the child reader has become linked with indifference to high standards of literary achievement and with populist ardour on behalf of the three political missions which are seen as most urgent in contemporary society: anti-racism, anti-sexism and anti-classism.

If this is the general divide between book people and child people amongst the critics, a matching divide is said to exist between writers. The book people amongst authors – those who are said by hostile commentators to have produced the prize-winning, dust-collecting, adult-praised, child-neglected masterpieces of the illusory 'golden age' – are those who write 'to please themselves', or 'for the child I once was', or, in C.S. Lewis's famous remark, 'because a children's story is the best art-form for something you have to say' (Lewis 1980: 208). The child people amongst authors, on the other hand, would accept Robert Leeson's analogy between the modern author and the oral storyteller of days before the printed book:

> is the public, the consumer, obliged to accept such a take-it-or-leave-it attitude, being grateful if the artistic arrows shot in the air find their target? What happened in the old story-telling days? If the audience did not appreciate the genius of the storyteller, did that individual stalk off, supperless, into the night? Actual experience of story-telling suggests something different. You match story to audience, as far as you can. (Leeson 1985: 161)

The trouble with this packaging of attitudes is that it over-simplifies, trivializes and restricts the boundaries of debate. Admittedly most writers on both sides of the notional divide have at times unwisely offered hostages to fortune. One may take for instance Fred Inglis's remark:

> Irrespective of what the child makes of an experience, the adult wants to judge it for himself, and so doing means judging it for *it*self. This judgement comes first, and it is at least logically separable from doing the reckoning for children. *Tom's Midnight Garden* and *Puck of Pook's Hill* are wonderful books, whether or not your child can make head or tail of them. (Inglis 1981: 7)

This carefully formulated and entirely sensible statement offers an important distinction between equally valid but separate ways of reviewing literary experience. Yet I have seen the last sentence removed from its context and made to seem like a wanton dismissal of the child, a typical instance of the book person's negligent aesthetics.

On the other side of the chasm is Bob Dixon, who follows an assault on ancient symbolic and metaphorical uses of the word 'black' by a paragraph which seems ready on ideological grounds to consign Shakespeare and Dickens to the incinerator:

> Adult literature, as might be expected, is full of such figurative and symbolic usages – when it isn't openly racist. Shylock and Fagin, Othello and Caliban all deserve a second look, for there's no need for anyone to accept racism in literature, not even if expressed in deathless blank verse. (Dixon 1977: 95)

This is quite true. Any individual is free to elevate political judgement above literary judgement, and to be contemptuous of all literature which offends a political criterion. The converse is also true. Any individual is free to like and admire a great work of literature, even if its ideology is repellent. These are the private freedoms of a democratic society, and I hope that any commentator would defend both with equal enthusiasm. I make the second choice myself in the case of D.H. Lawrence, whom I admire as a great writer and whose ideology I detest. Neither principle is much use when we confront the problem of introducing children to great works of the past which do not entirely accord with current moral priorities. But if anyone says, 'We should not introduce them; we should ban them', I begin to hear the boots of Nazis faintly treading, no matter what colour their uniforms.

My particular concern in this article is to argue that, in the very period when developments in literary theory have made us newly aware of the omnipresence of ideology in all literature, and the impossibility of confining its occurrence to visible surface features of a text, the study of ideology in children's literature has been increasingly restricted to such surface features by the polarities of critical debate. A desire on the part of the child people for a particular set of social outcomes has led to pressure for a literature to fit them, and a simplistic view of the manner in which a book's ideology is carried. In turn, this inevitably leads to a situation where too much stress is placed on *what* children read and too little on *how* they read it. At the very point in history when education seemed ready to accept the reading of fiction as a complex, important, but teachable skill, the extremities of critical opinion have devalued the element of skill in favour of the mere external substance.

Diversity and individuality

Things can be made to sound very easy, as they do in Robert Leeson's reassuring comments:

> This *is* a special literature. Its writers have special status in home and school, free to influence without direct responsibility for upbringing and care. This should not engender irresponsibility – on the contrary. It is very much a matter of respect, on the one hand for the fears and concerns of those who bring up and educate children, and on the other for the creative freedom of those whose lives are spent writing for them. I have generally found in discussion with parents or teachers, including those critical of or hostile to my work, that these respects are mutual. (Leeson 1985: 169–70)

I should like to think that this was true and generally accepted. But it cannot, no matter how true, be so simple. In a socially and culturally, politically and racially divided country such as Britain (and most Western countries to some extent or other) there is not a uniform pattern of 'fears and concerns' on the part of 'those who bring up and educate children'. The 'fears and concerns' of a teacher in a preparatory school in Hampshire are likely to be substantially different from those of a primary school teacher in Liverpool; those of an Irish Catholic parent in Belfast will differ from those of an Asian parent in Bradford. I wish to make only the obvious but neglected point that the same book, read by four children in the care of these four adults, will not in practice be the same book. It will be four different books. Each of these children needs and deserves a literature, but the literature which meets their needs is unlikely to be a homogeneous one.

It is of course important too for the writer's creative freedom to be respected. But in order to be respected it must be understood, and on that score also I do not share Robert Leeson's optimism. There is too much evidence of pressure on writers

24

(from all points of the politico-moral spectrum) to conform to a predetermined ideology issuing in visible surface features of the text (Inglis 1981: 267–70; Leeson 1985: 122). Here, for example, is Nina Bawden, a writer widely admired by critics of very different approaches.

> Speaking to people who care, often deeply, for children, I have begun to feel that the *child* I write for is mysteriously absent. . . . 'Are you concerned, when you write, to see that girls are not forced into feminine role-playing?' 'What about the sexuality of children?' 'All writers are middle class, at least by the time they have become successful as writers, so what use are their books to working class/deprived/emotionally or educationally backward children?' 'Writers should write about modern [*sic*] problems, like drugs, schoolgirl pregnancies. Aren't the books you write rather escapist?' 'What do you know about the problems of the child in the high-rise flat since you have not lived in one?' To take this last question. The reply, that you project your imagination, is seldom taken as adequate; but what other one is there? (Bawden 1975: 63–4)

Leeson's dictum, 'You match story to audience, as far as you can', is less straightforward than it seems. A diversity of authors exercising their 'creative freedom' – as they must, if they are to write anything worthwhile at all – will *only* match story to audience '*as far as they can*'. If there were indeed a single, uniform audience, a theoretical 'child' who stood for all children, there would be few problems. Either a writer would be able to match her story to this 'child', in which case her credentials as a children's writer would be proved, or she would not be able to, in which case she might have to settle for being a writer of those other children's books supposedly beloved of the book people, the ones admired by literary adults but unread by actual children.

However, one point I hoped to make with my opening anthology of truisms is that the most conspicuous truisms of all are ones which many adult commentators are in practice loth to accept. When Leeson says 'you match story to audience', he must surely be postulating many possible audiences, whether individual (parent reading to child) or socially grouped (teacher or visiting author reading to school class). It is clear that these audiences will differ greatly from each other, whether in age, or sex, or race, or social class, and that these different audiences will perceive the same story in different ways. Otherwise there would be no need for Robert Leeson to do any 'matching'. He is not suggesting that a writer who adjusts and improvises in order to make his story work with one group of children can then sit back, assured of its success with every other group thereafter. And yet at their own self-caricaturing extremes this is precisely the assumption on which both book people and child people seem to act.

For the caricatured book person (a *rara avis*, perhaps) the distinguished children's book has a quality of verbal imagination which can be shown to exist by adult interpretative analysis, and this is a transferable objective merit which the 'ideal' child reader (though unable of course to verbalize his experience) is capable of appreciating and enjoying. The good literary text has an external existence which transcends the difference between reader and reader, even between child and adult. Consequently there is an implicit definition of children's literature which has little *necessarily* to do with children: it is not the title of a readership but of a genre, collateral perhaps with fable or fantasy. Ideology will be admitted to have a place in it, but since the child audience and hence the teaching function are subordinate to literary and aesthetic considerations, it is a small part of the critic's responsibility to evaluate it.

For the caricatured child person the book exists chiefly in terms of audience response. The distinguished children's book is one which the 'kids' will like and which will aid their social growth. Historical periods will differ in the forms of social growth they cherish, but it is an article of faith that the current period will be wiser than its predecessors. The child audience, by some ideological sleight of hand, will be virtually identical or at the very least highly compatible with the preferred social objectives. In an age which desires to propagate imperialist sentiments, children will be an army of incipient colonizing pioneers. In an age which wishes to abolish differences between sexes, races and classes, the readership is a composite 'child' which is willing to be anti-sexist, anti-racist and anti-classist, and does not itself belong to any sex, or race, or class other than those which the equalizing literature is seeking to promote. The 'kids' are a Kid, who is sexless but female, colourless but black, classless but proletarian. Children's literature is implicitly defined as being for this Kid: it is not the title of a genre but of a readership. Ideology is all-important to it. Literary merit will be admitted to have a place, but it is a minor part of the critic's responsibility to evaluate it.

Both these caricatures exist. Both are extremely intolerant of anything which lies outside their preferred agenda. The first kind is the one which says 'I am almost inclined to set it up as a canon that a children's story which is enjoyed only by children is a bad children's story' (Lewis 1980: 120). The second is the kind which says, as someone did of Robert Westall's brilliant anti-totalitarian story *Futuretrack 5*, 'The book will appeal greatly to teenage boys, which is the best reason for not buying it.' Both (though naturally for very different reasons) will abominate Enid Blyton, and perhaps it is true to say that both understand the effective working of ideology less well than she did, in practice if not in theory.

My purpose here is emphatically not to argue for or against any single ideological structure in children's books (and certainly not to vindicate Miss Blyton's), but to contend that ideology is an inevitable, untameable and largely uncontrollable factor in the transaction between books and children, and that it is so because of the multiplicity and diversity of both 'book' and 'child' and of the social world in which each of these seductive abstractions takes a plenitude of individual forms. Our priority in the world of children's books should not be to promote ideology but to understand it, and find ways of helping others to understand it, including the children themselves.

Three levels of ideology

Ideology, then, is present in a children's book in three main ways. The first and most tractable is made up of the explicit social, political or moral beliefs of the individual writer, and his wish to recommend them to children through the story. An attractive example is this, offered by the late Henry Treece:

> I feel that children will come to no harm if, in their stories, an ultimate justice is shown to prevail, if, in spite of hard times, the characters come through to receive what they deserve. This, after all, is a hope which most of us share – that all may yet be well provided that we

27

press on with courage and faith. So in my stories I try to tell the children that life may be difficult and unpredictable, and that even the most commendable characters may suffer injustice and misery for a while, but that the joy is in the doing, the effort, and that self-pity has no place. And at the end and the gods willing, the good man who holds to the permanent virtues of truthfulness, loyalty and a certain sort of stoic acceptance both of life's pains and pleasures, will be the fulfilled man. If that is not true, then, for me, nothing is true: and this is what I try to tell the children. (Treece 1970: 176)

This is the most conspicuous element in the ideology of children's books, and the easiest to detect. Its presence is conscious, deliberate and in some measure 'pointed', even when as with Treece there is nothing unusual or unfamiliar in the message the writer is hoping to convey.

It is at this level of intended surface ideology that fiction carries new ideas, non-conformist or revolutionary attitudes, and efforts to change imaginative awareness in line with contemporary social criticism. This causes difficulties both for writers and critics, which can be exemplified from present-day concern with the depiction of sexual roles. There are hundreds of books which passively borrow and reproduce the sexual stereotyping which they inherit from earlier fiction. No one notices, except radical adult readers (and perhaps some children) who are alert to it and offended by it. On the other hand, any novel which questions the stereotypes and sets out to reflect anti-sexist attitudes will almost inevitably do so conspicuously because it depicts surprising rather than customary behaviour. Ironically, the astonishing effect of *The Turbulent Term of Tyke Tiler* as an anti-sexist story is largely due to its ingenious self-disguise. Much the same is true of anti-racist or anti-classist fiction. In so far as it diverges from stock assumptions about race or class, it may seem crudely didactic. If on the other hand the author seeks to present as natural a society without racial prejudice or class division and to leave out tutelary scenes of conflict, she risks blunting the ideological content and presenting happenings which readers simply do not believe. The writer faces a dilemma: it is very difficult in contemporary Britain to write an anti-sexist, anti-racist or anti-classist novel without revealing that these are still objectives, principles and ideals rather than the realities of predictable everyday behaviour. If you present as natural and common-place the behaviour you would *like* to be natural and common-place, you risk muting the social effectiveness of your story. If you dramatize the social tensions, you risk a superficial ideological stridency.

The writer may opt for more circuitous methods. The more gifted the writer, the more likely to do so. If the fictional world is fully imagined and realized, it may carry its ideological burden more covertly, showing things as they are but trusting to literary organization rather than explicitly didactic guidelines to achieve a moral effect. Misunderstandings may follow if you are unlucky or too trusting. The hand of anti-racist censorship has begun to fall occasionally on the greatest anti-racist text in all literature, *Huckleberry Finn*. Twain's ideological error is to be always supremely the novelist rather than the preacher, to present his felt truth uncompromisingly rather than opt for educative adjustments to it, and to trust the intelligence of his readers. Perhaps the most luminous moment in anti-racist storytelling comes when Huck, arriving at the Phelpses' farm and being mistaken for Tom Sawyer, has to fabricate an excuse for late arrival by inventing a river-boat mishap:

'It warn't the grounding – that didn't keep us back but
a little. We blowed out a cylinder-head.'
'Good gracious! anybody hurt?'
'No'm. Killed a nigger.'
'Well, it's lucky; because sometimes people do get
hurt . . .' (Chapter 32)

This snatch of dialogue is a devasting sign of what comes naturally to Huck's mind as soon as he begins to role-play Tom, but its full effect depends on its late placing in the novel, in the wake of all we have seen already of Huck's 'sound heart and deformed conscience'. It is a crucial point: you cannot experience the book as an anti-racist text unless you know *how to read a novel*. In modern children's writing the consciously didactic text rarely displays such confidence in its readers, with the unhappy result that reformist ideological explicitness is often achieved at the cost of imaginative depth.

The inference is clear: in literature as in life the undeserved advantage lies with *passive* ideology. The second category of ideological content which we must thus take into account is the individual writer's unexamined assumptions. As soon as these are admitted to be relevant, it becomes impossible to confine ideology to a writer's conscious intentions or articulated messages, and necessary to accept that all children's literature is inescapably didactic:

> Since children's literature is didactic it must by definition be a repository, in a literate society almost the quintessential source, of the values that parents and others hope to teach to the next generation. (Musgrave 1985: 22)

This is merely to accept what is surely obvious: writers for children (like writers for adults) cannot hide what their values are. Even if beliefs are passive and unexamined, and no part of any conscious proselytising, the texture of language and story will reveal them and communicate them. The working of ideology at this level is not incidental or unimportant. It might seem that values whose presence can only be convincingly demonstrated by an adult with some training in critical skills are unlikely to carry much potency with children. More probably the reverse is true: the values at stake are usually those which are taken for granted by the writer, and reflect the writer's integration in a society which unthinkingly accepts them. In turn this means that children, unless they are helped to notice what is there, will take them for granted too. Unexamined, passive values are widely *shared* values, and we should not underestimate the powers of reinforcement vested in quiescent and unconscious ideology.

Again I will take a pleasant example. It occurs in Richmal Crompton's *William the Bad*. Henry is summing up the salient features of British party politics before the gang hold their elections:

> 'There's four sorts of people tryin' to get to be rulers. They all want to make things better, but they want to make 'em better in different ways. There's Conservatives, an' they want to make things better by keepin' 'em jus' like what they are now. An' there's Liberals, an' they want to make things better by alterin' them jus' a bit, but not so's anyone'd notice, an' there's Socialists, an' they want to make things better by takin' everyone's money off'em an' there's Communists an' they want to make

30

things better by killin' everyone but themselves'. (Crompton 1930: Chapter 3)

This is fun, and not to be taken solemnly, but it is not exactly even-handed fun. I do not think Miss Crompton is deliberately making propaganda, but there is not much doubt where her own sympathies lie or where she tacitly assumes that the reader's will follow. The joke about Conservatives and Liberals is a joke about *our sort*, and the joke about Socialists and Communists is a joke about a *different sort*. The interest of the example lies in the gentle, unconsidered bias of the humour. Behind it lies an assumption of uncontroversial familiarity. It can be an instructive exercise to recast the joke, so that its bias dips in the opposite direction – suppose, for example, that it began its list with 'There's Conservatives, an' they want to make things better by makin' rich people richer an' poor people poorer.' It might still be funny, but it would at once acquire a shading of aggressive propagandist intention. As a character remarks in another, more recent and more radical children's book, Susan Price's *From Where I Stand*:

'Ah. It'll be something left-wing, then, if *he* calls them "political" in that voice-of-doom. The Tories aren't political, you know. They just are.' (Price 1984: 60)

This is a very small instance, introduced simply for illustration's sake, of something which is present to some degree in all fiction and intrinsic to its nature. There is no act of self-censorship by which a writer can exclude or disguise the essential self. Sometimes, moreover, the conscious surface ideology and the passive ideology of a novel are at odds with each other, and 'official' ideas contradicted by unconscious assumptions. Since this is by no means true of fiction only, the skills of analysis applied to different levels of a text should form part of teacher training in any society which hopes for adequate literacy. By teaching children how to develop an alert enjoyment of stories, we are also equipping them to meet linguistic malpractices of more consequential kinds.

To associate the ideology of children's books with ideology in its broader definitions, we need to consider the third dimension of its presence. This is the one to which developments in literary theory, by now familiar and widely accepted, have introduced us, and the one from which domestic skirmishing between book people and child people has tended to distract our attention. In order to affirm its general nature, I take a convenient summary of its position from a study not of children's literature but of sixteenth-century poetry:

> How does ideology affect literary texts? The impact of ideology upon the writings of a particular society – or, for that matter, on the conventions and strategies by which *we* read those writings – is no different from the way it influences any other cultural practice. In no case, in Macherey's words, does the writer, as the producer of the text, manufacture the materials with which he works. The power of ideology is inscribed within the words, the rule-systems, and codes which constitute the text. Imagine ideology as a powerful force hovering over us as we read a text; as we read it reminds us of what is correct, commonsensical, or 'natural'. It tries, as it were, to guide both the writing and our subsequent readings of a text into coherence. When a text is written, ideology works to make some things more natural to write; when a text is read, it works to conceal struggles and repressions, to force language into conveying only those meanings reinforced by the dominant forces of our society. (Waller 1986: 10)

If this is true, as I believe it is, we must think in terms which include but also transcend the idea of individual authorship, and reappraise the relationship between the author and the reader. In the case of children's literature, our thinking may be affected by an oversimplified stereotype of possible authority and influence. The individual writer is likely, as we have seen, to make conscious choices about the explicit ideology of his work, while the uniqueness of imaginative achievements rests on the private, unrepeatable configurations which writers make at subconscious level from the common stock of their experience. Our habit is so much to cherish individualism, however, that we often overlook the huge commonalities of an age, and the captivity of mind we undergo by living in our own time and place and no other. A large part of any book is written not by its author but by the world its author lives in. To accept the point one has only to recognize the rarity of occasions when a writer manages to recolour the meaning of a single word: almost all the time we are the acquiescent prisoners of other people's meanings. As a rule, writers for children are transmitters not of themselves uniquely, but of the worlds they share.

For modern children's writing this has many implications, but I would pick out two. First, the writer's ability to reshape his world is strictly limited. It is in his power (and may be his duty) to recommend an improved world, reflecting not what it is but what he hopes it might be. But this undertaking is bound by the same constraint as the literature of warning, which depicts a corrupted world as the author *fears* it truly is or might be. The starting point for each must be a shared understanding of the present, and an actuality which the young reader believes in.

The second point is that we may live in a period when our common ideology has many local fractures, so that children in different parts of the same national society are caught between bonding and difference. If children who are citizens of one country live in worlds within a world, discrete subcultures within a culture, they will need different storytelling voices to speak to them – voices which can speak within an ideology which for them is coherent and complete. As I hope this discussion has indicated, ideology is inseparable from language, and divergences of language within a national culture point to divisions and fragmentations in its shared ideology. In Britain as in other countries there is indeed a common language, but when that is said it must be qualified. Britain is also a country of many languages, many Englishes, and the children who speak them ideally need both a common national literature and local literatures which speak to and for themselves. Robert Leeson makes this point in his case for 'alternative' publishing for children. He begins by referring specifically to the spoken language and to dialect.

> The very richness of non-standard English is in itself a challenge to the whole system of education and literature, but a challenge that must be met. London schools at the moment are grappling (or not grappling) with new streams of language like Creole. (Leeson 1985: 179)

He goes on to argue that 'alternative' publications need not be subject to the orthodox scrutiny of critics 'provided [they] can meet the critical response of [their] readers'. Interestingly he then goes on to make two significant conflations of ideas:

first, he associates linguistic and literary subcultures with the literature of 'progressive' values, and second, he associates alternative publishing of books *for* children with publishing of books *by* children.

So far the alternative publishers have not made great inroads into the field of fiction for the young. There have been some feminist stories for small children, some teen-age writings, original and re-told folk stories from ethnic minorities. These are modest beginnings. (Leeson 1985: 189)

The point which is half made here can be fully understood in its general implications if we define 'ideology' largely and precisely enough. The two points are crucial: subcultures of language are inseparable from the climate of ideas and values which are at work in them, and children inhabiting a subculture need to create a literature of their own, not merely be supplied with one. Leeson's ideas on this point are important and helpful but unnecessarily restricted in their scope. Like many other commentators, he is in practice most concerned with the London community of ethnic minorities and progressive groups. Such critics tend to write as if other places, other social groupings, other sites of active dialects, other schemes of ethical values did not exist, or had no comparable needs. If our thinking about ideology is clear enough, it is apparent that the same considerations apply to *all* children in any part of society (and in practice this probably means all parts of society) where there is tension between a common ideology and local circumstances. To appreciate the implications for children's literature demands acceptance that we do indeed inhabit a fragmented society, where each of the fragments needs and deserves to feel a confident sense of its value. As Leeson argues – but with a wider inference than he draws from it – we need a national children's literature (not to mention an international one) but also local literatures for particular racial or regional or social or (why not?) sexual groups, and also a literature made by the children themselves. Only when we have a coherent definition of ideology does this become adequately clear.

The reader as ideologist

Above all, it emerges from this argument that ideology is not something which is transferred to children as if they were empty receptacles. It is something which they already possess, having drawn it from a mass of experiences far more powerful than literature.

In literature, as in life, we have to start from where the children are, and with their own (often inarticulate) ideology. This offends some commentators, who prefer the literature to begin where they wish the children were, or assume that easy transformations can be made by humanely open-minded critical inquiry, whether based in classrooms or elsewhere. Rob Grunsell, describing his experiences in running an alternative school for chronic truants in London, reports the discomfiting consequences of moving too rationally and openly beyond a pre-existent teenage ideology:

> At lunch they had opinions in plenty, particularly about the blacks and the Pakis. It seemed to me such an obvious place to start, so I planned out a lesson on racial attitudes – a straight survey of what they thought, with no judgements and no 'right' answers. They designed the questionnaire with me, enjoying filling in their answers. From that point on it was a disaster. The answers weren't the same. 'Was Jimmy right?', why were they wrong? I couldn't convince them, because they couldn't listen, that there were no right answers. Here, in a lesson, hating Pakis because they're 'dim' and 'chicken' was obviously wrong. They sensed what I thought, even though I hadn't said it. They had lost, as usual, and more hopelessly than usual since they could do nothing about it. My prize-winning lesson in open-ended exploratory learning produced five miserable, depressed people. (Grunsell 1978: 50)

A similar result is produced by much over-confident surface didacticism in modern children's books, as it is by much persuasive rationality in classroom discussion. Where the ideology is explicit, it does not matter how morally unanswerable the substance is if it speaks persuasively only to those who are persuaded already, leaving others with their own divergent ideology intensified by resentful bemusement. Susan Price's

From Where I Stand, which I referred to earlier, is a passionately anti-racist story which operates very much at the level of conscious authorial intention. At one point a highly intelligent Bangladeshi teenager, Kamla, is interviewed by the headmistress of her comprehensive school about an anti-racist pamphlet she has helped to compose. The headmistress tries to reason with her:

'You are going to tell me that Asian and black children are often teased and bullied by white children in this school. This isn't news to me, you know. I am quite aware of it. Whenever I can, I intervene, I punish children who are caught bullying or robbing others – but I punish them for bullying, for blackmail, for theft, not for racism. You see, it isn't always wise to tackle these things head on, my dear; I wonder if you can understand that? These attitudes are entrenched. Unfortunately, many of the children here have parents who are racist in their views. In that case, if you attack the opinion, then you attack the parents, and you are telling the children that their parents are bad people – now, that doesn't help. It only antagonizes them, reinforces their beliefs . . . And they are only *children*, Kamla.' (Price 1984: 119)

Susan Price's storytelling is very skilfully organized to discredit the headmistress by presenting her as one who is at best evasive and negligent in her efforts to subdue racist behaviour, and at worst has racist sympathies herself. The speech quoted above is thus placed in a context designed to undermine it. Readers are intended to conclude that the reasons for inaction given in the last sentences – reasons which are put forward often by real teachers in the real world – are merely disreputable rationalizations of unprincipled tolerance, if not something worse, with the implication that such reasons usually are. Susan Price is using literary skills to checkmate her opponents in an ideological chess game. But in the imperfect world these are genuine problems for teachers who try to educate children in anti-racist morality. It is unfortunately true that well-disposed ideological enthusiasm can be counter-productive in school classrooms; and it can be likewise in stories. So the likely effect of Susan Price's storytelling is to deepen children's entrenched attitudes, good and bad alike. If it were not so, the stresses on our social fabric would be a great deal easier to deal with.

Locating the ideology of individual books

I have argued, therefore, that we should accept both the omni-presence of ideology and the realities of fragmentation, diver-gence, passivity, inertia, conservatism, invisibility, unreason-ingness, in much of its expression and reception by the author and the child. Although it is easiest to illustrate the ideological process from the repertoire of *active* ideology in progressive modern fiction, that is only because didactic content is more obtrusive there, not because it is present on a larger scale than it is in traditional fiction. On all sides, in numerous commentaries on children's fiction (not to mention many novels themselves) a customary error is to make the wrong implicit analogy, by treating ideology as if it were a political policy, when in fact it is a climate of belief. The first can be changed, and itemized, and imposed, and legislated into reality and (though not always!) vindicated by pure reason. The second is vague, and holistic, and pliant, and stable, and can only evolve.

The first priority is to understand how the ideology of any given book can be located. Above all, such an understanding is important for teachers, especially primary school teachers and English specialists. Their task is to teach children how to read, so that to the limits of each child's capacity that child will not be at the mercy of *what* she reads. I shall conclude, then, with some examples of the kind of question which teachers in training might usefully be taught to ask about children's books, in order to clarify the ideology which is work-ing in them. They are mostly questions which adults generally might find interesting in order to test their own recreational fiction, and which can easily be modified for use in classrooms. The purpose, as I have tried to indicate throughout, is a modest one: not to evaluate, discredit or applaud a writer's ideology, but simply to see what it is.

The questions are only examples, and teachers and others will readily be able to augment them.

1. What happens if the components of a text are transposed or reversed (as I suggested might be done with Richmal

Crompton's political joke in *William the Bad*)? Does examination of the negative, so to speak, show unsuspected blights in the published picture? In particular, do we observe that a book which seems to be asserting a principle is only attacking a symptom? Is this 'anti-sexist novel' in fact sexist itself, and merely anti-male? Does this war story attack the Germans for atrocities which are approved when the British inflict them?

2. Consider the denouements of some books, and the happy (or unhappy) ending. Does the happy ending of a novel amount to a 'contract of reaffirmation' of questionable values which have earlier seemed to be on trial? Is the conclusion imaginatively coherent, or does it depend on implicit assumptions which are at odds with the surface ideology? Are there any loose ends (not so much of plot but of thought and feeling)? (Although it is not a children's book, students may find a particularly interesting example in the closing paragraphs of Richard Hughes's *A High Wind in Jamaica*.) If some 'happy endings' reconverge on the dominant ideology, is it also true that an unhappy ending is a device for denying such reconvergence, and hence for reinforcing a blend of ideological and emotional protest? (Students might consider the brilliantly effective unhappy endings of Susan Price's *Twopence a Tub* and Jan Mark's *Divide and Rule*.)

3. Are the values of a novel shown as a 'package' in which separate items appear to interlock? For example, does one story condemn racial prejudice and social class prejudice as if they were automatically interdependent, and does another in the same way celebrate a seemingly inseparable threesome made up of patriotism, courage and personal loyalty? (*Biggles* books are a good source of study on 'packaging' of various kinds.) Are these groups of virtues or vices necessarily or logically connected with each other? Are they being grouped together in order to articulate some larger, aggregated virtue or vice, such as 'white Britishness'? Students may find it interesting to bring this exercise to bear comparatively on the work of W.E. Johns and some current socially progressive fiction. Is it in fact a mark of quality in a book that it differentiates its values rather than fusing them in composite and (perhaps fraudulently) homogeneous groups?

4. Is it a noticeable feature of some major 'classic' children's books that they test and undermine some of the values which they superficially appear to be celebrating? (I think it is. Stu-

dents may find it interesting to perform this experimental inquiry on *Treasure Island*, *The Wind in the Willows*, and *Stalky and Co*, as well as *Tom Sawyer* and *Huckleberry Finn*.) Are there any modern children's books which seem to work in similar ways? Readers may find, for example, that the novels of John Christopher (notably *Fireball*) and Peter Dickinson (notably *Healer*) are more complex than they seem.

There is an important general point here. As recent studies based in modern critical theory have convincingly shown, many major works will sustain more radical and subversive readings than we are accustomed to. Critiques of children's literature which concentrate on surface ideology tend to ignore such possibilities. They observe only the external conservative values detectable in some major children's books, and overlook the radical questioning to which the text exposes them. The fallacy (as I have earlier suggested in the case of *Huckleberry Finn*) often lies in treating the novel as if it were some other kind of writing, and so ignoring narrative procedures which are basic to its meanings. If critics can make such mistakes, so can children: they need our help in learning how to read. But that is no excuse for suppressing or reclassifying the books.

5. Are desirable values associated with niceness of character, and vice versa? Is it really true that a given attractive philosophy or action could not believably be held or performed by someone whose character was in other ways unpleasant? How much allowance is there (and how much should there be in a children's book) for inconsistency, or for dissonance between ideology and temperament? How far is a book's ideology conveyed by 'moral symmetry' in character delineation?

6. Does anyone in a story have to make a difficult *choice* – of behaviour, loyalties, values, etc. – in which there is more than one defensible course of action? Or does the plot hinge merely on a predetermined choice, and interest depend on whether or not it is successfully carried out?

7. Is any character shown as performing a mixture of roles, especially roles with sharply differentiated contexts of friendship, safety or prestige? Does any character belong as an accepted member in more than one subculture or group, and move without stress between them? If any character does so, is one such group presented by the author as deserving higher value than another? The groups may be as simple as school (both staff and peer group) and family. They may, on the

other hand, extend to differences of race, culture, religion, political affiliation and social custom, as they do for example in *Kim*. *Kim* is an excellent text for students to consider, because it exposes the need for caution in using the vocabulary of political judgement, in this case 'racist', as a generalizing critical terminology.

8. Last and most important in this selection is the question of omission and invisibility. Who are the people who 'do not exist' in a given story? This may mean people who are present but humanly downgraded, as if inscribed above the writer's desk were the words 'All human beings are human, but some are more human than others.' Downgraded groups include servants, but may also in a given case include teachers, or even parents. More seriously, they may include criminals and policemen. More seriously still, they may include foreigners, soldiers, girls, women and blacks. These last groups are more serious invisibilities because they do not plausibly represent mere story conventions, but curtailments of humanity embedded in an ideology. Omission takes many forms: for example, the performance of important life-supporting tasks for children without any reference to the workers (such as mothers) who carry them out. Invisibility may take many forms, for example, the denial of names, the identification of people by what they do rather than what they are, and the absorption of individuals into social and racial groups. It can be helpful again to take an 'adult' text before considering children's books with students, and the most rewarding one I know to introduce this inquiry is Conrad's *Heart of Darkness*.

Taken together, questions such as these may serve effectively to lift ideology 'off the page' and bring it from obscure and unexpected places into the light, but it need not and should not suppress the uniqueness of individual stories, or convert them into cadavers for pedagogic dissection or for classroom autopsy. What we call 'ideology', as I have tried to argue, is a living thing, and something we need to know as we need to know ourselves. Very much like that, because it is a part of us.

2

Criticism: the state of the art

The three essays in this section illustrate the application of current critical techniques and terminologies to aspects of children's literature. They have in common a link with the Modern Language Association of America: Geoff Moss and Lissa Paul delivered versions of their essays at the MLA Convention in New Orleans in 1988, while Sarah Gilead's work was published in *PMLA*. Otherwise, their approaches and tones of voice are very different: Moss comes closest to the accessible yet scholarly attitude that is becoming characteristic of the mainstream, synthesizing children's literature criticism; Paul's discourse, as befits her material, is experimental; while Gilead's selection of language is characteristic of the dialect of critical theory (and as such, perhaps less immediately approachable by the layperson). Together, however, they give a good impression of the range, diversity and essential commonality of contemporary criticism.

'*Metafiction* is a term given to fictional writing which self-consciously and systematically draws attention to its status as an artefact in order to pose questions about the relationship between fiction and reality' (Waugh 1984: 2). As such, it might be supposed that we are dealing with a sophisticated form quite alien to children's literature. But the reverse is true; children – developing readers – live in a world which is far more conscious of and ambivalent about the relationship between fiction and reality than the world of the skilled reader, and children's writers have responded to this, perhaps more than is generally acknowledged. As Anita Moss suggests:

> Many novelists have been acutely concerned with the process of creating narrative and with the narrative forms of ordinary life which are embedded throughout fiction. The nature of narrative itself often becomes the real concern in novels and stories. Why characters tell stories and

how they tell them, as well as to whom, become major themes in Paula Fox's *How Many Miles to Babylon?* (1967), Natalie Babbitt's *Knee-Knock Rise* (1971), Charles Dickens' *A Holiday Romance* (1868), and E. Nesbit's *The Story of the Treasure Seekers* (1899). To a greater or lesser extent all of these books may be considered as 'metafictions', works in which the imagined process by which the story is created becomes a central focus of the book. This metafictional quality is implicit in the first two works and explicit in the last two, as both *A Holiday Romance* and *The Story of the Treasure Seekers* actually feature fictional child authors as narrators.

How stories within stories interlace to form an overarching structure; how characters function as both tellers and listeners; how children's writers choose to end their stories; and how they conceive of the process of storytelling itself through their fictional child authors are literary issues which recent narrative theory has addressed in significant ways. (Moss 1985: 79–80)

This is even more true of the picture book, a point made very neatly by David Lewis, in 'The constructedness of texts: picture books and the metafictive':

Imagine a conversation around the dinner table. The subject is books. You overhear someone enthusiastically describing what they have recently read, but you miss the titles and authors. You hear of a story where the main character is a compulsive tale-teller misleading the other characters and redescribing insignificant events in outrageous detail. Someone else recounts the astonishing exploits of a character who, when threatened by adversaries, can step out of his role as a fictional character and re-create his circumstances in authorial fashion so that his enemies are foiled. Staggering! A third voice chips in with the outline of a book where a young girl appears to be simultaneously a character within two stories and then goes on to describe another book by the same author where the reader is given so much repetitive, trivial detail that the narrative seems submerged in a welter of information.

This sounds pretty avant-garde stuff. . . . [Y]ou hear praised to the skies a book whose richness and humour arises from diverse fragments of text which must be

physically lifted out of the fabric of the book itself and
unfolded in order to be read. . . . (Lewis 1990: 131)

This description of Jill Murphy's *On the Way Home* (London:
Macmillan, 1982), Anthony Browne's *Bear Hunt* (London:
Hamish Hamilton, 1979), John Burningham's *Come Away from
the Water, Shirley* and *Where's Julius?* (London: Cape, 1977,
1986), and the Ahlbergs' *The Jolly Postman* (London: Heinemann, 1986) indicates, perhaps, the complexity of the theory
that would be necessary to account for, or adequately describe,
these texts. This is especially the case in the context of the
child audience, a problem addressed by John Stephens:

> An important aspect of contemporary children's fictions
> is the positioning of the audience as a subject. The whole
> notion, needless to say, is fraught with conceptual diffi-
> culties, but in order to proceed I am going to assume one
> central philosophical position: that our individual subjec-
> tivity, our selfhood as acting human agents, is con-
> structed *in dialogue* with the culture we inhabit. From that
> I extrapolate the argument that narrative fictions simul-
> taneously represent forms of that dialogue between self
> and society, and are themselves objects engaged with by
> readers as a part of that dialogic process. This is especially
> crucial with reference to children's fiction where the nar-
> rative modes employed are usually restricted to two
> types: either first person narration by the main character;
> or what I refer to as the one-plus-one structure, third
> person narration of a series of events *focalised* by the
> central character.
>
> My argument is that in most modes of narration the
> representations of interaction between characters and
> society, whereby a character 'discovers' its own subjec-
> tivity, is reproduced on another level in the audience
> engagement with the text, which is largely on terms
> determined *by* the text. This has the effect of constructing
> a specific and restricted subject position for the audience.
> My concern in this paper is with narrative strategies
> which constitute narrators and audiences as agents in the
> production of significance and hence potentially replicate
> the production of subjectivity in the world. This different
> kind of dialogue is brought about by means of a metafic-
> tional foregrounding of the processes which produce a

story – especially through a focus on the gap between signs and things and the differences between expectation and performance in retelling a story. It should be stressed, though, that the audience is never a free agent but operates in a dialogue between the inferences constructed within discourse and its own prior knowledge and expectations. (Stephens 1991: 63–4)

The essay that follows is by a writer who perhaps epitomizes the new children's book critic. Geoff Moss is a teacher in an English school, and his writing stems from his MA in Children's Literature from Bulmershe College (now the University of Reading), one of the new postgraduate qualifications which are fruitfully bringing together children's literature, theory and practitioners. The first part first appeared in *Children's Literature Association Quarterly* as part of a special section on Narrative Theory and Children's Literature in Summer 1990, the second part has been especially edited for this volume.

Metafiction, Illustration, and the Poetics of Children's Literature
Geoff Moss

1
Extending the limits: metafiction and postmodernism

My starting point is the question: 'Do metafictional texts have any place in children's literature?' – This is a little like asking: 'should children be exposed to postmodernism . . .?' To which the answer from children's literature circles might be either, 'what on earth are you talking about?' or more likely, 'Not bloody likely!' However, there is a Chinese proverb which goes like this: 'If you draw your sword against the prince you must throw away the scabbard.' And it is in this spirit of revolutionary (and probably foolhardy) zeal that I want to answer my first question against the background of how we might arrive at and understand the underlying systems of convention which make literary meaning – or a poetics of children's literature.

One way to approach work in this area is through looking

at texts which seem to fit unproblematically into the category of children's books. *Charlotte's Web, The Wind in the Willows, The Secret Garden* or *The Eighteenth Emergency* may be books that are problematic in other ways, but it is never argued that they are not fiction for children. Another approach is to look at books which *don't* fit, books which seem to defy the rules. Perhaps the most useful way to describe such works could be as 'counter texts' – a term I borrow from Barthes. Counter texts are aberrations within the body of a plot structure which, when recognized, shed light on functional norms at play within the whole text. Here, I want to use the term not within a single text, but to signify individual texts within the broader 'text' of children's literature.

At the limits of children's literature there are a number of innovative or experimental texts. Robert Cormier, Alan Garner and Jill Paton Walsh have written novels which place considerable demands on teenage readers. In picture books David McKee, John Burningham, Fulvio Testa, Anthony Browne and others have toyed with the interplay of language and picture in radical ways. However, the form of writing generally exemplified in fiction for children invites the reader to accept that the author has expressed his or her personality in a unique vision or interpretation of the world and that the reader has direct access to that personality. Technique and structure are backgrounded so that the message of the text is conveyed through an apparently neutral or transparent medium which allows the utmost identification with the author's intention, provided that the text is read carefully. The majority of the fiction aimed at the teenage market is 'closed'; it aims to deny the plurality of meaning and might be termed 'readerly' after Barthes (Barthes 1975). Such texts assume a form of innocence, especially about the medium of language, on behalf of the reader who is invited to accept, without question, an established relationship between signifier and signified. It is this assumed innocence of the reader which gives us a clue as to why this is the dominant form in children's literature.

At the other end of the continuum (although Barthes did not truly intend his terms to be classificatory) the 'writerly' text has the tendency to foreground technique and structure and propounds no simple mimetic connection between fiction and reality, between signifier and signified. Metafiction is a term that can be applied to some writerly texts. Patricia Waugh describes it thus: 'Metafiction is writing which consistently displays its conventionality, which explicitly lays bare its conditions of artifice, and which explores thereby the problematic relationship between life and fiction' (Waugh 1984: 4). My 'counter texts' are all varieties of metafiction, but I would like to draw the distinction here between the texts I shall examine and those texts which have characters telling stories within their own narrative. Although often worthy of study, the story within the story tends to follow in the tradition of self-reflexivity in the novel as a form, but it is rarely self-consciously questioning enough to come under the radical umbrella of metafiction.

Before I look at these counter texts, I want to look at the reasons why there are so few metafictional texts for children. There does seem to be a resistance to experiment in certain quarters. John Rowe Townsend, for example, quoting Isaac Bashevis Singer, proclaims that 'while adult literature is deteriorating, literature for children is gaining quality and stature' and he sees 'the modern novel giving the impression of slinking into a corner: narrow, withdrawn, self-occupied' (Townsend 1971: 12). Clearly the influence of Fowles or Calvino must not be allowed to pollute the purity of children's literature. Townsend would far rather see child readers 'enter into things and live the story'. David Rees, too, is intent on judgement. Alan Garner's *Red Shift* is 'very nearly impenetrable' (Rees 1980: 61) and 'not a children's book' (ibid.: 65). Departure from the narrative norm, such as in *I am the Cheese*, is viewed with suspicion and perhaps even distaste. Steve Bowles, a young British critic, probably sums up this kind of evaluative stance when he condemns Aidan Chambers's *Dance on my Grave* as the kind of 'arty farty stuff' which 'has plagued British teenage fiction for years' (Bowles 1987: 17). These critics provide useful examples of the attitude that metafiction is undesirable and too difficult for children.

So are metafictional texts for adults only? Are they just too difficult for children? Charles Sarland, looking at the structure of popular novels by Dahl and Blyton concludes that 'children are remarkably competent at handling all sorts of technical devices of story telling provided that the story is clearly of their culture, for them' (Sarland 1983: 170). He argues that there might be a case for children being able to cope with quite complex forms. For Sarland, 'modern adult fiction may be infinitely more complex [than children's fiction] but the difference is quantitative not qualitative' (ibid.: 169). Hugh Crago claims that 'our creative and publishing practice has denied many child readers the chance to experience anything but the simplified'. Furthermore, he takes Sarland's arguments about competency a stage further when he wants us to perceive two important consequences of looking at response: 'first, that children's responses to literature do not differ in any significant way from adult responses given that the comparison is made between individual children and adults whose articulacy and sophistication is roughly equivalent; second that critics and educationalists have no more right to predict the responses of "child readers in general" than they have to predict that of "adult readers in general" ' (Crago 1979: 148).

If it is inappropriate to assume that children will find metafictional texts difficult or uncomfortable we have to look elsewhere for an answer to the mystery of the paucity of such texts. Jacqueline Rose observes that many commentaries on children's literature praise the qualities of the readerly text; she goes on to argue that children's fiction is impossible because it is always an adult construct which 'sets up the child as an outsider to its own process, and then aims, unashamedly, to take the child in' (Rose 1984: 2). She argues that the child is portrayed as a pure point of origin in relation to language, the state and sexuality and that through this conceptualization of the child and the world as knowable in a direct and unmediated way, adult relationships towards them are made safe. If this ideological reading of literature is accepted then we can see that metafiction, which denies that language is invisible and prevents total absorption in or identification with a book, subverts this framing or repetition of the child which has become canonical in children's literature. If Rose is right, then the tendency is for adults to promote closed rather than open texts for children, to cut the child off from the experiment lest it should be dangerous and to deny metafiction because it turns the reader into a self-conscious collaborator rather than an easily manipulated consumer.

Recent literary theory has presented a view of the self not as unitary and whole, but as problematic, a fiction which arises from a polyphony of discourses (see Belsey 1980). Children's literature, perhaps because of its early didacticism and late liberal humanist tendencies, has continued to promote and privilege the status of the subject except in a very few cases. *Breaktime* by Aidan Chambers is one of these rare examples. It traces the journey of an adolescent boy named Ditto, to manhood through his first sexual experience, his relationship with his ill father and his desire to escape the suffocation of home life. In this, we have nothing especially different from the run of the mill realism of the teenage novel. However, the ways of telling this story are as important as the story itself. In fact, the book begins with a framing device which calls into question the whole process of fiction writing. Ditto's friend, Morgan, believes that literature is useless and too logical to be lifelike so Ditto challenges this with a record of his 'jaunt' which will 'take what form I feel like giving it at the time of writing. I do this because you feel fiction is contrived, designed to fit certain pre-set ends. I shall use whatever styles of prose or verse or writing of any kind I wish to use and which seems best for what I want to say' (Chambers 1978: 31). What then follows in the book is Ditto's account of his travels; he uses dialogue, playscript, typescript, stream of consciousness, first person, third person, cartoon, lists, reports, graffitti, letters, jokes, guidebooks, historybooks, quotation, footnotes and any amount of self-conscious cliché.

Breaktime emphasizes rather than suppresses its intertextuality and consequently is, in Bakhtin's phrase, 'dialogic' (Bakhtin 1981). Thus, the voices within the novel are relativized so that no one form is given a privileged position – such as when the suspense of a burglary scene is fractured with the contrasting effects of inane jokes and quotations from Dickens and Chaucer. At other times the reader's journey becomes what Chambers calls 'graphematic as well as linguistic' (Chambers 1985: 96) as drawings, letters and even blank pages help the story along. And there *is* a story which is easy to follow through the realistic conventions within the text. As Waugh points out: 'very often realistic conventions supply the "control" in metafictional texts, the norm against which the experimental strategies can foreground themselves' (Waugh 1984: 18), thus keeping the readers from extreme dislocation. When Ditto takes Helen back to his tent with the intention of seducing her, the episode is recounted in the first person by Ditto – a common technique in many realist novels. But the seduction itself suddenly disrupts any feeling of being at home in a 'transparent' text when the text on the page splits into two columns. The right hand column is Ditto's reaction to the sexual act; it, in turn, is split into two voices: in italics are his initial attempts at self-control ('ten nines are ninety') which are gradually transformed into the Molly Bloom-like rhythms of sex ('. . . is this what makes the body is this the howdyado the I'm all right jack . . .') (Chambers 1985: 124); in normal type are the more observable events ('her hands ran down my chest') (ibid.: 123). The two voices become one at the moment of climax. On the right hand side of the page is a dry factual account of sexual intercourse from an educational book by Dr Spock. The effect is a distancing from Ditto's involvement in the event because, although we see clearly his feelings and thoughts, we also have to read the section three times and at each reading Ditto's position seems more amusing and absurd because it is so self-conscious.

This section is typical of the novel. The alternating perspective shows us how much the character of Ditto is constructed by the novelist and the reader rather than by reference to reality. Another section is entitled 'Who is Ditto?' and we are given a range of descriptive devices through which Ditto constructs himself. At the end, however, we are given a space to add 'any other attributes you think are important and which you note or deduce from a study of these pages previous and to come' (ibid: 34). As Ditto is, apparently, obsessed with identity, we, as readers, are abruptly shown that he is exactly what we make him to be. Ditto's many escapades all apparently enable him to come to a greater awareness of self. As he gains sexual and emotional maturity we see some hope for his relationship with his father. But the irony of this is that the change in him is itself a construct realized through fiction. When the novel ends there is perhaps a confirmation of Barbara Hardy's celebrated phrase 'narrative is a primary act of mind' when Morgan asks: 'Are you saying I'm just a character in a story?' Ditto replies: 'Aren't we all?' (ibid.: 139).

Breaktime, then, is a major metafictional novel for teenagers just as Chambers's other books *Dance on my Grave* and *Now I Know* also make use of experimental technique to subvert not only our view of the teenage novel, but also our own attitudes to homosexuality and religion.

Peter Hunt's *A Step off the Path* seems to be another kind of metafictional novel which works both as 'fabulation' which Scholes has defined as fiction which 'offers a world clearly and radically discontinuous from the one we know and yet returns to confront that world in some cognitive way' (Scholes 1975: 12) and also as 'historiographic metafiction' which, Linda Hutcheon argues, explores history as text, deconstructing the continuities of narratives about the past (Hutcheon: 1988). With its passing references to the popular 'Famous Five' adventures of Enid Blyton, it can be read simply as a time-slip story in which a group of children get caught up in an Arthurian legend. But behind this conventional device is the idea that the whole adventure is apparently actually 'told' by another character in the book who is not caught up in the main storyline. We are warned at the start that there is 'a long weekend of storying ahead' (Hunt 1985a: 18). Jo, the young storyteller, seems to be structuring what is happening in the main story, but sometimes this is in doubt, and we are called upon to question the authority of the author or storyteller in any story. The relationship between the Arthurian story world and the real world is constantly questioned through positing alternative storylines, through confusing telephone calls from one world to the other and through the storyteller herself losing interest in a story which seems to be telling itself. Through making Merlin a villain and a woman, Hunt makes us reread cultural history and in doing so he shows us that reality and history are fictive constructs. He allows us to read conventionally, but warns us to question this involvement: 'No,' Matt said. 'You're getting mixed up with real life. You can change what happens in real life but you can't change stories.' He stopped, thinking. 'Or is it the other way round?' (ibid.: 139).

The book is less self-conscious than *Breaktime* but it might well give teenagers a thought-provoking introduction to the playfulness of metafiction just as *The Book Mice* by Tony Knowles might do the same for younger readers. The mice in this book draw attention to the conventions of sequence, pagination, linearity and suspense as they crawl through holes in the book, climb over the edges of the pages and even clamber out of the book on to the desk on which it is resting. 'Leave the book, how can we possibly do that?' 'Easy,' says Kipps, 'just climb out like this' (Knowles 1980: 10). On the desk they spill some ink, which seeps into the book and grows as a black splodge on the later pages. When they return to the book they are frightened by their own inky footprints on the blank page. Of course, at the end of the book they decide to turn over a new leaf. Clever and playful as it is, it is interesting how, in the world of picture books and young readers, where conventions are easily challenged because they are newly learned, not so ingrained, *The Book Mice*, despite its metafictional thrust, is not a counter text in the same way as *Breaktime* and *A Step off the Path*.

Metafictional texts do seem to me to have a place in the field of children's literature. Firstly, because children do have an interest in these kinds of texts – certain kinds of readers find them fascinating. Secondly, because such texts may well have the function of providing an active criticism of more mainstream texts, of defining the limits of poetics; and finally because children's literature, like any form of literature, will inevitably build on, toy with and perhaps even destroy conventional forms as it develops. Perhaps provocation is as important as satisfaction for children. That's why it is worth throwing away the scabbard.

2
'My teddy bear can fly': postmodernizing the picture book

When Margaret Meek speaks of the picture book as having 'plenty of artistic and iconic intrigue, imaginative verve in texts and pictures, and inventive formats' (Meek 1983: 50) she voices a commonly held view that contemporary picture books for children are often a site for radical and demanding experimentation. In the last twenty years the picture book has shed its image of having importance only for the very young reader as the first stage along the route to 'real' reading, and has, as Jane Doonan claims, taken on 'themes which are challenging and are rich with underlying messages, some of which would formerly have been associated with adult experience' (Doonan 1986: 159). According to Egoff, the current state of picture books within the field of children's literature exemplifies a double paradox: first that 'the picture book, which appears to be the cosiest and most gentle of genres, actually produces the greatest social and aesthetic tensions in the whole field of children's literature' (Egoff 1981: 248) and secondly that 'the genre which seems to be the simplest actually is the most complex, deploying two art forms, the pictorial and the literary, to engage the interest of two audiences (child and adult)' (ibid.: 248). I would like to explore these oppositions of cosiness and tension, simplicity and complexity, and to suggest a more detailed framework for looking at a number of texts which seem to extend the limits of children's literature.

Picture books: codes and conventions

Adults master the complexity of picture books quickly and easily. They usually have an awareness of the range of conventions deployed in a picture book text and can decode the pictorial, cultural and linguistic codes with considerable competence. Young children have to learn these codes. Research indicates that children of two to two-and-a-half years of age often tend to ignore the spatial relationships in pictures, with the result that they look at books upside down or fail to separate the trivial from the important.

Up to the age of around four years children do not tend to make narrative links between series of actions in different pictures. Instead of seeing a story, they tend to see a group of objects, they make an inventory; even seven-year-olds may have difficulty with sudden changes in background or period or with objects not coloured in a conventional way. In general, children under six years of age tend to see 'wholes' and are not always capable of making completions of complex pictures (Cass 1984; Whalen-Levitt 1984).

These developmental observations are broadly derived from the pattern of cognitive development outlined by Piaget, whereby the child moves from pre-operational through concrete operational thought to formal operations (Sarland 1985). In addition to these developmental stages, Moebius suggests that there are graphic codes associated with the picture book which need to be assimilated by children in order to 'enhance the reader's feeling comprehension of events and emotions', and he goes on to show the complexity of the combination of word and image: 'a kind of plate tectonics of the picture book, where word and image constitute separate plates sliding and scraping along against each other' (Moebius 1986: 143) suggesting that textual codes as well as graphic ones are of equal importance.

Although there are many picture books which tell perfectly straightforward narratives, this does seem to be the richest area of experimentation in children's literature. Much of this has to do with the fact that the primary audience for such texts is still learning the codes and that, through the playfulness of the text, those codes are tested, inverted, altered and finally assimilated by their readers. Very often, artists play with conventions deliberately in order to make their 'readers' more aware of how the text is operating. As Whalen-Levitt puts it: 'When we read a picture book that compels us to break through the complacency of patterned responses, we are provided an opportunity to develop a more intimate awareness of our own expectations' (Whalen-Levitt 1984: 6).

Whalen-Levitt proposes a number of ways in which picture books 'play' with conventions. Initially, she cites those pictures which violate our commonsense view of the world and which use the idea of visual nonsense. An extension of visual nonsense is the picture which is 'impossible'. Such pictures make use of the kinds of techniques seen in the drawings of M.C. Escher or in Anno's *Upside downers* (1988), which employs the visual trick of the Moebius strip so that the figures on the landings and stairways are trapped in a constant circuit of two apparently conflicting planes. Because western aesthetic tradition encourages perceptual completion in visual reception, picture book artists have seen the possibilities of toying with the discovery of missing forms to make use of this convention. Fold-over pages and pop-up books draw upon early traditions to do this. Jan Pienkowski's *Haunted House* (1979), a very complicated pop-up book, draws upon our curiosity to find out what is inside the refrigerator, under the stairs and even inside the toilet bowl, in order to satisfy our sense of gaining a complete picture.

Another form of picture play is in the manipulation of viewpoint. Charles Keeping's books constantly use the counterpoint of alternating viewpoint. In *Intercity* (1977), the diversity of views seen through the train window are in colour, which is contrasted with the monochrome interior views of the carriage where there is nothing to do but read (one of the books, held by the little girl, is Keeping's own *Joseph's Yard*, 1969), eat chocolate or fall asleep. In *Sammy Streetsinger* (1984) we see Sammy on stage as the audience sees him, tiny and remote, and then we see the audience, monochrome and uniform stretching away into the distance. The overall effect is of the distance and anonymity of this previously vibrant performer understood through these alternating viewpoints.

As well as playing with point of view, artists can use camouflage to extend the range of play with readers. This may be seen in Satoshi Kitamura's *Lily Takes a Walk* (1984) where Lily's dog, Nicky, sees the disturbing things in the urban landscape which Lily misses – such as the lampposts and tunnel which become a threatening monster. The developing reader may delight in empathizing with Nicky's open-mouthed fear; for the more widely read reader there is pleasure too in spotting allusions to other works of art. Anthony Browne's work is a particularly fertile ground for references to other artists; *Through the Magic Mirror* (1976) refers to the paintings and ideas of René Magritte; *Gorilla* (1983) features the Mona Lisa, gorilla style, Superman and King Kong, and, as Jane Doonan (1986: 164) points out, *The Visitors Who Came to Stay* (McAfee 1984) makes allusions to both Manet and McGill.

Undoubtedly, this is a useful framework with which we can build an understanding of some of the ways in which picture books allow us to derive pleasure and make meaning through play. By looking at visual nonsense, impossible pictures, discovery for completion, point of view, camouflage and allusion, we can understand the ways in which authors of picture books have disrupted codes and conventions in radical ways. However, there seems to me to be quite extreme and complex patterns emerging in picture books which go beyond this framework and which have some things in common with the categorization of radical postmodernist texts whose primary audience is adult. This is clear from the way in which commentators on picture books are often uncertain about the audience for books whose genre suggests a very young readership but whose content implies an adult or sophisticated interpretation. It is this area of tension and contradiction that I now want to explore by focusing on the way in which a small number of picture book artists have handled their material in such a fashion that it can be illuminated by the critical theory associated with postmodernist writing.

This is not the place to enter into a close definition of the term 'postmodernism'. Kermode (1968), Brooke-Rose (1981), Hutcheon (1984, 1988), Eagleton (1986) and McHale (1987) all provide some working definitions. Broadly speaking, postmodernism pictures a subjective, relativistic world which is so full of contradiction and so dependent on individual observers for its definition that there is little certainty about anything. Building on poststructuralist thinking, it also posits a view of this observing self as decentred, as a product not of individual consciousness but as the meeting point of a plurality of discourses so that the human being is not a unity, not autonomous, but a process, perpetually in construction, perpetually contradictory, perpetually open to change.

McHale sees this as a part of postmodernism's general concern with ontological rather than epistemological matters. Rather than being concerned with knowledge about the world by asking such questions as: 'How can I interpret this world of which I am part?', postmodernism is more interested in problems of modes of being, with such questions as: 'What is a world? What kinds of world are there? How are they constituted and how do they differ? What happens when different worlds are placed in confrontation or when boundaries between worlds are violated?' The result of this shift from the ways of modernism to postmodernism is an increased self-consciousness in art and writing, an exploration of the limits and possibilities in art and of the past which informs it.

Now, this may seem a long way from children's literature. Postmodernism is often attacked for its obscurity and narcissism or for its nihilism in presenting a view of the world which is often ironic or parodic. The underlying thrust of work written for children is the resolution of contradictions or the balancing of basic sets of oppositions (see Nodelman 1985). The focus is very often on the unified subject and on the child interpreting the world in order to arrive at a state of self-awareness. Because of their primary audience, most children's texts are allusive only in limited ways and are rarely ironic, parodic or self-conscious. However, what I want to argue here is that some picture books do exhibit some of the characteristics ascribed to postmodernist works and that, because the primary audience is very young and has a limited grasp of the narrative and graphic codes for decoding picture books, artists have used the playfulness of this audience to produce works which are at the limits of children's literature.

There are two analyses of the poetics of postmodernism which I have found most useful in looking at picture books. The first is Lodge's (1977, 1981) breakdown of postmodernist characteristics into contradiction, permutation, discontinuity, randomness, excess and the short circuit. The second is Wollen's (1982) investigation of the contrast between Godard's 'counter-cinema' and the values of the Hollywood movie.

For my purposes, I want to propose a synthesis of these two approaches to the categorization of postmodernist art. That one author is a novelist and critic of literary texts and that the other is primarily concerned with the visual image seems to make their contributions particularly applicable to an examination of postmodernist elements in children's picture books. I intend to look at such texts under the following headings: Narrative discontinuities; Short circuitry; Multi-diegetic, polyphonic worlds; Attacking the coherent self; Playing with words; and The pleasure of the text.

Narrative discontinuities

Most of the picture books I have looked at tell a story in the simplest sense. Even the most complex, David McKee's *I Hate my Teddy Bear* (1982), tells the tale of an argument between a boy and girl over the relative merits of their teddies. When the focus is largely on the *text* as informed by the pictures, it seems invalid or pointless to discuss the degree to which picture book authors have broken the emotional spell of the narrative. However, some works do play with this idea. John Burningham's two books *Come Away from the Water, Shirley* (1977) and *Time to Get Out of the Bath, Shirley* (1978) show, on facing pages, two distinct narratives. One is the world of the nagging parent and the other is Shirley's fantasy world of pirates or knights. What is happening here is described by Rasmussen:

> A kind of dialectic is set up across the page fold showing the rules and 'look of' the two opposing kinds of reality. The usual conventions of the picture book format (or art form) are violated purposefully in this ironical treatment, where seeing is no longer believing – at least not in a literal sense. (Rasmussen 1987: 184)

This discontinuity or narrative intransitivity is seen in a more complex way in Fulvio Testa's *The Paper Aeroplane* (1981). On the first page a boy launches a paper aeroplane from a window. The second picture shows him in a small aeroplane – an echo of the text on the opening page: 'I feel like I'm flying' – accompanied by a friend who appears here for the first time. The third picture shows two children standing by a telegraph pole against a barren landscape. One child is pulling a kite shaped like a bird and on the telegraph wires there are five birds, with another three about to land. The accompanying text is:

Suddenly there are birds all round me, flying with me across the sea. Now they are skimming just above the waves and I know I shall soon see land.

The text therefore disturbs the reader into asking a number of questions which the convention of the picture book implies will be answered by reference to the picture: Which of the children is the 'me' of the text? In what way are the birds 'all round me'? How is he or she flying? Are we given any clues about the land which is to be seen? In this case, however, the answers are not supplied. We seem to be a frame further on in the story – we have actually landed. Between this picture and its text, the causal links have been restricted and we are forced into a more active construction of meaning than in the first picture. Lodge argues that 'one quality we expect of all writing is continuity' (Lodge 1977: 231) and yet this text denies this, and considerable emphasis is placed upon the readers' active participation in recuperating a meaning from the sequence.

At the end of *The Paper Aeroplane* we are given a final image which is a repetition of the opening picture but from a different angle. As viewer, we now see the aeroplane being launched from inside the room rather than outside it. In this book there is no closure but rather a self-reflexive, circulatory pattern inasmuch as the book is about to begin again, and within the room are reminders of the elements of each of the preceding pictures – a kind of narcissistic intertextuality found in post-modernist texts. There is, for a children's book, a considerable amount of narrative disruption and no eventual resolution because of the repetitive structure of the text. Indeed, the reader is actually invited to become part of the text in the exhortation: 'If you want to travel through the world and beyond it, just make a paper aeroplane' and on the back cover is the enabling device for this: a visual recipe for your own aeroplane.

Testa exploits disjointed narrative in another of his books: *Never Satisfied* (1982). The device is familiar from Kitamura's *Lily Takes a Walk*: the two boys are bored with the fact that nothing ever seems to happen to them, whilst in the background of each picture in the book extraordinary events are taking place. One of the most bizarre of these is that objects are being thrown out of the window of a house on the very first page, culminating in the final picture where the house is beginning to be buried under its own strange contents. One of the boys is oblivious to this in the same way that we cannot help but fail to find any causal explanation for what is taking place. With echoes of the excess which Lodge claims is a feature of postmodernist fiction's desire to dwell upon the banal, the trivial or the superfluous, Testa leaves us being buried under a last image which is puzzling and which fractures our narrative expectations – we are never satisfied. In children's literature in particular, we are used to texts which are easily recuperated or naturalized. Culler defines these terms in this way:

> 'Recuperation' stresses the notion of recovery . . . it is thus a central component of studies which assert the organic unity of the text and the contribution of all parts to its meanings and effects. 'Naturalization' emphasizes the fact that the strange or deviant is brought within a discursive order and thus made to seem natural. (Culler 1975: 137)

The odd thing about *Never Satisfied* and *I Hate my Teddy Bear* (which I will look at later) is that both of them seem to make recuperation and naturalization problematic to their readers. I am sure that most readers, of any age, would agree with Seymour Chatman when he argues that: 'I cannot accept a text as plurisignificational until I make at least one satisfying sense of it' (Chatman 1980: 27) for it seems that we have a desire to make even that which appears incoherent have significance. No doubt we make our own meaning from the enigmas of such texts, but what interests me is the challenge that these kinds of narrative discontinuities set both child and adult readers alike – a challenge to become a more active, reflexive reader.

Short circuitry

Using the language of the electrician, Lodge talks of the postmodernist writer wanting to give the reader a shock through exposing the conventional gap between the text and the world, between art and life. Wollen, referring to a similar process in Godard's films, prefers to explore this through the binary opposition of the two qualities of transparency and fore-grounding: 'Language wants to be overlooked v. making the mechanics of the text/film visible and explicit' (Wollen 1982: 82). In Godard's films his desire to show the constructed, as opposed to 'natural', quality of cinema resulted in the appear-ance of the camera on screen; the scratching of the surface of the film and the excessive amplification of noise on the soundtrack.

Within the genre of the picture book there are examples of the short circuit which function in similar ways to metafictional devices. By highlighting and drawing attention to the conven-tions or means of production within the text such devices produce readers who are both capable of emotional involve-ment in a text and aware of how that text has been constructed.

Many children's texts require active involvement in the material substance of a book in ways in which I have pointed out earlier. Eric Carle invites the young reader to explore the holes eaten by his *Very Hungry Caterpillar* (1970) and the Ahlbergs want us to play *Peepo!* (1981) through the even larger holes in theirs. The young reader, through the deconstructive devices found in what Margaret Higonnet has called 'the play-ground of the peritext' (1990), comes to learn narrative struc-tures through experimental play and the subversion of the adult conception of fictional works: the page after page of standard typography which has become so fully automatized in our own reading.

What makes *The Book Mice* (which I discussed in the first part of this article) particularly interesting, and particularly close to many postmodern texts is that the attention drawn to the materiality of the book is completed entirely through fictive or illusory means. The hole in the page is not real, as in Carle's or the Ahlbergs' books, but an imitation of a hole, and thus it foregrounds the boundary between the book as real world object (which shares our world with us) and the fictional objects and world which the book projects. In *The Book Mice* this boundary is blurred as our attention is not only drawn to the mice in the book but to the (fictional) book itself as material object.

McHale argues that: 'the material book . . . although in a sense it does not belong to the text's ontological structure, nevertheless constitutes a kind of ontological sub-basement or foundation, without which the structure could not stand' (McHale 1987: 180). In many respects, what *The Book Mice* is doing is highlighting this relationship and illustrating the notion that picture books have come under the influence of the short circuitry which enlivens the reading of many adult texts and which draws the process of reading closer to the process of writing.

Multi-diegetic, polyphonic worlds

There seems to me to be a more productive place in children's literature to search for multi-layered narrative than in picture books. The form itself, the combination of picture and text, at once reveals a conflict of interests and, as I have shown, writers have explored this essential contradiction to develop narrative discontinuities. Often, however, writers have utilized the structure to create two or more different narratives by using the text for one purpose and the pictures for another. Anthony Browne's illustrations and Annalene McAfee's text to *The Visitors Who Came to Stay* does just this. Against McAfee's cosy text about Katie and her father's life without her mother, we are presented with a series of bleak, harsh illustrations depicting Katie's inner turmoil. Elsewhere, Browne creates a deviation from the written text through incongruent and absurd images appearing in the background of predominantly realist illustrations. The pictures and the text do work together but the detail forms a surrealistic scattering of visual jokes. *A Walk in the Park* (1977) features a man taking a pig for a walk, park benches wearing shoes, a dog in a pram, a man taking a tomato for a walk, Tarzan swinging through the trees of a suburban park, and a host of other bizarre happenings. Here we have what Wollen would call a text which 'becomes a composite structure, like that of a medieval macaronic poem, using different codes and semantic systems' (Wollen 1982: 85).

A text which takes this further and becomes what Wollen believes is an example where 'instead of a single narrative world, there is an interlocking and interweaving of a plurality of worlds' is McKee's *I Hate my Teddy Bear* (1982). This is a book which seems to exist at the very limits of children's literature because of its insistence on making the reader struggle for meaning through the opposition of simple text with very complex pictures.

The simplest narrative level of *I Hate my Teddy Bear* is the written text itself. Read without reference to the pictures it does constitute a self-enclosed story; as Brenda visits John, and they go for a walk, the text is a gentle linear narrative, full of repetitions. As we focus on their progress along the streets, through the park and back to John's flat again, we see a journey which is both physical and metaphorical – a journey through time and place and also through the emotions of anger, jealousy, friendship and reconciliation. The story of this journey, and the emphasis this places on recuperation, establishes a surface level of the text, a level normally associated with what young children desire in a book. Where McKee deviates from this convention is in the detail of his pictures and in the creation of a multi-diegetic world against which this simple story can take place.

Each picture in McKee's book contains the simple story of John and Brenda as well as a number of other narrative lines which invite, but often fail to allow, recuperation of meaning. The narrative of the large hands being carried by groups of people in many of the pictures, which functions as a running joke throughout the book, is resolved on the final page as we find out through the focalization of the teddy bears (not the humans) that these hands form an outdoor exhibition of modern sculpture. But other stories remain open to interpretation. Throughout there are instances of harmony, discord and confusion in male/female relationships. Brenda and John's mothers are troubled by a letter and a photograph of a bearded man. Is this the same man who appears later in the book taking a photograph of a photograph of a woman? Or appears on a park bench reading his own palm when he could have consulted the fortune teller who earlier told the fortune of a woman who looked like John's mother? Why are the old man and woman constantly unravelling a ball of wool, and why is the woman in pink spying on the jogger? Who are the couple who dance together in an upstairs window and ride together on a bicycle?

Elsewhere, mysterious characters appear: a gangster with a violin case; a tramp carrying a carpet; a woman knitting a scarf which dangles into the fishpond, and so on. People from other times also appear, being photographed in Edwardian costume as a family group or dancing in 1920s flapper dresses. Ten women on one page are dressed identically, teapots appear in

61

the middle of the street and McKee plays with perspective, especially in the interior scenes where he tends to squash rooms flat so that walls and floors appear to be on the same plane.

It is noticeable that characters in the pictures are oblivious to the absurd world that surrounds them. That this world is taken for granted, that the strangeness is considered banal, is another feature of much postmodern writing. It is, for instance, a central feature of Marquez's *One Hundred Years of Solitude* (1970) where plagues of insomnia, ghosts and apparitions are accepted quite matter of factly, or of Salman Rushdie's *Midnight's Children* (1981) with its India so pervaded by miracles that they seem routine. McKee actually uses this characteristic motif of postmodernism again in a later book, *Snow Woman* (1987). Here the primary narrative reflects on male and female roles as a brother and sister decide on whether to build a snowman/woman. Again, this element of the text is straightforward, although it does utilize the pictures to make some witty comments on its main theme: the mother and father, for instance, are androgynously alike with their identical clothes and hairstyles. However, in almost every picture there is a work of art, usually a drawing or painting hanging on the wall, which, in odd or unexpected ways, comments on the problematical nature of male/female relationships. In a sense, these pictures provide an ironic counterpoint to the main narrative, but their very oddness is ignored or overlooked by the characters. Within the cosy, middle-class home portrayed by McKee with its hi-fi, dimmer switches and real fireplaces, we find violent and disturbing images – and no one but us notices.

Texts such as *I Hate my Teddy Bear* and *Snow Woman*, therefore, give children the opportunity to experience multi-layered narrative, to read and write a text at the same time in that they can be entertained by a text on its simplest level as well as becoming engaged in the active pursuit of complex meaning. Such books are saying: there is not one story, one voice here, but many.

Attacking the coherent self

Much poststructuralist theory (which might be said to articulate the basis of the postmodernist outlook) attacks the humanist ideology of the unified and autonomous individual. Rather than seeing 'man' as the centre of meaning around which the world is oriented and the self as the essential core of being which transcends the environment itself, poststructuralism has

> sought to disrupt this man-centred view of the world, arguing that the subject, and that sense of unique subjectivity itself, is constructed in language and discourse; rather than being fixed and unified, the subject is split, unstable and fragmented. (Rice and Waugh 1989: 119)

Such ideas would not appear to have a role to play in the domain of picture books, because they attack the very strong focus made within them on the emergent and triumphant self. However, the unity and fluidity of the picture book are illusions created through an easy acceptance of convention and narrative patterns. Peter Hunt toys with the idea that child readings or 'misreadings' may differ from adult readings:

> The adult critic tends to seek firm connections between elements to build up coherent wholes from what must be (most obviously in the picture book) a repetitive and continually variable experience. Not only do we not read sequentially, but our concept of text is perpetually being revised. (Hunt 1985b: 120)

Because the picture book is a series of frames, materially marked by borders or page edges, and the portrayal of character or landscape is necessarily fragmented, it follows that each picture relates to a different subject position; each picture gives a new viewpoint. If, as Hunt points out, reading is a constant process of revision and change, it can be argued that, on one very important level, picture books actually present the discontinuity of the self and render it problematic. Cultural history generally prevents us from allowing this notion to have a dominant position and we fall back on our awareness of generic convention to reach a point of closure which leads to unity and the completion of a work. Because fragmentation is disruptive we resist it and prefer to view a picture book as we do a film, as a series of still images giving the illusion of movement.

Fulvio Testa's books do not present a view of the coherent self. In *Never Satisfied* it is not really clear whether the two boys are the same two boys in each picture, because their clothes are constantly changing. The postmodern position argues that even if they are the same, they are *not* the same because the subject is a process and not a fixed point. Satoshi Kitamura shows the disunity of the self within individual frames. In *Angry Arthur* (Oram 1982), Arthur is split into numerous personae as he travels through space fragmented by his rage. This is, of course, the visual convention for movement but this text does stress the disunity arising from anger when images are cracked into pieces like shattered glass and the multi-bodied Arthur does seem to be indicating the subject's disintegration rather than unification.

Despite its unpromising applicability to children's picture books, the decentring of the self may well prove to be central to a deconstructive reading (or misreading) of them.

Playing with words

Because postmodernism highlights the construction of the world through language and shows the relationship between the signifier and the signified to be random and arbitrary, many postmodernist writers have played with the invention of new languages.

In *Riddley Walker* (1980), Russell Hoban portrays the alien world following a nuclear holocaust through the fragmented and unstable language of his central character. Dipple argues that: 'From beginning to end of its experimental procedure, *Riddley Walker* questions the major issues of reality and knowledge within any civilization (text) as it gropes towards expression or meaning' (1988: 171). The novel investigates the way in which language builds a world. Hoban draws upon this postmodernist stance in his children's books too. The world of the child is shown to be given structure through the invention of words and the formulation of language. Hoban plays with words in just the same way that new language users, young children (and readers of picture books), play with words to explore their limitations. In Hoban's books we understand what Wendi Husa is, where the Gar Denshed is to be found, what womble, muck and sneedball might be, and why we should eat a Guit Frum. (See *The Great Fruit Gum Robbery* (1981), *The Battle of Zormla* (1982), *The Flight of Bembel Rudzuk* (1982), *How Tom beat Captain Najork and his Hired Sportsmen* (1974) and *A Near Thing for Captain Najork* (1975)). What is important in terms of the text, just as it becomes important in the metafictional novel, is that the reader stops to think about how we are able to recuperate that meaning and is, therefore, more aware of the rule-governed nature of language as a system.

That language is related to context is shown in Oram and Kitamura's *In the Attic* (1984) when the boy in the story talks to a tiger. Both talk a different language, and this is shown through the use of speech bubbles. The bubbles do not contain words, but the stripes of the tiger and the pattern of the boy's jumper. Here language is shown most clearly to be an arbitrary system of signs, which is an idea at the heart of postmodernist thinking. When the boy speaks of finding a game 'that could go forever because it kept changing' he seems to be speaking of the flexibility of language which is highlighted in picture books through the endless games that are played with words.

The pleasure of the text

Picture books are undoubtedly very entertaining. Visually and linguistically, they are full of humour and life, whilst the genre is also capable of carrying observations about the darkest aspects of humanity, such as in Maruki's *Hiroshima Story* (1983) and McEwan's *Rose Blanche* (1985). In another field, Wollen sees the revolutionary cinema as challenging the conventional cinema's pursuit of pleasure through provocation. The aim is to dissatisfy and hence change the spectator (Wollen 1982: 87). In a sense, picture books do this. Their primary audience is most frequently young children, often those learning to read, and through presenting radical challenges to adult conceptions of the shape of stories by employing some of the threads of postmodernist writing and film-making, these children are invited to toy with forms before assimilating them. They are texts of pleasure because they can comfort and re-present culture in an unthreatening way. But they can also be what Barthes calls 'textes de jouissance' – texts of bliss:

> the text that imposes a state of loss, the text that discomforts (perhaps to the point of a certain boredom), unsettles the reader's historical cultural, psychological assumptions, the consistency of his tastes, values, memories, brings to a crisis his relation with language. (Barthes 1975: 33)

What seems to be captured here are all the tensions that can exist within the picture book and that postmodernist theory can help us to understand. Picture books have an odd position at both ends of a simple/complex continuum and, as such, can be both comforting and disturbing. It is in the area of picture books that we can find the greatest number of texts which might be said to be testing the limits of children's literature.

Lissa Paul introduced an article in 1990 with the disarming words: 'This is not really a critical essay – more like an item from a gossip column. But as I am writing and circulating it myself, it also has the quality of a leaked document' (Paul 1990: 55). Her tone of voice, highly engaged and engaging, personal and conversational, marks a radical change from the conventional abstract and impersonal voice adopted (until very recently) by the majority of critics. It also belies a formidable range; Paul continued in 1990:

> I'm working on a poetics of children's literature, one that moves out of the realm of criticism as interpretation. These new poetics are shaped by the nonlinear patterns of 'chaos' theory of physics, and by revisionist approaches to the Aristotelian concepts of mythos (plot), mimesis (imitation), and anagnorisis (recognition): the first major shifts in Western perception since Euclidean geometry and Platonic philosophy first shaped it. (1990: 55)

The essay reprinted below (first published in *Signal* in May 1989) is one of a fascinating series, and, commenting on it, Lissa Paul observed that 'I think I've caught a glimpse of a form of discourse, a poetics, that will be of value to children's literary critics – though . . . I suspect I don't quite know what I've caught' (Paul 1990: 57).

Intimations of Imitations: Mimesis, Fractal Geometry and Children's Literature
Lissa Paul

If Plato had known anything about fractal geometry, he wouldn't have been so hard on mimesis. At least that is the thought that occurred to me as I tried, painfully, to negotiate twenty-five hundred years of representation theory. Fractal geometry, you see, is a mathematical method of describing irregular shapes in nature – forests, coastlines, snowflakes. It works through a process of something called 'self-similarity'.

Descriptions of self-similarity in fractal geometry, it occurred to me, are very much like descriptions of mimesis as imitations, in the sense that imitation is produced (especially in oral formulaic poetry) by repetitions of self-similar acoustic and stylistic structures. Both mimesis and fractal geometry, I thought, are about recognizing the world through imitation rather than through the cause-and-effect rational discourse that has dominated Western thinking since Plato.

My mind kept sticking on connections between repetition, recollection and recognition. The point I want to make is that repeated patterns are imitations. And the reason repeated patterns are important is that they enable people, especially those who live in largely oral cultures (children for example), to remember and recognize what they hear.

I should explain that the reason I was thinking about mimesis and fractal geometry in the first place is that I couldn't shift my mind away from two books for children that are intimately concerned with imitation: *The Bat-Poet* by Randall Jarrell (Jarrell 1977) and *What is the Truth?* by Ted Hughes (Hughes 1984): both are about mimesis, about poems that are like animals.

Now, I do know that the proper way to organize a paper for the MLA is to outline the theory first, and then use examples to

---

This paper was originally given at a session on Narrative Theory in Children's Literature at the Modern Languages Association (MLA) Conference held in New Orleans at the end of December 1988. The MLA is a monster conference. It bills itself as the largest Humanities conference in North America, annually drawing between ten and fifteen thousand delegates from universities all over the world, though primarily from Canada and the United States. Everything – and everyone – 'hot' in literary studies comes sooner (rather than later) to the MLA. What goes on there is the good gossipy stuff of novels (for further information, read *Small World* by David Lodge).

The MLA is a kind of Mecca for English professors, though Adrienne Rich is perhaps more accurate when she calls it 'both marketplace and funeral parlour for the professional study of Western Literature'. She ought to know. She makes the remark in a 1978 introductory essay to a published version of her paper, 'When we dead awaken: writing as re-vision', which she gave at

demonstrate, but I'm going to work the other way around. Instead of discussing the theoretical ground of mimesis and fractal geometry first, I'll talk about why my mind kept turning, like a broken record, to *The Bat-Poet* and *What is the Truth?*, then I'll explain how the theory taught me to read the texts.

I was initially struck by a number of similarities between the two books. Both contain spoken poems embedded in prose narratives – both foreground the presence of 'the oral in the written', as Peter Brooks says in 'The storyteller' (Brooks 1987: 21). In both books, the poems are set to be delivered orally by specific characters. Both have pictures (the Jarrell illustrations are by Sendak, and those in the Hughes book are by R. J. Lloyd). They are both about being awake when you are supposed to be asleep: *What is the Truth?* occurs between two and six in the morning, *The Bat-Poet* is about a bat with insomnia who insists on staying awake in the daytime. But the most important similarity is that both books are concerned with representation: the bat-poet wants to know owls, mockingbirds and chipmunks and to make them into poems. God's son in *What is the Truth?* wants to know the 'Truth' – and versions of 'Truth' are put to him in the various animal poems spoken by individual villagers. As I have said, both books are about likeness between animals and poems.

In *The Bat-Poet* the insomniac bat longs to imitate the mockingbird's capacity to imitate (fittingly the mockingbird is the poet laureate of the forest). Jarrell even sets up an ideal mimetic listener for the bat's poems, a chipmunk, who shivers when he hears the bat's poems about a narrow escape from

---

the MLA in 1971. The paper is a marker in the history of feminist criticism. It is often cited as one of the places where the feminist programme of literary studies is first named and made visible. 'Re-vision,' she says, is 'the act of looking back, of seeing with fresh eyes, of entering an old text from a new critical direction' (Rich 1979: 33). Both mimesis and fractal geometry (and chaos theory, which I will get to later) have similar re-visionary agendas – though their reference points are to mathematics, and natural and physical phenomena, rather than to texts.

There is good reason for this lengthy description of the MLA. Because my paper was originally intended for an audience of academics *au courant* with poststructuralist literary theory (or 'a congeries of old-boys networks', as Rich says), I knew I had to negotiate a Scylla and Charybdis course between the fashionable and the unfashionable. Mimesis is unfashionable, so, as you will see, I had to write an apologia for my use of it. Fractal geometry, on the

the owl. Unlike those of us trained to maintain the polite, critical distance of a literate audience, the illiterate chipmunk listens like a member of an ideal pre-literate culture. He identifies personally with the narrow escape described in the poem. The chipmunk exhibits what Eric Havelock, in *Preface to Plato*, calls identification, for the re-enactment of 'polymorphic vivid narrative situations' (Havelock 1963: 200).

Appropriately, it is the chipmunk who innocently gives the bat-poet – who is having difficulty making a cardinal poem – friendly advice on representation. The chipmunk tells the bat-poet to 'just say what he's like'.

In *What is the Truth?* likeness is also at issue, this time as being the way to find the 'Truth' – with a capital 'T' in the text. The lesson in Truth turns out to be a lesson in mimesis. God and his son land on a hillside and summon various villagers – the farmer, his wife, son and daughter, the vicar, the shepherd and the poacher – to tell them the Truth. The Truth takes the form of variations on animal poems, variations that differ in terms of the perceiving subject.

Take cows. The farmer's wife offers a maternal approach to cows: 'There's comfort in the Cow, my dear, she's mother to us all./ When Adam was a helpless babe, no mother heard him call'. The farmer however sings about cows 'as if he had a pint glass of ale in his hand': 'The Cow is but a bagpipe,/ All bag, all bones, all blort./ They bawl me out of bed at dawn/ And never give a thought/ a thought/ they never give a thought'. The farmer's daughter hears this and thinks her father has made a mistake in his attempt at Truth, so she tries

---

other hand, is so fashionable it doesn't even officially make the list of proposed MLA discussion topics until next year. My interest in both mimesis and fractal geometry comes from a conviction that they will soon inform major changes in the way we see the world and the way we understand the process of learning.

Instead of simply providing footnotes to fill in the gaps of my oral paper, I've written this literal 'subtext', one that places my oral presentation in a written context. I've borrowed the form (though not the content) from Jacques Derrida, who uses it in an essay called 'Living on: border lines' (Derrida 1985). I hope that this subtext provides the kind of authority for my re-visionist fractal and mimetic readings that Adrienne Rich provides for her feminist readings.

Mimesis means an imitation or a copy. Aristotle uses the term, in a positive way, in the *Poetics* to explain what is valuable about poetry: that it is a good

something closer to her own more reflective, gentler temperament: 'And there's a ruined holy city/ In a herd of lying down,
cud-chewing cows –/ Noses raised, eyes nearly closed/ They
are fragments of temples – even their outlines/ Still at an angle
unearthly'.

The Truth of cows varies. The likeness of a cow is not
one poem but several. But all the poems are, nevertheless,
recognizable likenesses of cows. I'm reminded of what Michael
Riffaterre says in *Text Production*, that there is 'something
invariant that we recognize in variation' (Riffaterre 1983: 12).
But it is not the Truth. In fact, the question of likeness as truth
keeps coming up throughout the poem: 'Are we getting any
Truth yet?' asks God's son repeatedly. But the question of
Truth, you see, really doesn't have a lot to do with the poems.
The poems about cows, and about the other animals, require
mimetic, personal identification, the kind the chipmunk experiences in *The Bat-Poet*. They are not about objective Truth at
all. So in the end, the attempts to find the Truth are pointless
anyway, because all the variations on the Truth of cows, or
whatever, are spoken by the same subject – God. It is God
who says he is all of the animals: ' "And the Truth is", God
went on, "that I was that Fox. Just as I was that Foal. As I
am, I am. I am that Foal. And I am the Cow. I am the Weasel
and the Mouse. The Wood Pigeon and the Partridge. The
Goat, the Badger, The Hedgehog, the Hare. Yes, and the
Hedgehog's Flea." '

What I particularly like is the way Hughes plays out the
tensions between abstract to-tell-the-truth discourse and

---

thing that art imitates life because through art we begin to understand what
it means to be human. Aristotle wrote his *Poetics* essentially as a defence of
mimesis against Plato's attack on it in *The Republic*. Plato objects to mimesis
because it is not about ideas. And he devalues mimesis because it is removed
from his ideals of the True, the Beautiful and the Good.

Mimesis has been having an image problem ever since – for the last twenty-
five hundred years. Now, especially since the Romantic period, we value
originality, so we tend to think of copies as fakes, like imitation Gucci hand-
bags. This is one of the points made by M.H. Abrams in *The Mirror and the
Lamp*, an important book on the literary theory of the Romantic period.
Abrams defines the mirror and the lamp as two 'antithetic metaphors of mind,
one comparing the mind to a reflector of external objects, the other to a radiant
projector which makes a contribution to the objects it perceives' (Abrams 1953:
vi). You can see which one Abrams favours: he sees nothing 'radiant' about

mimetic imitative discourse. The ostensible search for 'Truth' in the book, is, of course, an echo of Plato's programme. But the search for Truth has nothing to do with poetry. The joke is on those misguided seekers after Truth. The book ends up in a celebration of variation where there is something invariant.

In my examples from the *The Bat-Poet* and *What is the Truth?* I've been trying to show that both Jarrell and Hughes are intimately concerned with representation, especially with the presence of oral representation in written texts. Now I'm ready to make the disorderly theoretical connections between repetition, recollection and recognition that kept pursuing me through my reading on mimesis, fractal geometry and the books by Hughes and Jarrell.

My problem, as a critic thinking and writing in a poststructuralist age, is that mimesis is out of fashion. In a cultural context where fragmentation and infinitely deferred meaning are the order of the day, here I am, unable to subdue an interest in the self-similar structures of mimetic discourse. As Abrams knew long ago, critical interest shifted from mirrors to lamps. What Abrams doesn't say, incidentally, is that that shift also reflects a gender bias (Abrams 1953).

Mirrors belong to the (lower) female order of re-production and re-creation, to mimesis, to imitation, not to the male order of original production and creation. Although this is not really the place to go into it, I must mention that, according to people like Walter Ong and Eric Havelock, who work out of a context of communication theory, mimesis is female and has its source in the oral poetry of the pre-literate Greeks (see Ong 1982;

---

reflection. But poets (Ted Hughes and Randall Jarrell, for instance) still wonder how to make art like life, how to make it mimetic.

Hughes talks about mimesis (though he doesn't call it that) in *Poetry in the Making* when he says that ultimately words can't capture 'the infinite depth of crowiness in the crow's flight'. He tries a whole series of enviable descriptions, referring to 'the ominous thing in the crow's flight, the barefaced bandit thing, the tattered beggarly gipsy thing'. He goes on for a while but gives up in the end, saying that the descriptions fail to capture the 'instant glimpse knowledge of the world of the crow's wingbeat' (Hughes 1967: 119–20). In linguistic terms, Hughes believes that his collections of signifiers (sound images) don't add with his signified (his mental concept of the crow's flight) to equal an adequate sign for what he saw and felt when he looked up at the crow flying. But that doesn't mean that Hughes believes that the whole enterprise of writing poetry is a lost cause. In fact, he believes the opposite: that 'it is

Havelock 1986). It is the language of Mnemosyne (memory) and her nine daughter muses. All cultural codes were stored in oral formulaic poetry – hence the need for readily repeatable and memorable forms. But with the rise of the phonetic alphabet, mimetic forms became obsolete. Cultural codes were no longer stored in poems, they were stored in texts. And in a straight male line from Plato to Derrida, mimetic forms were devalued.

But even though we live in what Terence Cave calls a 'post-mimetic age' (Cave 1988), children's literature traditionally functions as the preserve of mimetic narrative, oral narrative – in accordance with Aristotle's (sweeping, vague, but pervasive nevertheless) assertions that imitation is natural to humans, innate from childhood, that there is pleasure in repetition (Aristotle 1961: 1448b). Repetition is valued because it makes narrative memorable, both in traditional oral forms like nursery rhymes, fairy tales and playground rhymes, and in books written for children, especially for young children just learning to read. Mnemonic patterns – particularly the structural and acoustic repetitions of poetry – are important, because, as Walter J. Ong says in 'From mimesis to irony', unless an oral culture thinks in mnemonic patterns, it 'is only daydreaming' (Ong 1982: 24).

The idea that mimesis is about repetition and recollection seems straightforward enough, but as a critic in a post-mimetic age, I still find myself in the unhappy position of having to admit that I want to talk about signifieds. I can't maintain a

---

occasionally possible, just for brief moments, to find the words that will unlock the doors of all those many mansions inside the head and express something . . . of the crush of information that presses in on us'(ibid.: 124). For Hughes, then, poetry tries to grasp the complexity and multiplicity of the world, to make it memorable and recognizable. The equations of fractal geometry, it occurred to me, operate in the same manner: they too make the complexity of likeness visible.

Plato, unlike poets, was not interested in mimesis. At least he was not interested in admitting a world that acknowledged unexplainable complexity. He wanted to evolve a form of discourse that could explain everything in orderly, cause-and-effect terms. His philosophy set the tone and direction for what we now think of as the scientific method. The only way to find the True, the Beautiful and the Good, he believed, was to break the world down into little bits. If the most basic bit could be found, the order of the universe would be revealed. We have taken that principle on faith ever since and have

safely poststructuralist position of endlessly deferring meaning and talking only about interrelations between signifiers.

At first, I thought I was just going to have to accept being in a permanent dilemma. But, luckily for me, Christopher Prendergast, in *The Order of Mimesis*, provides a way of resolving mimesis with contemporary critical thinking. He reminds us that 'the order of mimesis and the order of "reality" confront each other as homologous systems of signification' (Prendergast 1986: 68); that is, they bear a kind of intertextual relationship to each other. Mimesis, then, becomes a kind of recognition scene (ibid.: 216) that 're-presents not the world but the world as already organised in discourse'. It is not about producing 'a semblance of the real world, but a semblance of true discourse about the world' (ibid.: 68). That helps. What he means is that mimesis is not exactly about making poems like animals, it is about how the language of poetry makes animals recognizable.

But I'm still in trouble with poststructuralist orthodoxy. What mimetic narrative recognizes – according to critics from Aristotle, through Auerbach, Abrams, Havelock and Frye – is a kind of commonly held cultural code. So mimesis is still problematic for poststructuralist critics because it is vague and smacks of soft-centred humanism. The difficulty is that mimesis tends towards unity, what Auerbach calls the 'elementary things which our lives have in common' (Auerbach 1968: 552) and Havelock calls our 'personal identification' with a spell (Havelock 1963: 26). It is the element that makes the chipmunk shiver at the sound of the owl poem, and the

---

regarded examples of randomness as uninteresting or unimportant – or simply invisible.

The problem is that the world never can be reduced to a most basic bit. 'Deterministic predictability' turns out to be, as James Gleick says in *Chaos*, a 'fantasy' (Gleick 1987: 6). Tiny, essentially immeasurable variations make enormous differences in the order of the universe. For example, people predicting the weather have found that no matter how precise their readings, no matter how frequent, their predictions are still accurate to no more than a few days in advance. They give a kind of scientific koan that says 'a butterfly stirring the air today in Peking can transform storm systems next month in New York' (Gleick 1987: 8). That phenomenon is known as 'sensitive dependence on initial conditions'. It is a mark of what is now commonly called *chaos theory*. *Fractal geometry* is the mathematical language that describes those phenomena.

I should explain something about chaos theory here, especially as it is

element that makes us recognize that all the cow poems are about cows, even if they are very different cow poems.

Prendergast, again, provides an escape clause. He argues that mimetic recognition is not as unified as it appears. It includes, by its very deference to nature, the possibility of multiplicity – the range of fickle emotion and experience. Mimetic recognition with its apparent fusion of subject and object turns out to be a very fractured and irregular form of knowledge. It turns out to be the very opposite of orderly, logical, Platonic cause-and-effect discourse. It is not mimesis that is built on the nice smooth planes and curves of Euclidean geometry, but philosophy. Mimetic narrative is actually taken up with fractured and fractional irregularities. And so I come – finally – to fractal geometry.

Fractal – a kind of portmanteau word suggesting both fractured and fractional – was coined by a mathematician, Benoit Mandelbrot, in 1975 to describe his new geometry of irregular shapes. Mandelbrot had been fed up with the inadequacy of conventional Euclidean geometry to explain or even recognize the irregular forms of nature: 'clouds are not spheres,' he says, 'mountains are not cones, coastlines are not circles, and bark is not smooth, nor does lightning travel in a straight line' (Mandelbrot 1977: 1). Whereas conventional Euclidean geometry can't explain trees, for example, Mandelbrot wanted to argue for forests. So he invented a mathematical set of instructions to explain the regular irregularity of forests – and trees – through something he calls 'self-similarity'. When I first read about self-similarity, it occurred to me that mimesis encoded exactly the same kind of self-similar descriptions.

---

something of a misnomer. Chaos theory is not about disorder. It is about order we haven't previously been able to recognize. It is really about 'nonlinear dynamical systems' and it has two basic tenets: 'simple systems give rise to complex behaviour' and 'complex systems give rise to simple behaviour' (Gleick 1987: 304). That is, apparently simple systems like pendulums are unpredictable, yet systems that don't conform to prediction, no matter how accurate the data – like the weather, or wildlife populations – do have an order that is only visible when the relationships between scales are compared. It is just that we never noticed that pattern of regularity before. We were too busy trying to find a Euclidean and Newtonian order in the universe, too interested in the order of straight lines and bell curves.

So we missed the order in the relationships between scales. Mandlebrot saw those relationships and described them, and suddenly the order in the

Self-similarity involves a series of regular substitutions of one pattern for another – exactly the sort of task suited to computers. Mandelbrot found that he could tell a computer to repeat huge numbers of self-similar patterns at different scales. No matter how much the pattern was magnified, no matter how small a piece observed, the same pattern was visible. To find order in chaos, Mandelbrot looks at scales, and relationships between scales, rather than length. He likes to cite the length of the coastline of Britain as an example. If you measure the length of the coastline by going around every grain of sand, your line will be longer than if you measure the length from an aerial photograph. It is not the length that changes, but the scale. Italo Calvino, in the 'Exactitude' lecture from *Six Memos for the Next Millennium*, makes a similar observation when he describes Leonardo da Vinci's discussion on the telling of a fable of how fire's pride is extinguished by water. Leonardo apparently tries three versions of the fable, each with different details, but finally breaks off 'as if becoming aware that there is no limit to the minuteness of detail with which one can tell even the simplest story' (Calvino 1988: 78).

But if you do repeat enough details, as Mandelbrot found when he used a computer to generate pictures of his self-similar sets, regular repetitions went critical in unexpected ways. They revealed pictures that were incredibly accurate descriptions of forests, coastlines, moss – exactly the kinds of irregular formations in which Euclidean geometry wasn't interested.

The point I want to make is not that Mandelbrot sets con-

---

patterns of snowflakes and moss and ferns revealed themselves. Once physicists discovered chaos theory, says James Gleick, they were able to return 'without embarrassment to phenomena on a human scale' (Gleick 1987: 7).

The point of this précis of chaos theory is not to extrapolate that cause-and-effect discourse is wrong, but that it doesn't tell the whole story. A contemporary focus on chaos theory and fractal geometry helps us re-know some of the ways of looking at the world to which we have grown oblivious. I'm back to Adrienne Rich's re-visionary programme of feminist theory as a way of re-knowing what literature is about. Re-visionist accounts of mimesis belong in the same cluster of ideas. We have been so concerned with looking at mimesis as an orderly, linear system that we haven't been able to see the relationships among its varieties of disorder. Christopher Prendergast's book, *The Order of Mimesis*, makes the disorder of mimesis visible, especially in the discussions about the fickleness and unpredictability intrinsic in likeness to life.

struct a semblance of reality, but that – as Prendergast says about mimesis – they construct a semblance of *discourse* about reality. Both fractal geometry and mimesis demonstrate that repetition of self-similar structures can make the world recognizable, memorable, that it keeps us from letting the world pass by us in a daydream. The chipmunk recognizes the owl and feels fear. The farmer, his family, and readers, recognize variations on cows.

I know I've only briefly touched the territory that links principles of repetition, recollection and recognition with mimesis and fractal geometry – I was warned strictly to keep my talk to fifteen minutes. But I do just want to collect some of the ideas I've been ranging through. Mandelbrot says that questions long asked without response tend to be 'abandoned to children' (Mandelbrot 1977: 3). The questions Jarrell and Hughes ask about how to make words like things are among those questions long abandoned to children. The answers are still problematic, but it is possible to recognize that mimesis is to verbal representation what fractal geometry is to visual representation. Both allow for the recognition of multiplicity, variety and irregularity in the repetition of self-similar patterns.

So, what am I left with? An intimation, a hint, I think, that mimesis and fractal geometry are worthwhile ways of recognizing the world. Poets are concerned, like it or not, with signifieds as well as signifiers. Self-similarity, in mimesis as in fractal geometry, does reveal the surprising fractured and fractional face of the world. And the principles of repetition, recollection and recognition that inform twenty-five hundred years of representation theory are more than just mnemonics.

Those principles have important pedagogical implications. Instead of focusing on the logical cause-and-effect sequence of learning as the organizing principle that enables us to recognize the world, we can turn instead to fractal and mimetic

---

The title of my paper contains an echo of Wordsworth's 'Intimations of Immortality'. Wordsworth's preference for lamps over mirrors in the poem means that he does rather bemoan the imprisoning growth of his child 'trailing clouds of glory' into 'The Little Actor' who lives his life 'As if his whole vocation / Were endless imitation'. So it seems to me fitting that it should be a contemporary 'nature' poet, Ted Hughes, who celebrates mimesis: 'I am each of these things. The Rat. The Fly. And each of these things is Me. It is. It is. That is the Truth.'

recognition, to the capacity to see repeated patterns, and the capacity to recall them at will, and experience pleasure in that recognition of pattern – exactly as children who recognize the pleasure of hearing a story again and again.

The relationship between fantasy and other literature, and between fantasy and children's literature, has been highly ambivalent. Its undoubted importance in children's literature has tended to be in inverse ratio to its critical acceptability. It is commonly seen as characteristic of (and appropriate to) childhood, and, consequently, of relatively small interest to adults. Glenys Smith has summed up the general attitude of child-psychologists:

> The impulse to imagine, to fantasise, is evident in children from an early age. James Britton (1977: 42) defines children's fantasy as 'the handling of images as play' and sees it as a developmental activity in children which goes beyond the purely cognitive. Play is a voluntary activity which frees children from the need to equate their 'play' images with their experience of reality and by so doing enables them to be in some sense 'more themselves'. Britton sees daydreams . . . occupying in the child's life a space between the verifiable external world . . . and the inner psychic world. (Smith 1987: 260)

Historically, the development of criticism has been complex, and it is striking that fantasy has flourished in British children's literature in the periods before the First World War, and after the Second – which may have some interesting sociological implications. As Wolfe observes, in the nineteenth century, 'despite occasional essays by George MacDonald, William Morris, Oscar Wilde and others, fantasy for the most part was treated by critics and reviewers as an anomaly'. He goes on:

> Fiction, like technology, was incorporated into the Victorian ideal of Progress, and fantastic fiction often seemed a throwback. . . . An anonymous essay in *The Westminster Review* in 1853 (titled, appropriately, 'The Progress of Fiction as an Art') argued that 'a scientific, and somewhat sceptical age, has no longer a power of believing in the marvels which delighted our ruder ancestors'. The fantas-

tic, when it was mentioned at all, was usually mentioned in the context of children's literature. . . .

The major exception to this trend could be found in essays by practicing authors. George MacDonald's 1893 essay 'The Fantastic Imagination' disputed the notion that fantasy was only for children . . . G. K. Chesterton's . . . 'The Ethics of Elfland' [1908] . . . argued for the moral and ethical significance of the fantastic. E. M. Forster's influential *Aspects of the Novel* (1927) elevated fantasy (and what he called 'prophecy') to the status of a major fictional technique or mode, an idea which has since been echoed by Eric S. Rabkin (1976) and Kathryn Hume (1984). (Wolfe 1990: 371–2)

One result of this has been that books on fantasy have tended to treat fantasy marketed for children, and for adults, on the same terms (for example, Sale 1978 and Swinfen 1984). More recently, attention has been given to the linguistic formulations and implications of fantasy, notably by John Stephens:

One of the more curious sides to the criticism of children's literature is the urge to polarize fantasy and realism into rival genres, and to assert that children prefer one or the other, or 'progress' from fantasy to realism (or vice versa). Felicity Hughes has persuasively argued that much of this rivalry originates as a special problem in the history of the production and reception of the novel, specifically in the desire to make it a literary form acceptable to high culture, 'art's traditional élite audience of educated adult males' (Hughes 1978: 28). By the mid-twentieth century, this desire had solidified into an identification of seriousness with realism and a concomitant consigning of fantasy to non-serious or popular literature for those audiences, such as children, deemed incapable of complex aesthetic responses. An interesting consequence of this, as Hughes points out, is that many extremely fine writers whose bent is towards fantasy have written for children, with the further consequence that there exists both a strong tradition of fantasy writing and a large body of very high quality texts.

Those who would defend the reading of fantasy can thus argue from a position of some strength, though the actual bases of defence tend to be surprisingly slight, largely undemonstrable, and essentially dependent upon ideological presuppositions. A defence characteristically includes the following: fantasy gives pleasure and delight; it aspires to the realm of poetry and cultivates the imagination; it renders experiences in sharp focus, untrammelled by the tangential complexities of the real world, and thereby deepens understanding of the world; it enables readers to experiment with ways of seeing, and so reveals how reality itself is a particular social construct which may carry the further implication that 'realist' writing is restricted to surfaces. On the other side, it is claimed that realism typically illuminates life as it is, presenting social and personal concerns in a context which includes a range of human desires and responses; it reflects society, and in doing so by means of a fictional construct, or representation, can offer its audience new experiences and help children mature intellectually and emotionally by enabling them to experiment with subject positions by engaging with them at one remove from consensus reality. All fiction is, of course, at least one remove from reality – fantasy is presumably at least twice removed, in that it is a representation of something which does not exist in the actual world. (Stephens 1992: 241–2)

Sarah Gilead's 'Magic abjured: closure in children's fantasy fiction', reprinted below, seems to me to be valuable not only because it treats of 'children's' texts with academic seriousness and rigour, but because it successfully integrates aspects of psychological, reader-response and textual criticism so that each, unobtrusively, illuminates the other. Her justification of the validity of her study in this essay is very brief; she had explored the issues in more depth in an earlier piece:

It is commonly assumed that children's literature properly simplifies moral, social, psychological complexities so as to suit the limited intellects of children. In this view, authorial comprehension and control over the literary product is complete, and the author's sense of the reader is unambiguous. Both these assumptions are highly debatable. The first implies that literary meanings directly reflect the author's intentions and are manifest in the primary text; the second implies that the literature that academic tradition or publishers' promotions designate as 'children's' is indeed for children, and that there is unanimity between the author's and the community's sense of audience. Such simple identities constitute a theoretical utopia, a closed system like *hortus conclusus* that most critics would recognise as unrealistic. . . . We may even say that such claims are ontologically uncertain because of the tendency of literary texts to deconstruct the overt patterns of meaning. (Gilead 1988: 145)

Magic Abjured: Closure in Children's Fantasy Fiction
Sarah Gilead

Children's literature, like any literature, bears examining from the viewpoint of adult readers. Even its child-directed projects reflect the adult writer's intentions and satisfy adult readers' notions about children's tastes and needs, as well as fulfilling the needs of the adult societies to which the children belong. In addition, the works are shaped by conscious or unconscious goals that diverge from the conventional (one might say official) child-directed ones. Unless otherwise specified, therefore, the term *reader* in this essay refers to the adult reader.

As U. C. Knoepflmacher has observed, the socializing tendency in children's literature consorts with its appeal to adults' 'regressive yearnings'. Works of fantasy in particular

can be said to hover between the states of perception that William Blake had labeled innocence and experience. From the vantage point of experience, an adult imagination re-creates an earlier childhood self in order to steer it towards the reality principle. From the vantage point of innocence . . . that childhood agent may resist the imposition of adult values. (Knoepflmacher 1983: 497)

In a particular work, the differing perspectives may be manifest in a dramatic clash between characters, in the protagonist's internal conflict, in patterns of imagery or symbol, or in narrative structure. A return-to-reality closure tends to concentrate these dramatic, psychological or figurative expressions of the work's opposing purposes and themes.[1]

80

Such a device recurs in many classic works of children's fantasy fiction: the adventurers return home, the dreamer awakens, or the magical beings depart. Often the ending completes a frame around the fantasy, reestablishing the fictional reality of the opening. Despite its commonness, indeed its seeming naturalness, the pattern is surprisingly varied in dramatic mode and in meaning. So familiar is the return-to-reality closing, embedded as it is in literary tradition and convention, that the reader's interpretive query is disarmed by the satisfaction of formal expectations.[2] Though apparently paralleling the initial frame segment, the return may in fact undo the narrative work of the opening: the first segment justifies as well as generates the ensuing fantasy or dream; the conclusion may question that justification. The simple aesthetics of parallel or circular narrative framing may function for obvious interpretations but falter on closer scrutiny. The familiarity and self-evident validity of both process (return) and ontological locus (reality) reassure the reader. At the same time, the return almost inevitably requires a reinterpretation (even a radical one) of the fantasy and may embody a metaliterary comment on the work's cogency or purpose.[3]

While officially resolving and fixing meanings (offering, in particular, the 'correct' interpretation of what precedes), the return seems in fact to pose many more questions than it settles. It may legitimize the fantasy narrative as a necessary lapse from structured reality, a lapse that paradoxically supports reality. But often such a reading noticeably simplifies the fantasy's rich and multiple meanings (the misprision tending to give itself away by a patronizing or sentimental tone). From the vantage point of the return, is the fantasy a socializing, ego-forming expression of anxieties, fears, or grievances? or is it a stimulus to subversive desires or cognitions and hence a threat to socialization? Does the fantasy plot yield knowledge, consolation, or moral significance and thus fit the concept of children's literature as comforting and educative? or does the return assert such purposes only to imply more dubious ones? Does the return neutralize the social criticism implicit in the fantasy? Does the frame, as a 'safe' container, enable the fantasy to challenge the norms of reality? or does it, in swerving from such criticism, paradoxically reveal an even more profound disaffection with reality? Does the return imply faith that a coherent and mature self can abjure the crutch of escapist fantasy? Indeed, the return may be viewed as resolving a narrative rivalry between realism and fantasy and thus as analogous to a self that has worked out internal conflicts. But what if the return instigates this rivalry even as it appears to offer resolution? Does the framed narrative imply a self that is fragmented into dream self and waking self? or into child and adult? Perhaps the overall narrative, like the self, acquiesces to the ideologies that fix its patterns and meanings but, at the very point of acquiescence, registers discomfort with such constraints. Indeed, the strange blending of acquiescence and resistance may account for the dramatic power of the return, at once a positivist assertion of fantasy's usefulness, of fantasy as reality's tool, and a demonstration of narrative's dependence on nonreality, since storytelling energy lapses when reality returns.

The works of children's fantasy literature that feature the return-to-reality closural frame can be classified into three basic types. In the first, the return completes a history of psychic growth and interprets the fantasy narrative as a salutary exposure of forbidden wishes and emotions. The exposure neutralizes antisocial impulses. Obsessive inquiry, resentment, anger, or anxiety is symbolically enacted in the fantasy and thus reduced to an acceptable level, so that the formerly fragile or threatened ego returns as a more fully formed social entity. Examples of this type include *The Wizard of Oz*, by L. Frank Baum, and two picture books by Maurice Sendak.[4]

The second type features a return that rejects or denies the fantasy by misreading it sentimentally and ignoring its subversive force. This return simulates the closural effects of the first type but disrupts rather than smoothly concludes a linear socialization plot. Implied is a conflicted and unsuccessful straining toward such a plot. Examples are Lewis Carroll's *Alice* books and Edith Nesbit's *Enchanted Castle*.

In the third type, the return neither normalizes fantasy as socializing therapy for the protagonist (and implicitly for the child reader) nor rejects fantasy as fostering a neurotic avoidance of social and psychic realities. The return turns against fantasy but, unlike the second type, acts in a tragic mode that reveals, without an assuring sense of mediation, both the seductive force and the dangerous potentiality of fantasy. Examples of the third type are J. M. Barrie's *Peter Pan* (the prose-narrative version) and P. L. Travers's *Mary Poppins*.[5]

The return as *Bildung*

The end of *The Wizard of Oz* fulfils the heroine's conscious and frequently uttered wish to return home. In Chapter 15, Dorothy dreams of Kansas and of her Aunt Em's 'telling her how glad she was to have her little girl at home again' (Baum 1958: 106). This dream anticipates the ending, where Aunt Em finally becomes Aunt M, that is, a mother with an abundance of maternal affection. Has Kansas, ordinary reality, similarly altered? And, if so, does this indicate a transformation in the child protagonist's consciousness or emotional state?

The Kansas of the initial framing segment reveals an adult world oppressively ruled by the reality principle, a world in which the orphaned Dorothy is apparently doomed to follow Aunt Em's destiny. Once young and hopeful, Aunt Em has withered and shrunk in the pervasive greyness and dearth of reality. In view of this joyless prospect, Dorothy's escape (whether consciously desired or not) appears necessary to her survival. Her journey from Kansas to Oz is dreamlike: she falls asleep on the way, as the cyclone recalls the visionary breezes of the aroused romantic imagination, which transport the individual out of waking consciousness into a trancelike heightened awareness. Oz is a wonderland full of colour, surprises and magical adventures. But Kansas is never far off, for it remains overtly in Dorothy's repeated wish to return home, more subtly in reality-echoing patterns of enslavement and immobilization. The Scarecrow and Tin Woodman are 'frozen' until Dorothy releases them; Dorothy and her four companions, as well as the Munchkins, the Winkies and the Winged Monkeys, are at various times imprisoned or enslaved by the wicked witches.

Yet her escape from Kansas is simultaneous with guilt as, newly arrived in Oz, Dorothy is credited with killing the Wicked Witch of the East (the house 'accidentally' lands on the witch – the house symbolizing, as a house often does, self). Evidently, magical journeys are fuelled by power that can be murderous. The Good Witch of the North, who initiates Dorothy into fantasy, must first rationalize fantasy's destructive effects: the Wicked Witch of the East 'has held all the Munchkins in bondage for many years, making them slave for her night and day' (1958: 7). Dorothy's fantastic journey has freed them, just as it frees her. What has been murdered for the sake of freedom appears to be the reality principle itself, which cannot be eliminated permanently and is soon resurrected in the form of the witch's double, the Wicked Witch of the West, who must be killed too. The first killing is unintentional, though expressing an unconscious and inadmissible escapist wish, while the second is somewhat more intentional. Dorothy and her friends accept it as a necessary task imposed by the Wizard himself, the presiding spirit of fantasy, who makes it a condition for helping Dorothy get back to Kansas. The act rectifies the relation between fantasy and reality by justifying her sojourn in the fantasy world. The killing replaces the finding of the Wizard as the object of the quest and enables Dorothy to fulfill her conscious wish to return to reality. But if the wicked witches symbolize the reality principle, why must they be killed to effect Dorothy's return to reality?

Dorothy's desire to return home seems mainly to reflect a primitive ego ideal rather than to emerge from a fully integrated conscience: 'I am anxious to get back to my aunt and uncle, for I am sure they will worry about me' (1958: 9). This motivation is too shallow; her maturer imaginings must also wish for return. Thus, the yellow-brick road can lead her home only by first immersing her deeper in fantasy; and the silver slippers of the dead Witch of the East take her on her real quest, to accommodate her fantasy self to the exigencies of reality. The slippers' hidden power is finally discovered to be the most arcane of all the powers of the imagination – the ability to make reality tolerable. As reality's counterrealm, fantasy becomes only one mode of a complex consciousness capable of dwelling in either fantasy or reality (or in both); fantasy in fact becomes a tool for confronting rather than evading reality.

Dorothy cannot relinquish the green world of fantasy until she learns the limits as well as the uses of enchantment. The heart of the green world is the Emerald City, whose inhabitants and visitors, including Dorothy, wear green spectacles: altered perceptions, altered reality. In Chapter 16, 'The magic art of the great humbug,' Dorothy's friends, with the help of the Wizard's illusions (actually symbolic props), acquire belief in themselves and in the imagination's creative and healing powers. Even a false belief (that an ex-balloonist is a powerful wizard) can cause a whole civilization to arise and prosper. The false belief turns into a potent though indirect form of truth. Dorothy earns a return to reality by killing the witch, who is 'wicked' because she threatens the fantasy kingdom, forging mental manacles that prevent the imagination from finding its true power. Like Aunt Em, she is a domestic enslaver and imprisoner who makes Dorothy clean pots, sweep the floor, and feed the fire. Just as Aunt Em is desiccated, seared by reality, so is the witch dried up, unable to bleed where Toto has bitten her (1958: 88). To return to reality, Dorothy must first make the fantasy kingdom safe. That is, she must make reality endurable by ensuring that it can sometimes be transcended. The power that Dorothy must recognize and use is twofold and paradoxical: she must allay reality's crushing force and must act out her loathing and fear of reality in order to accept it after all.[6]

Once expressed, Dorothy's angry fear of the witch has a cathartic as well as a murderous effect: it melts the witch and frees Dorothy, her friends, and the other enslaved Ozians. With discontent safely drained off, Dorothy is freed from enslavement both to reality and to fantasy. The two can now align properly, and Dorothy can revert to her customary placidity. The Wizard, Oz's Barnum-and-Bailey entrepreneur and Baum's double as fantasist, is unmasked as a humbug only to be revealed in his true powers as a maker of symbolic solutions for real problems. Dorothy returns home to a Kansas transformed by her new perceptions. The farmhouse destroyed in the storm has been rebuilt, and Aunt Em, now physically and emotionally energized, welcomes Dorothy effusively, no longer as an orphan and a stepchild but as a beloved daughter. Both house and aunt have absorbed a modest, healing dose of Oz's green force. Dorothy's loss of the dreamworld is fully compensated by the reality she regains when she returns newly matured through the magic of fantasy.[7]

Like *The Wizard of Oz*, two of Maurice Sendak's picture books for children, *Where the Wild Things Are* (Sendak 1963) and *In the Night Kitchen* (Sendak 1973), enclose fantasy narratives in realistic frames whose closural segments confirm the fantasies' therapeutic function. The dissolution of the dreamworld implies that the dreamer has introjected the messages conveyed and can now achieve intrapsychic and communal integration. In each of these works the child hero enters a fantastic kingdom, performs symbolic tasks, and returns to his own room. In *Where the Wild Things Are*, Max is introduced as a rebel in a wolf suit. The suit's great shadowy tail, almost as big as Max, trails him like a formless animal self, an emblem of primal desire not yet shaped by culture. In the first and second illustrations Max hangs a stuffed toy by its neck, pounds a huge nail into the wall, and brandishes a fork at a small dog. But oral aggression is his forte, heard in the threat 'I'll eat you up!' that he directs to his mother, the authority figure (and, perhaps, the object of frustrated Oedipal desire). The mother's symbolically appropriate punishment for the 'wild thing's' verbal assault is food deprivation ('he was sent to bed without eating anything'), which demonstrates his dependence on family and society for both physical and emotional nourishment – demonstrates but does not, in the proper sense, teach him until his return from the fantasy voyage. Max responds to his punishment with fantasy rather than with more rage: fantasy channels rage into aesthetic or symbolic forms that dramatize the conflict between infantile desire and the newer, socially imposed need to moderate or deflect such desire. Not only does fantasy replace violent emotion, it turns destructive force into narrative energy. Max discovers the art of sublimation.

This narrative energy is first evident in the progressive transformations of the realistic locale. The room, which symbolizes Max's changing self (as the house symbolizes Dorothy's), becomes a moonlit forest, then an ocean with a boat (named 'Max') taking Max on his interior voyage, and finally the titular location, a magical island inhabited by comic-grotesque beasts. On the island, Max is both 'wild thing' and social being capable of devising symbolic strategies against the projected forms of his animal self. As king of the heavily toothed, clawed and tailed beasts, Max is both their *semblable* and their master. He calls for and joins a 'wild rumpus' that is not only a defiant reenactment of his earlier wildness but a cathartic restaging of it. His violence is here held within a double frame consisting of the fantasy itself and the ritual within the fantasy. Max determines the beginning and the end of the rumpus, which spends his anarchic energy and leaves him and the wild things exhausted. The beasts' ensuing threat ('Oh please don't go – we'll eat you up – we love you so!') recalls Max's earlier cannibalistic threat but now lacks self-destructive force. Max has already 'sent the wild things off to bed without their supper'. Having tamed his transgressive desires, he has earned the right to enjoy the 'cooked' pleasures (in Lévi-Strauss's sense) of culture and society. Like Dorothy, he effects a return to reality by reinventing it, that is, by altering his own relation to it. The hot supper awaiting him in his room symbolizes his mother's forgiveness and love and, perhaps, her recognition that Max has successfully internalized social values and behavioural norms. As in *The Wizard of Oz*, the journey out is really the journey in.

In the Night Kitchen repeats the basic plot of *Where the Wild Things Are*. Disturbed by night noises, Mickey falls into another realm, the 'night kitchen', a surrealistic synthesis of the kitchen and New York City. The now naked Mickey looks infantile, if not foetal; his journey is in quest of his origins, and his adventures enact conception and birth. The triplet 'Oliver Hardy' bakers, at once moustached fathers and pregnant-bellied, kitchen-bound mothers, mix a helpless Mickey into a batter and threaten to bake him (Sendak 1973: 13–15). Mickey saves himself by poking up through the batter, asserting that he is more than its ingredients ('I'm not the milk and the milk's not me! I'm Mickey!' (ibid.: 17) and then leaping into the bread dough and shaping it into a private airplane. He will actively cooperate with the baking rather than let himself be moulded by outside agents.

Diving into a giant milk bottle, he resembles a foetus in the birth canal; singing 'I'm in the milk and the milk's in me' (ibid.: 31), he envisions a mystical, embryonic union between substance and spirit, self and container. As he swims up out of the milk bottle, he pours his own substance into the unfinished cake batter below. He has worked his way back to conception to become an active participant in it and in his birth. He helps the bakers finish baking the cake and confirms his triumphant fantasy appropriation of his own paternity-maternity by crowing like a rooster (ibid.: 36), then sliding down the side of the milk bottle-birth canal, not ignominiously expelled into the postpartum world but playfully, wilfully entering it.

The fantasy of self-making allows him to wrest his being from the grip of biological processes; instead of being devoured by them, he becomes their master. Returning to reality, he is reborn, reclothed, 'cakefree and dried' (ibid.: 39) – that is, carefree and comfortably rid of his clinging fears about birth, sexuality and mortality. Fantasy allows him to reduce his apprehensions by obviating or at least postponing the need to confront them directly. Creating an idiosyncratic version of his own birth, Mickey obtains a consoling sense of his uniqueness and autonomy. On his return, the room is free of its initial anxiety-produced disturbances, the 'racket in the night' (ibid.: 6–7).

In *Where the Wild Things Are*, fantasy encourages self-confrontation and exploration; the self is controlled in a tale of taming, comically accomplished. The fantasy of *Night Kitchen* enables an equally salutary deferment: ego is reinforced in a tale of self-assertion, the hero vanquishing fearsome giants by appropriating their power. Just as aggression is reduced to manageable levels in *Wild Things*, passivity and a sense of helplessness are reduced in *Night Kitchen*, but here the problem is more diffuse: the 'night noises' of anxiety are only remotely menacing, so that the solution is more playful, less invested with the ritual solemnity of Max's fantasy. But in both stories the protagonists renounce dreamworlds and choose the security and familiarity of home, of reality made more more tolerable, and indeed subtly altered, by fantasy.[8]

In *The Wizard of Oz* and the two Sendak books, fantasy demonstrates its reality-ordering power and purposes. The closures, however, hint at the possibility of undoing the *Bildungsroman* linearity that they themselves establish. Since the Romantics, the conceptual status of the child has been unstable. The child as embodiment of the creative imagination does not easily comport with the traditional notion of the child as naturally subject to superior adult authority. In children's works with a manifest socialization plot, the adult writer and reader may at once approve and resent the thinly concealed didacticism, the appropriation of fantasy for the uses of social control; the concealment alone suggests ambivalence. The return closure establishes a clear ontological and narrative hierarchy wherein dream becomes secondary to the ordinary reality of consciousness and social life, with fantasy serving as a necessary detour in a schematic *Bildung*. The return regulates the world of imagination, the place where the wild things *were*. Internalized and transformed, imagination disavows its anarchic, escapist energies. But the titles, dramatic centres, and, often, cover illustrations, as well as the sheer narrative-pictorial bulk, invert this official hierarchy; in fact, they foreground the fantasy realms where the wild things are and will always be: the fantasy locales frame the closural frames, which revert to the status of perfunctory formal devices. If Oz is in one sense merely a means to return to Kansas, Kansas is, even more persuasively, merely a setting and an excuse for the invocation of Oz.[9]

The return as narrative repression

In Lewis Carroll's *Alice's Adventures in Wonderland* and *Through the Looking-Glass*, realistic framings enclose Alice's complex dream journeys. Do her 'awakenings' instruct the adult reader in a consoling strategy of misreading that makes it possible to ignore or sanitize subversive messages from the political or personal unconscious? Peter Coveney suggests that 'the "dream," the reverie in Dodgson, becomes in *Alice in Wonderland* the means of setting the reader's senses more fully awake. . . . *Alice in Wonderland* releases the vitality of an intelligent and sensitive commentary on life.' In contrast, at Alice's awakenings the reader 'feel[s] the work turn towards unfulfillment, and . . . death'. Coveney implies that the frame indicates a lapse of Carroll's creative courage (Coveney 1967: 245–6). More recently, William A. Madden has argued that the dream narratives instruct the dreamer and the reader as dreamer in the nightmarish nature of reality. The frames' function is to interpret properly that 'dark central vision' and to convert it to 'profoundly instructive comedy' (Madden 1986: 371). The frames affirm the works' therapeutic effects on both protagonist and reader: the reader's vision is cleansed, just as Alice awakens with her former 'inner restlessness' assuaged and with a renewed perception of 'what is necessary to happiness' (ibid.: 368). Awakening thus transforms the potentially dangerous lessons of the subversive dreams into tonic confirmations of the dreamer's and the reader's potential wholeness and sanity. The frames confirm the stories' linearity and transform what would otherwise be chaotic nonsense or nightmare into a *Bildungsroman* plot of psychic testing and maturation.

The following brief examination of the awakening scenes in the *Alice* books calls into question Madden's view; indeed, the scenes at once invite and undercut his reading. For Madden, Alice's awakening from Wonderland confers on ordinary reality the full, vision-renewing force of her dream; the 'conventional view of the world' held by Alice's sister is shattered by the 'overwhelmingly vivid reality of Alice's dream' (Madden 1986: 364); the sister's interpretation of the dream points to the dullness of ordinary reality and reveals the need to transcend it by renewed perception (ibid.: 367–8). But in fact the sister is not led to a heightened sense of reality; her conventional, sentimental outlook rewrites and softens the vivid reality of Wonderland, enabling her to escape the dream's frightening social and psychological truths. Like the ordinary adult reader of children's literature, the sister is dismissive: 'It *was* a curious dream, dear, certainly; but now run in to your tea: it's getting late' (Carroll 1960: 162). Having heard Alice recount her dream, the sister is inspired to a sweetened redreaming of Alice's nightmare. If Alice's dream is a child's uncomprehending but lucid view of mad adult reality, the sister's is a sentiment-dimmed adult's view of childhood's idyll. In the sister's nostalgic reverie, Alice becomes 'little Alice' with 'tiny hands' and 'bright eager eyes' (ibid.: 162). The sister's version of Alice's dream is a pleasant escapist fantasy filled with exotic creatures performing for the dreamer's amusement but not, as in Alice's dream, interacting with the dreamer in disturbingly intimate ways. The White Rabbit hurries through the long grass, the Mouse splashes through the pool, the March Hare sits at a never-ending tea: the sister's Wonderland is a vacation from reality, not a revelation of reality's substance and meaning. Her version is further vitiated by rationalization: it is a dull translation of 'dull reality'. The long grass of the dream merely transposes the real grass of the riverbank, the Hare's rattling teacups are merely tinkling sheep bells, and so on. The sister's fantasy has its own closural frame: the dreamer pictures Alice's future as a mother who, like other adults, purveys harmlessly amusing tales to children. The purpose of children's literature is imaged here as both simple and benevolent: to beguile, amuse and soothe the child. Before dreaming of Wonderland, Alice is bored and restless; afterwards she is cheerful – and obedient. The closural framings of *Wonderland* thus assert the conventional functions of children's literature and disavow the notion of children's literature as a locus of dissatisfaction with the logical (or illogical) order of adult reality – disavow, that is, our own and Alice's experience of Wonderland.

According to Madden, at the end of *Through the Looking-Glass* the dream 'has shaken Alice out of her preoccupation with attaining queenhood' (Madden 1986: 369); it has also stimulated her intellect, so that she demonstrates a newfound ability to ask philosophical questions about reality. Once again, however, Carroll invites an ironic alternative reading of Alice's misreading of her own dream: 'oh! such a nice dream!' she chirps in response to her melancholy dream encounters, filled with images of death and loss. The adult reader may understand the import of the philosophical question she poses, but Alice does not ('Now, Kitty, let's consider who it was that dreamed it all. This is a serious question, my dear' (Carroll 1960: 343)). In the dream, the confusion between nightmare and reality is frighteningly immediate, threatening Alice's sense of her own permanence and coherence; appropriately, she weeps (ibid.: 238). But in the frame segment Alice is relentlessly cheery and playful, in ironic contrast to the seriousness of her question. Prattling on, she gets into deep philosophical waters without realizing that her feet are wet. The closing frames of *Alice in Wonderland* postulate, though with ambivalent sentimentality, that the adult can recapture childhood or that childhood innocence can persist in the adult's storytelling imagination. In contrast, the return frame of *Looking-Glass* reveals a wide gap, indeed an impassible one, between the reader's understanding and Alice's. As U. C. Knoepflmacher has demonstrated, *Looking-Glass* treats the adult's idealization of childhood ironically and disparages the values both of socialization and of the desire to retain childhood innocence. Childhood and adulthood are discontinuous (Knoepflmacher 1983: 512, 517). In the return segment, the adult reader may be awake, but Alice slumbers on unaware, though we sense that soon she will truly awaken to adult comprehension – but only at the price of losing her ingenuous joy.

The return presents no stable interpretation of the foregoing fantasy; indeed it permits the reader to focus, as Madden does, on the work's 'cover story', a fictive representation of the maturation process. Alice's naïveté may be read as unconscious, commonsense armour against the existential tension produced by the dream.[10] An equally strong interpretive effect of the frame transforms the fantasy into an evocation of childhood's idyll as inviolably, savingly separate from the adult realm of anxiety. Finally, the frame establishes an ironic difference between its own somnolent, indeed escapist 'reality' and the dark wakefulness of the dreams.[11] Alice's posing of philosophical chestnuts, far from indicating her newfound maturity, swerves away from the instructive though poignant morbidity of the dream. The closing frame of *Looking-Glass* banishes the emotionally needy adult figures of the fantasy (the Gnat, the White Knight, the dying Wasp of the suppressed episode of the eighth chapter (see Carroll 1977)). Child and adult can only 'dream' each other, remaining 'half a life asunder'; they cannot meet even on the conventional, sentimental ground proposed at the end of *Wonderland*.

In both *Alices*, the closing frames satisfy adult didactic and escapist impulses but also cast an ironic shadow on these inclinations. The endings suggest the successful maturation of the child protagonist – they put Alice into an adult 'frame'. In *Wonderland*, we glimpse a future Alice grown up enough to tell stories to her own children, as if that capacity in itself demonstrated maturity. In *Looking-Glass*, Alice asks serious questions about reality. At the same time, these returns sentimentalize the preceding dream narratives and the child protagonist, romanticizing the child and childhood as unattainable other rather than incorporating the child into adult reality. Such romanticizing itself reflects adult escapist, perhaps antisocial, proclivities. But sentimentality also conceals this adult appropriation of childhood. Paradoxically, then, the awakened Alices at once embody and evade grown-up desires. Just before she awakens, Alice comes dangerously close to revealing herself as a product of adult ideas and emotions. At the ends of the fantasy sections of both *Wonderland* and *Looking-Glass*, Alice herself momentarily attains a sharply critical consciousness: she perceives that courtiers and kings are 'nothing but a pack of cards' and that induction to queenhood is entry into a world of chaotic violence. Awake, she loses this consciousness. When Alice 'grows' into an unmistakable dream image of adult iconoclastic rage, she must be banished, to return to a safer image of childhood.

In Edith Nesbit's *Enchanted Castle* (1907), magic represents the power and dangers of desire, as it does in many other fairy tales, including Nesbit's better-known *Five Children and It* (1902). The plot traces the effects of the children's use and final renunciation of a wishing ring. Simultaneous with this renunciation is the achievement of the book's secondary 'adult' plot, a rather predictable romance of thwarted but true love between an English lord and a French governess. The episodic magic plot is replaced by a more conventional linear plot of courtship and marriage. The two stories are linked causally and thematically: the first produces and completes the second, and both are based on wish fulfilment. This double plotting invokes the familiar process of socialization, in which an anarchic childhood realm is replaced by a social world dominated by middle-class events and morality. In the Hall of Psyche, also the Hall of Granted Wishes, Psyche speaks through the governess's lips and teaches the children that wishing exacts a deadly price: death or madness. 'Granted wishes' organize the fantasy plot, but here Psyche renounces the misrule of desire in favour of inner organization by retributive guilt. The main plot has repeatedly demonstrated that children pay a severe though lesser price for wishing. The only free wish is the last, at once renouncing unregulated desire and turning it into a different sort of magic. The governess's final wish is to undo all the magic that the ring has performed and to convert the ring into 'a charm to bind [her and her lover] together for evermore' (Nesbit 1956: 252).

The children's discovery of the ring reflects their deep wish to diversify and enliven reality. On holiday, as the protagonists so often are in children's literature (and in Nesbit, in particular), the children long to loosen or defer the tightening ties to social reality that characterize growing up. The ring they find also embodies narrative desire and energy, producing story patterns without tedious repetition, as various individuals wear the ring, have adventures, and get into trouble. Narrative thrust and the wishing ring disappear simultaneously.

Each fresh episode is at first deliciously unmoored from the ordinary constraints of reality. But if the ring dissolves the barriers between desire and reality, it also operates against desire by showing the crude and troublesome ways that desire obtrudes on reality. A wish-created episode leads to its own return to reality and demonstrates reality's intractability. The children are relieved to return to the familiar. A child becomes invisible, or four yards high, or turns to stone; dummies made of household junk come importunately alive (the 'Ugly-Wuglies'). Each incident, at first pleasurable in its strangeness, ultimately proves the greater desirability of the ordinary. Yet desire returns, too, to generate another equivocal release from the ordinary. The ring's magic produces experiences of transcendent beauty and exaltation (the Edenic interlude with the living-myth statues, lyrical counterparts of the hideously living dummies); but elsewhere, as with the Ugly-Wuglies, the children are punished for meddling with powers that they do not understand and that threaten both their own world and the adults'.

Where is magic's residue in the ordinary reality that follows the renunciation of magic? After an oneiric feast with the statue gods, the children awaken to a chill, grey day; they stand in brambles and coarse grass. 'There was no smooth lawn, no marble steps, no seven-mooned fish ponds. . . . [I]t was very cold' (Nesbit 1956: 211). But only a few pages later they enjoy a real but idyllic picnic: 'a tea for the gods!' (ibid.: 225). Is unenchanted reality capable after all of engendering its own enchantments? When the wishing ring is replaced by a wedding ring, is egotistical childhood replaced by a satisfying adult moral and social (and sexual) reality? While empowered by the ring, the children enjoy a kind of comical authority over governesses, police officers, aunts and servants. Without the ring, the adults take over the story and resume their customary dominance over the children. The return to reality is also a turning to sentimentality: do adult wishes only arbitrarily replace the child's? Does the transparent wishfulness of the cliché-ridden romance plot compensate for the loss of the ever-changing fantasy world? Is ordinary reality shown to be intolerable unless softened by such romance? Given its most polarized interpretation, the ending on the one hand insists that desire must be renounced but that the sacrifice is recompensed by personal maturity and social integration and on the other hand provides, more implicitly, covert valorization of anarchic desire; for without anarchic energy, all that is left of desire is a sentimentalized, softened version. The opening framing segment shows the children playing 'The Sleeping Beauty'. The concluding romantic plot is an obvious version of 'Cinderella' (see page 122, where the governess is transformed from sad spinsterhood to beauty and luxuriant sexuality). Thus, the socialization plot the children complete by abjuring magic is itself a fairy tale combined with popular romance. Officially, the ending defines wishing as puerile, dangerous and useless, except as a tool for promoting adult projects such as marriage. But the narrator mocks the reader's naive expectations that the ending will satisfy and exposes the fictionality that underlies all literary realism: 'it is all very well . . . to pretend that the whole of this story is my own invention: facts are facts, and you can't explain them away' (ibid.: 253). 'Facts' refers to the mysterious disappearance, reported in the evening newspaper, of 'Mr. U. W. Ugli', the Ugly-Wugly 'who became real' at the Hall of Granted Wishes, then unreal when wishing was abjured. Playfully addressing the fantasy-reality crux of her own story, Nesbit links the 'realistic' conclusion to an entirely fictional-fantastic 'factuality'. If the socialization plot finally conquers escapist fantasy, fantasy continues to exert ironic pressure on that plot. Like the *Alices*, *The Enchanted Castle* holds in uneasy equilibrium the realms of frame and fantasy.[12]

The return as tragic ambiguity

The third type of children's fantasy narrative is perhaps the most problematic. In the first type of closural return we considered, fantasy's energies are appropriated for socializing purposes and are thus defined as controllable and usable. In the second type, fantasy is misread through the interpretive screen of sentimental comedy. But the tragic mode of return is dominated by a sense of loss unmitigated by a playful or softened tone. Indeed, the meaning of the return remains indeterminate. Ironically, such indeterminacy leaves the value of fantasy intrinsic, independent of other frames of reference. Missing is the closural translation of fantasy or magic into some readable, culturally encoded set of religious, moral or psychological meanings.

Throughout J. M. Barrie's prose version of *Peter Pan*, the titular hero is an emissary from the fantasy world (Neverland) and thus the children's and reader's guide in a symbolic flight from reality. Yet Peter is magnetized by that reality, to which he constantly returns. Forever young, he embodies the adult obsession with time and death. Peter is at once the idealized child and the regressive, impotent adult who is compelled to kidnap the very concept of childhood to alleviate the intolerable burden of adult existence. Free of mortality, sexuality and social responsibility, Peter is imprisoned by his inability to grow up. Condemned to repeat the same story of denial with each generation and insatiably hungry for new stories, Peter exemplifies the unacknowledged power of children's literature over adults.[13]

In the initial framing segment, the narrator locates the Island of Neverland in a child's mind. Like the derivative figure Mary

Poppins, discussed below, Peter represents the child's escapist imagination – more properly, the adult's romantic view of childhood as the liberated imagination itself. Peter also reveals the adult's fearful or even guilt-laden desire for the idealized imagination of the child. Mrs Darling dreams 'that the Neverland had come too near and that a strange boy had broken through from it. . . . [S]he thought she had seen him before in the faces of many women who have no children' (Barrie 1985: 9). What escapes repression here is the adult desire not only for children but for childhood. Peter, then, embodies both repressed adult wishes and the absence or loss of childhood, the lack that breeds regressive desire. That desire, while exposed and partly satisfied in fantasy writing, requires the assuring frame structure of children's literature, with the genre's nominal but official child audience and purposes. But here the initial frame invokes only to repudiate the dream of eternal childhood and thus educates the adult reader in the elusive ways of desire that perpetuate lack even as they promise to assuage it. In keeping with the familiar Romantic model, only death – literal or metaphoric – makes Barrie's child eternal; only after childhood ends can the adult reconstitute it as the object of desire, so that the concept originates in loss. The return to childhood through fantasy narrative inevitably traces the route toward childhood's end: the way back turns into the way forward once again. With inevitable logic, then, the close must mirror the beginning. Escape into an idealized past cannot, as in the works examined above, fuel even an illusory progress toward adult consciousness but must, rather, collapse into cyclicality.[14]

Thus, Peter is death itself as well as the desire for eternal childhood. Death is the strategy of refusal in the self's war against biological, generational processes. Through a familiar slippage of psychic signifiers, the fear of death becomes a death wish. Peter is the product of a guilt-ridden, self-consciously sentimental swerve from adult fears of sexuality and death. We remember that in Mr Darling's economy children are threats: they cost too much. In fact, they cost one's own life. The existence of the next generation guarantees the expendability of the present. In Mr Darling the adult's fear of mortality is expressed as thinly concealed hostility toward and envy of the child. For the child, adults are threatening examples of ageing and mortality. Peter's strategy is to short-

circuit those species-serving systems that collaborate with nature's indifference toward the individual: socialization, marriage,
the family (at one point, Peter rejects three importunate
females: Tinker Bell, Tiger Lily and Wendy (1985: 100)). But
that means taking the shorter route to the same end and
enduring constant hauntings by the returned repressed, nicely
imaged in Peter's haunting of the nurseries he has escaped.
His very presence turns Wendy into a little mother, linking
her to the adult future he abhors and fears (ibid.: 24, 31, 67).[15]

Not surprisingly, *Peter Pan* is a morbid book, rich in themes
of guilt, revenge, obsession and murder. The adult's regressive
desires produce the idealized fantasy figure of the child, but
the fantasy reveals itself to be a self-defeating and paradox-
ridden strategy against the fear of death. Peter's charm, his
immortality, his flight, his realm – all are death-ridden. The
true paradox of the 'never' in Neverland is in its double meaning of stark denial – on the one hand, the refusal of the self
to conceive of its own end and, on the other, the absolute
reality of death. When Peter first appears, he is described as
'lovely' but 'clad in skeleton leaves and the juices that ooze
out of trees' (ibid.: 10). Both boy eternal and rotting corpse,
he arrives like a dream of immortality come true but also like
a plague deadly to children – like ageing and death, he empties
the nursery. As he kidnaps the Darling children in retaliation
for their father's childish bullying, he fulfils both the child's
revengeful wishes to punish powerful parents (like the other
'lost boys', he is a victim of and an escapee from adult reality
in general and from parental neglect in particular) and the
parents' unconscious wishes to rid themselves of children,
evidence of their own ageing and mortality. As in the Romantic
paradox discussed above, the real child must give way to the
symbolic substitute. Like the author of children's literature,
Peter kidnaps the child to escape the nursery, gravity and
other limitations and burdens of ordinary reality; but he takes
us to a world infused with morbid reminders of that reality.[16]

Neverland is a realm of death under the cover story of
boyish fun and adventure. The boys live underground, each
in a house whose entrance fits him exactly, like a coffin. Peter,
like death, changes the boys to fit the entrances. When they
shoot Wendy, they build a tiny house around her, like a tomb.
The ticking crocodile is death itself (when the clock runs down,
the prey is caught) or it is ourselves, doomed to the brief

lifespans measured by our ticking hearts. Neverland is a stew of murderous rivalry or revenge (Tink against Wendy, Hook against Peter). Hook is a comic-melancholy and murderously resentful adult obsessed with Peter, the pristine image of childhood and the past: envied, desired and hated. An obvious analogue for Mr Darling (in productions of the play, the roles were often performed by the same actor), Hook is the time-burdened adult living with the painful consciousness of mortality and with a romantic sense of adulthood as the loss of perceptual and emotional force. For Hook, Peter and the ticking crocodile are doubles, each a living symbol of relentless temporality (ibid.: 135). In a metatextual sense, Peter exemplifies a vitiated or defunct psychocultural strategy against the fear of death. Hook is bemused by the image of the innocent and inviolable child, but his anxiety and anger are thereby deepened, not assuaged. In symmetrical fashion Peter hates Hook, the adult who seems to the child to embody the facts of generation, time and mortality. Not surprisingly, Pan slays Hook only to become him (ibid.: 148).

Though the Darling children and the Lost Boys are 'found' again by the powerful social realities and narrative conventions that appear to triumph at the end, the return does not bring stability but, rather, generates further losses and returns. The children lose their powers of flight, their belief in the possibility of escape through fantasy, and also, perhaps, their belief in the inviolability of childhood itself. Peter, forgetting the past, is entrapped in an eternal present without emotional or cognitive meaning. Those who have returned to reality are 'grown up and done for'. Mrs Darling is 'now dead and forgotten', and Nana, we are told bluntly, 'died of old age' (ibid.: 162). We glimpse the generations come and go (Wendy's, Jane's, Margaret's); and while Peter, as the resistant impulse, accompanies them, his unchanging presence only emphasizes and seems somehow to hasten the speed of generational process. And, of course, he himself only exists by means of – indeed, has come to epitomize – the narrative genre whose putative agenda he dismantles.[17]

Like Peter, Mary Poppins is associated with flight and nature (the wind, animals, heavenly bodies). Her 'pop-ins' appear spontaneous, like the wind that blows her into and out of the narrative. Mary is a semidivine 'Cousin' of the zoo animals; for the children who accompany her to the transformed, moonlit, 'upside-down' zoo, she is a teacher of truths transcending adult conceptual narrowness and selfishness (Travers 1934: 134). Defying gravity, she seems also to defy adult 'gravity' (see especially Chapter 3, 'Laughing gas', where comic fantasy temporarily defeats anxieties concerning loss and death). But Mary is also a governess, a socializing agent and at times even a repressor who denies magic or uses it for punishment of moral lapses. For example, at the end of Chapter 3, the scene of the hilarious, floating tea, she sniffily denies that the incident took place. In Chapter 6 she whisks the children off to hobnob with animals, only later to use this fantasy journey, in the form of a nightmare, to punish one of her charges (ibid.: 80–1). Thus, Mary embodies the ambivalence of fantasy writing for children, now escapist and frankly unsocial (or even antisocial), now framed by the justifying context of moral didacticism.

In the overall narrative's closural frame, the fictional world is restored to its original, prefantasy condition. When Mary departs, magic, fantasy and nature myths depart too. But the child protagonists experience this departure as loss, not as restoration. Further, the meaning of the departed fantasy is not established: no particular lessons have been learned, self-concepts are not strengthened, religious truths vaguely hinted at remain unrevealed. The closure points to an absolute barrier between fantasy and reality, between childhood and adulthood; Mary's presence obscures that barrier, but her absence makes it manifest. Oddly, though, when her magic disappears, the very sense of its loss suggests that magic is an intrinsic, though ambiguous, good – not justified by, and apparently not needing to be justified by, any other frame of reference.

Like Peter Pan, Mary and her magic come into the initial reality frame to fill a parental gap and, more broadly, to compensate for the multiple inadequacies of adult reality. In the initial frame, adult activities are presented as trivial, the adults as obtuse and selfish, remote from the children and indifferent to their needs; and these qualities are exacerbated in the closing frame (see especially pages 156–7, where Michael now fully comprehends his mother's selfishness). The closural loss of magic and of its consolations thus sharpens the critique of adults and of their version of reality and makes the loss of the fantasy world tragic. Reality is not rectified; fantasy and reality are not aligned.

The series of episodes and interpolated tales that make up the narrative mostly follow the reality-fantasy-reality pattern of the whole. Fantasy never becomes fully present; it is temporary, risky, and unstable in duration and meaning (ironically, adult reality is even more unstable and much less satisfying and comprehensible). For example, Chapter 2, 'The day out', repeats the general frame narrative in structure but opposes it in meaning. Mary's day off is indeed 'off' the plane of reality. Initially described in realistic terms, it soon enters the 'framed' world of fantasy – here, almost literally: she and her sidewalk-artist friend, Bert, 'enter' a picture he has painted, a pastoral landscape where they enjoy an idyllic tea. Returning to reality, Mary tells the children that she has been in a fairyland all her own, that is, one derived from her wishes. In the demarcated spaces of art, fantasy offers temporary gratifications for reality's omissions (the 'real' tea was foiled by Mary's and Bert's lack of money). In confusing contrast, Chapter 9, 'John and Barbara's story', shows infants outgrowing their ability to understand the speech of natural objects and creatures. In Chapter 2 Mary seems to offer fantasy as a compensatory resource. In Chapter 9 she presides over the 'natural' loss of the 'magical' delights of perceptual and cognitive unity with nature. Does her leaving reflect childhood's inevitable end? If so, why have her equivocal lessons in fantasy reinforced the children's sense of reality's inadequacy? As reality even more clearly resumes its initial shape of barren and joyless necessity, the children are left with a framed portrait of Mary and her hint of return ('au revoir'). That is, they hope that once again ordinary reality may be reduced to a mere frame around a more exciting and variable realm. Almost cruelly, Mary has forced them back to reality without reconciling them to it; she has, if anything, spoiled them for it by her tantalizing range of modes of escape and by her refusal or inability to define the uses of enchantment.[18]

In one sense, the return-to-reality closure asserts the conventional, ideologically mandated meanings and indeed relations between the concept pairs 'child' and 'adult', 'fantasy' (or 'dream') and 'reality'. But to do so, it must counter a potential obscuring of such meanings and relations: the initial narrative movement from fictional reality to fantasy raises the possibility of regressive slippage from adulthood to an idealized realm of childhood. But if the ending abjures such childhood, relegating it to a mere stage in the progress toward adult selfhood, the ending also confesses the attraction of childhood for adults. The return seems to relegate to the child (as subject and reader) the desire for fantasy, but at the same time it expropriates these desires, as well as the child as subject, for possibly conflicting adult projects, such as socialization and escape. Well or thinly concealed is the fact of fantasy as object of adult desires and as response to adult anxieties and wishes. The closural narrator may be an idealized adult purveyor of controlled fantasy – that is, fantasy as therapeutic or monitory for the nominal child audience or as merely playful entertainment. The same closural narrator may also be an image of the adult consumer of fantasy, with the child as a projection of the regressive adult.

M. M. Bakhtin's observation about novelistic closure may be applicable here. In postmythic literature, the 'absence of internal conclusiveness and exhaustiveness creates a sharp increase in demands for an external and formal completedness and exhaustiveness, especially in regard to the plotline' (Bakhtin 1981: 31). The official discursive thrust of children's literature in particular is toward linear plotting leading to a conventionally closed ending. Socialization plots tend to present life-process transitions as manageable; the traditional role of adults and of adult institutions *vis-à-vis* the child is virtually defined as the regulation of the transitional state of childhood. Writing for children thus permits the adult to recuperate the familiar – the authorized quality of folk, mythic and ritualistic discourse – and to link slippery modern culture to the lost wholeness and stability of an imagined (and largely imaginary) past. The self-doubt and anxiety behind such recuperative desire are particularly evident in the most problematic of the narrative transitions, the ending: the point at which we are invited to relax our attentiveness and interpretive energy and at which, for that very reason, the greatest demands are placed on our understanding.

The return seems to offer the reassuring concept of reality as that which is familiar and ordinary, that which loyally awaits our return even though we turn from it. But such a cosy view points to reality's idealized, simplified, fictional status. There is of course a never eliminable gap between extraliterary reality and the fictional reality of the realistic frame segments. The separate fictional realms of the frame and the central narrative may suggest a fixed hierarchy of realities, with extraliterary reality supreme, the fantasy narrative at the lowest level of reality, and the fictional reality of the frame segments in the middle and possibly mediating between the other two. But this hierarchy is unstable: the fantasy may satirize the reality claims of ordinary modes of perception and experience, and the frame reality may be more consoling and escapist than the preceding fantasy narrative. The return frame may establish the hierarchy of realities by classifying the foregoing fantasy as dangerously – or safely – remote from extraliterary reality; or it may, ironically, reveal the equal or even deeper fictionality of both literary and extraliterary versions of reality. Thus, instead of restoring or inverting conventional orders of significance, the return may function as the point at which the text most dramatically turns on itself to reveal its duplicities and discords.

Notes

1 Recognizing the double appeal that children's literature has for the adult reader, U. C. Knoepflmacher suggests that the superimposition of outward frames or bridges may reflect the author's conflicts of intention and selfhood (Knoepflmacher 1983: 500).

Humphrey Carpenter (1985: 11, 13) and Peter Coveney (1967: 31) characterize children's literature as an escapist exercise for adult authors. Christopher Clausen offers as a taxonomic criterion for the genre the thematics of home, often in the form of a closural return, and sees the homecoming as the fulfilment of an escapist impulse, a retreat to safe domesticity. So considered, is the return an escape from fantasy rather than from reality? I take up this question in discussing the *Alice* books later in this essay. Eric S. Rabkin defines literary fantasy as 'the continuing diametric reversal of the ground rules within a narrative world' (Rabkin 1976: 73). Fantastic reversal is both escape from and constant reminder of the world diametrically escaped (ibid.: 48), presumably the extratextual world as well as the narrative locus. He does not discuss the frame-narrative structure but does consider the use of a nominal child audience for adult fantasy projects (ibid.: 96, 97).

Tzvetan Todorov derives the literary fantastic from characters' and readers' 'uncertainty' regarding the laws that govern reality (Todorov 1973: 25). Presumably, a closural return to reality would eliminate the fantasy element by resolving the uncertainty. Todorov is in fact unclear in discussing closure as a generic determinant. At one point he seems to define the fantastic as an 'evanescent genre' whose attributes may well dissipate at closure – for example, at an awakening that dispels the fantasy (ibid.: 42). But, he also argues, by restoring the hero or the reader to reality's rule, the ending retroactively defines the foregoing narrative as the uncanny, not the fantastic (ibid.: 41). Even more problematic is Todorov's narrowly cognitive approach, which leads him to characterize the fantastic as evidence of, and thus somehow party to, premodern repressive discourse; the fantastic becomes anachronistic when replaced by a more liberal discourse, that is, by psychoanalysis (ibid.: 160). Clearly, his limited view of the usefulness of the fantastic seems to stem from the positivist notion that defines symbolic discourse as primitive and sees analytical-rationalist discourse as progressive and superior. Further, Todorov dismisses the capacity of the literary fantastic to question the normatively real and even insists, against massive evidence to the contrary, that the fantastic died with the nineteenth century. For him, the very positing of a dichotomy like language/reality or real/unreal is naive, so that fantasy writing cannot avoid postulating the very reality it attacks (ibid.: 166–8). In contrast, I believe that fantasy writing in general and children's fantasy writing in particular continue to flourish and to generate critical and theoretical responses such as Todorov's precisely because fantasy both collaborates in the ongoing invention of reality and teases us with the possibility of refusal.

2 Most critics of fantasy literature have minimized or misread the significance of the frame device. T. E. Apter believes that works set in a realm separate from 'our world' do not qualify as fantasy literature. He does not consider the possibility that the separation of the fantasy narrative from the realistic frame may heighten, not diminish, the effect of the fantasy. Rosemary Jackson is interested in fantasy's subversive thrust and in the dream of fantasy as a doomed escape from sociocultural reality. Jackson observes that fantasy texts often express desire first by manifesting it and then by expelling it (Jackson 1981: 4). Does the return to reality mark such a shift? Following Todorov, she excludes literary works that provoke no true ambiguity of response (ibid.: 144) or that legalize fantasy by a framing device that neutralizes its force. She does not examine how the frame, by providing a safe 'cover story', enables fantasy to function transgressively. J. R. R. Tolkien also excludes dream tales from true fantasy literature, because they 'cheat' the reader of 'imagined wonder' (Tolkien 1964: 19).

3 For Jacqueline Rose, the meaning of language in children's literature and the reality of cultural categories such as child and adult are open to question (Rose 1984: 1). Her study centres on the adult's desire revealed 'in the very act of construing the child as object of its speech' (ibid.: 2). She considers the 'cover-up' aspect in children's literature, as I do, and emphasizes the way children's literature conceals its instrumentality in repressing adult desire.

In an essay especially pertinent to the present study, Knoepflmacher discusses the endings in children's books centring on a journey and in adult books featuring child travellers (Knoepflmacher 1988). The closures of such works are inevitably problematic: while the journey provides a gratifying delay in socialization, the closural return 'necessarily reactivates questions about goals and directions, about the very teleology of growth' (ibid.: 48). 'Endings . . . inevitably compel us to reassess the journey we undertook with our child or childlike agents' (ibid.: 49).

4 In a much cited study of fairy tales, Bruno Bettelheim eloquently asserts the therapeutic power of the genre. Although he dismisses the bulk of children's literature (Bettelheim 1978: 4), his descriptive-prescriptive view of fairy tales clearly derives in part from a long tradition of writing for children that aims at helping them grow up in the way adults think they should. For Bettelheim, literary fantasy is a legitimate cultural-collective extension of a child's actual fantasizing; but since personal fantasy may be inadequate, the fairy tale may assist in carrying out the psychosocial work of fantasy. He points out that the fairy-tale hero typically returns to reality at the story's end ('a happy reality, but one devoid of magic'); thus the tale teaches the child that 'permitting one's fantasy to take hold of oneself for a while is not detrimental, provided one does not remain permanently caught up in it. . . . As we awake refreshed from our dreams, better able to meet the tasks of reality, so the fairy story ends with the hero returning, or being returned, to the real world, much better able to master life' (ibid.: 63).

D. W. Winnicott's concept of transitional objects and phenomena should be mentioned here. An intermediate state between an infant's inability to recognize reality and the child's growing ability to do so is at once illusion and creative play. Eventually, this transitional state is diffused into large cultural fields that are similarly between inner and outer reality: play, dreaming, the arts, drug addiction, fetishism, and criminality (Winnicott 1971: 2–6). Equally necessary for the infant's development is first the illusion of an external reality that corresponds to the infant's own capacity to create and then the disillusion of such an idea. Winnicott distinguishes between creative play, which carries on the never completed task of accepting reality, and escapist fantasy, which is regressive and dysfunctional (ibid.: 37). Literary and other forms of creative play are for Winnicott, as for Bettelheim, essentially therapeutic, necessary for discovering the self and for adjusting to reality. In this respect, the closural return of literary fantasy could replay the necessary illusion-disillusion process of the infant's education in the ways of reality. For the adult as reader, the literary fantasy could fuel the ongoing process of reality acceptance; for the adult as teacher, literary fantasy may proffer the reassuring notion that reality can be sufficiently mastered to be passed down, as a cultural endowment, to the next generation, to the child reader. The adult writer-reader could enjoy the transitional phenomenon while disavowing a need for it, defining the need as exclusively the child's.

John H. Timmerman's view of literary fantasy, its assumptions and effects (on adults and children), accords with Bettelheim's view of the fairy tale. Offering a relief from structured reality, fantasy in fact enables the reader to engage the ordinary world with clearer insight and sharper perspective, even with renewed faith (Timmerman 1983).

5 Since this essay is intended to be preliminary and suggestive rather than comprehensive or final and since space is limited, it evades the ticklish difficulties of classifying the frame effects of other major children's fantasy works. Some of these works use frame devices not discussed here and not included in the proposed tripartite taxonomy: for example, the absence of the expected return (as in E. B. White's *Charlotte's Web* [1952] or C. S. Lewis's final book of the Narnia series, *The Last Battle* [1956]).

6 In 'Roads half-taken', Knoepflmacher argues that Baum insistently renders Dorothy 'innocent and innocuous' despite her murder of the witch. Unlike Alice, Dorothy rejects 'the imaginative freedom and power accorded to her' by 'a fantasy that validates even more relentlessly than fantasies usually do the ordinary, everyday realm to which the child must return' (Knoepflmacher 1988: 50–1). My view of the Wizard is similar to Knoepflmacher's: '[t]he Wizard stands for a Baum aware of his own limitations as an illusionist humbug who presses chimeras into the service of a gray reality that cannot be evaded' (ibid.: 51); however, Knoepflmacher perceives a tragic subtext in the book, Dorothy's return implying that she will 'grow up as gray-faced as Aunt Em' in a farmhouse destined to be blistered into greyness. Dorothy's fantasy and return sacrifice her 'to a civilized adult reality which neither Dorothy nor Baum dares to repudiate' (ibid.: 52).

7 Gender is an important element in the treatment of the fantasy-reality nexus in children's literature (see such studies as Knoepflmacher's 'Of babylands and Babylons' (1987) and 'Avenging Alice' (1986); especially interesting is his argument that fantasy in Victorian children's literature written by women both permits a female reclaiming of male-colonized literary fields and serves antifantastic ideology (Knoepflmacher 1987: 301)). In *Wizard*, Dorothy's vexed relations with Aunt Em and with the good and bad witches (reminiscent of the good mother–evil stepmother doubles of fairy tales) suggest that the grimness of her perceived reality derives at least partly from her sense of female powerlessness and entrapment. Certainly fantasy, as the locus of satire or as a phase in a *Bildung* plot or as a mapping of a political or psychological unconsciousness, tends to raise a wide range of gender problems. More rarely, as in *The Wind in the Willows*, gender is thematically suppressed, though the suppressing itself is significant. Gender issues cannot be considered here, however, since they would both complicate and confuse the present argument.

8 In his acceptance speech on receiving the 1964 Caldecott Medal, Sendak explained that children use games to combat their vulnerability to their own emotions – emotions that 'they can only perceive as ungovernable and dangerous forces. To master these forces, children turn to fantasy: that imagined world where disturbing emotional situations are solved to their satisfaction.' Max, through fantasy, 'discharges his anger against his mother, and returns to the real world sleepy, hungry, and at peace with himself'. Sendak virtually defines fantasy as a tool for mastering emotions, and he ascribes 'whatever truth and passion' is in his work to his sensitivity toward 'the awful vulnerability of children and their struggle to make themselves King of All Wild Things' (in Cott 1981: 43–4).

9 Comparison between an illustrated text like *The Wizard of Oz* and picture books like Sendak's two works is somewhat difficult, though still possible. While pictures and illustrations both have visual framing contexts (including the frames of supplement and margin) that interact with the narrative frames, the pictures of a picture book produce their own narrative thust, equalling or surpassing that of the literary narrative (consider Beatrix Potter, Laurent de Brunhoff and Chris Van Allsberg). The frame effects of such pictures, forming part of the adult reader's understanding of the narrative, cannot be safely ignored; though I do not focus on the significance of the visual framings (including cover illustrations), no discussion of Sendak, for example, can avoid some mention of them. See Selma G. Lanes's remarks on the generic differences between illustrated text and picture books and on Sendak in particular (Lanes 1971: Chs 4 and 5).

10 Donald Rackin's argument intersects at some points with my own (Rackin 1982). In both *Wonderland* and *Looking-Glass*, Alice's 'progress' is toward denial of her frighteningly vivid dream perceptions (whose chaos and violence Rackin attributes to the sense of disorder and aimlessness associated with post-Darwinian concepts of nature). Alice stops dreaming to avoid further confrontation with the void. 'At the end of each book, she has the good sense . . . to run away, to deny and suppress her own true nightmares.' Denying 'the validity of adventures that have all the luminosity of our truest experiences' (ibid.: 18–19), the endings reject the vision of anarchy and choose reality. Yet because reality, the mode of civilized order (tea, pets), is isolated from and discontinuous with the truths of the dream vision (ibid.: 20), it is presumably an inadequate response to that vision. The awakenings define as mere nonsense what both Alice and the reader have experienced as reality; yet the frame realms are eggshell-fragile verbal structures that adumbrate the modern artist's efforts to shape a vision of horror into game and adventure (ibid.: 22–3).

Rackin's eloquent 'Love and death in Carroll's *Alices*' (Rackin 1987) focuses on the eighth chapter of *Looking-Glass* ('It's my own invention'), where Carroll as the White Knight prepares to lose his Galatea to adult reality. Rackin implies that the return effects a final anti-*Bildung* rupture between child and adult, a rupture in which fantasy is revealed as a doomed, ineffectual effort to appropriate childhood.

11 As William Empson points out, '[T]he triumphant close of *Wonderland* is that [Alice] has outgrown her fancies and can afford to awake and despise them'. *Looking-Glass* ends on a similar note. Both endings 'clearly stand for becoming grown-up and yet in part are a revolt against grown-up behaviour'. He adds, 'I remember feeling that the ends of the books were a sort of necessary assertion that the grown-up world was after all the proper one; one did not object to that in principle, but would no more turn to those parts from preference than to the "Easter Greeting to Every Child That Loves Alice" (Gothic type).' The endings have made some children cry 'at such a betrayal of the reality of the story' (Empson 1950: 270).

See Jan B. Gordon on the anti-*Bildung* aspects of the *Alices* (Gordon 1987: 26), though he still classifies *Wonderland* as a *Bildungsroman* (in contrast to *Looking-Glass* as a *Künstlerroman*). Nina Auerbach contrasts Alice to other Victorian heroines who do not truly develop. Even Jane Eyre and Maggie Tulliver remain idealized feminine figures, instruments of grace for their beloved men. Auerbach praises Carroll's sympathetic probing of the female psyche in Alice, who is allowed to remain 'hungry and unregenerate' (Auerbach 1987: 44). It is not quite clear whether Auerbach sees Alice as developing in some sense or as resisting conventional schemes of female *Bildung*.

12 *The Enchanted Castle* features a more extensive, complex and playful treatment of closural return than do Nesbit's better-known fantasies for children: *Five Children and It*, *The Phoenix and the Carpet* and *The Story of the Amulet*. Limited space precludes a comparison between the closures in these books and in *The Enchanted Castle*, rather a neglected classic. Julia Briggs notes that wishing in *The Enchanted Castle* is more dangerous than in *Five Children and It*, where the effects of wishes wear off at sunset (Briggs 1987: 265). Noel Streatfeild, herself a popular and prolific children's writer in a semirealistic mode, notes that in no other work by Nesbit is the nearness of a magic world to the everyday world so clearly felt as it is in *The Enchanted Castle* (Streatfeild 1958: 127); Streatfeild also stresses the book's uniquely macabre element, the Ugly-Wuglies (ibid.: 131). Again, space does not allow a fuller exploration of their significance, but they are clearly nightmarish, menacing adult figures, made up of the detritus of ordinary adult life (mops, brooms, umbrellas; politeness, respectability, the desire for a really good hotel) and mangling polite adult speech with their roofless mouths. More to the point here, they first appear as the audience and patrons of the children's home-made theatre. The figures are made by the children themselves, perhaps as a sly inversion of the adult 'manufacture' and colonization of childhood. Briggs suggests that they symbolize the malevolent dead, as well as another kind of horror, 'the

emptiness of the bourgeoisie' (Briggs 1987: 266). Either way, they represent adulthood as a monstrous emptying out of self, whether through socialization or ageing; the children regard these parodic human beings with fear and loathing, while the dummies' politeness toward the children thinly conceals an envious hatred.

Knoepflmacher defines Nesbit as an antifantastic fantasist whose ambivalence about the female imagination derives not from the moral concerns of earlier women writers but from personal fears stemming from her childhood (Knoepflmacher 1987: 302). In *The Story of the Amulet*, for example, Nesbit juxtaposes magic and the ordinary world of newspapers, thus mocking 'the impertinence of her own miracle-making'. In her wishful attempts to repair her sense of incompleteness and loss through the agency of a new female magic, 'the writer often saw herself as an impostress of sorts' (ibid.: 321). Briggs points to Nesbit's uncertainty about her own identity – now wanting to pursue 'the child's self-delighting freedom', now seeking 'the adult's greater power to compass her own ends' – and speculates that the origin of this uncertainty may lie in a deeper uncertainty about her femininity (Briggs 1987: xvii). Briggs also suggests that Nesbit's antifantasy, which coexists with celebrations of the fantastic imagination, is rooted in a sort of 'feminine realism' that sets Nesbit apart from male fantasy writers who 'escape into self-contained fantasy worlds' (ibid.: xix, 190).

13 Carpenter notes that *'Peter Pan* . . . manages . . . both to celebrate imagination, and to give a rather chilling warning of its limitations' (Carpenter 1985: 179). Elliott Simon also points out that Never-Never Land (the name of the fantasy locale in the play version) is finally not an antithesis of the adult world but an extension of it (Simon 1978: 227, 229), implying that the problem of how to link fantasy to reality is in fact not solved.

14 Carpenter, discussing the play *Peter Pan*, notes that there 'can be no ending, only a return to the beginning' (Carpenter 1985: 180).

15 On the notion of flight from death as producing an obsession with death, see Norman O. Brown (1959: esp. 88, 95, 249).

16 Simon discusses the sinister and violent quality of the magic of Never-Never Land and comments on Peter's fascination with death (Simon 1978: 228). Andrew Birkin's and Janet Dunbar's biographical studies (Birkin 1979; Dunbar 1970) reveal how Barrie's many versions of *Peter Pan* strangely reflect and even more bizarrely anticipate the deaths of children Barrie knew (the deaths, appropriately, are both literal and figurative, with Barrie himself providing the chief example of figurative death). For a traditional psychoanalytical view of Barrie's fantasy locales and figures, see Geduld 1971, especially pp. 53–67.

17 Jacqueline Rose argues that the adventures in *Peter Pan* are contained 'by the nursery which is the start and the finishing point of the whole story', so that here, as elsewhere in children's literature, the reality frame contains and neutralizes fantasy (Rose

1984: 33). We have seen that the frame may point to other, less reassuring interpretive possibilities, even while seeming to exclude them.

18 A topic for further consideration would be the ways that a particular author experiments with the frame device, either in a series of fantasy works or in separate works. The foregoing discussion of two Sendak picture books offers an abbreviated example of such a study (which, if expanded, should include *Outside, Over There*, the third part of what Sendak himself considered a loose trilogy). The fantasies of Nesbit (noted above) and Travers seem amenable to such a comparative approach, as do Baum's thirteen Oz sequels. Other fantasy serialists might include Mary Norton (the *Borrowers* series) and C. S. Lewis (*The Chronicles of Narnia*). There are of course many individual fantasy works with the frame structure; notable examples include Andersen's 'Snow Queen' and George MacDonald's *At the Back of the North Wind*, as well as the contemporary *A Wrinkle in Time* (Madeleine l'Engle) and Chris Van Allsberg's picture books (especially *Jumanji*, *Ben's Dream*, and *The Wreck of the Zephyr*).

The closural frame of the second Mary Poppins book, *Mary Poppins Comes Back* (1935), is far more consoling than that of the original *Mary Poppins* (1934); similarly, the third book, *Mary Poppins Opens the Door* (1943), where Mary's 'gifts' to the children (including the gift of renewed parental warmth) compensate for her departure. *Mary Poppins in the Park* (1952) and *Mary Poppins in Cherry Tree Lane* (1982) dispense with the frame device entirely and generate dramatic interest by intensifying the liminal quality of their incidents.

3

Internationalism

Because of its position in the literary system, children's literature leans towards internationalism and multiculturalism for several reasons. There is the supposed universality of at least some aspects of 'childhood' (or early youth), the educative/ acculturalizing role of children's literature in many societies, and the positioning of the 'universal' folk/fairy tale in children's literature. Consequently, the criticism has tended both to deal with the literature of many cultures, as with the Children's Literature Association in North America or the Institut für Jugendbuchforschung at Frankfurt am Main; or actually to organize itself internationally, as with the International Research Society for Children's Literature, the International Board on Books for the Young or the Internationale Jugendbibliothek at Munich.

Some of the pressures are, as Margaret Kinnell has pointed out, pragmatic – within the UK, teachers of children's literature (as well as teachers of children) are facing increasingly multicultural audiences. There are also 'questions about the cultural "ownership" of children's literature'. More positively,

> At the 'macro' level, children's books are seen as an invaluable means of spreading international understanding – what Paul Hazard termed 'the world republic of childhood' provides a powerful metaphor of internationalism, expressing the universal belief that children share much in common [Hazard 1947]. And more, their literature offers access to this sharing of values, norms, and experiences, just as it also offers a means of understanding cultural disparity.
>
> However, there is a real risk of – at best – platitudinising and at worst, manipulation of various kinds, when children's books are assessed in terms of their utility value in furthering the grand design of enhancing under-

standing. In any event, broad agreement at this level that comparative studies are to the general good can be assumed: the part they play in developing more clearly focussed insights at the 'micro' level of national literatures is however perhaps more contentious. (Kinnell 1987: 161, 162)

The issues involved are complex, ranging from the blandness of 'Europublishing' – that is, the production of (predominantly) picture books in large editions, allowing different languages to accompany the pictures – to the way in which different countries have widely differing concepts of childhood. As Birgit Dankert observed at the first international conference of the International Youth Library in 1988: 'Quite clearly and with few exceptions, the internationalism of research results in children's literature has been until now a form of peaceful but mutually oblivious co-existence – instead of a scheme of integrated projects, research focuses and reports' (Dankert 1991: 28). The fact that we must be very careful in assuming any cultural universals, or congruities of thought is illustrated by Dankert's description of the development of children's literature in Africa.

1. In addition to many other cultural 'achievements', the former colonial powers also introduced children's books to Africa. These cultural imports elicited then (and elicit still today) the same ambivalent mixture of respect and rejection which characterizes African reactions to so many other borrowings from former colonial powers.
2. The newly independent African states have placed great emphasis on expanding educational systems. School books, 'readers' and the like, which have always been a legitimate part of children's and youth literature, are therefore gaining considerable significance.
3. Increasing literacy leads to a growing book market. This attracts the interest of multinational publishing companies that export European, Anglo-American and superficially Africanized children's books to African countries, both for school use and for leisure reading (or they have them produced through their African subsidiaries). This kind of uncontrolled, which is to say strictly market economy governed, proliferation of originally English-lan-

guage children's books has been described by Sheila Ray in her study *The Blyton Phenomenon*. [Ray 1982]

4. African governments draw upon the oral tradition – also in its new printed form – to engender African awareness, nationalist feeling, and a sense of culture transcending tribal boundaries. Children's books are just one tool among others to this end.

5. African authors often emulate their colleagues in more prolific literary nations and therefore include children's books in their creative repertoires.

6. International organizations involved in developmental aid, cultural exchange, and the promotion of literature are avid supporters of African children's literature at their various conferences . . . without really ever considering whether this position is justified in an African context. If arguments in favor of children's books are brought up, then they resemble those of the early years of European children's literature: that children's books should educate, that they should preserve folk culture, that they should help guarantee Africa's transition to a culture of the written word, that they should support African cultural identity. (Dankert 1991: 23–4)

It would obviously take a whole book to unpack the literary and social implications of that statement. Dankert's view was that in the long term, children's literature – and especially its librarians – should emulate the sciences in establishing reliable international databases and information links, rather than making premature judgements about universals.

Certainly we should beware of assuming that psychological insights (Freudian, for example) have anything more than relatively local applications. Similarly, we should take note of Brian Alderson's observations on the relationship between the oral tradition and literary derivatives (given, interestingly enough, at another conference on cross-culturalism, held by the Children's Literature Association in 1987). There is, he notes, a gap

between folktale as told story and folktale as translated artefact – especially folktale as printed story. The intellectual 'processing' that went on (especially among the 'non-professional' participants) as a natural experience in one language was transferred to another, or as spoken word was seen to be acquiring the 'dignity of print', led to various encroachments on the storyteller's tale which inhibited its original spontaneity. Worries about the cruelties or the inequalities so rife in folktales threatened bowdlerization. The directness of speech rhythms was felt to be not dignified enough to appear in a printed book. In other words there was a perceived difference between 'traditional' works and more self-consciously 'composed' works which points towards a fundamental distinction that has to be made between what happens in the ever-approachable traditional tale and what happens in literature. (Alderson 1987: 6)

Cultural differences are profound; it may not even be possible to approach traditional stories directly, as Rhonda Bunbury has noted of Australia: 'Even today, there are groups of Aboriginal people who choose not to reveal the stories for publication in the Western world because they fear translation and print will reduce the meaning and significance of the stories once they are taken out of their cultural context. . . . The intricate and deeply symbolic secret sacred stories cannot be reflected in publications as they are not for "outsiders" ' (Bunbury 1988: 1, see also Bunbury 1986: 42–3).

Moore and MacCann, in their discussion of Harris's 'Uncle Remus' stories, quote Roger D. Abrahams's introduction to his *African Folktales*:

The very fact of collecting and codifying . . . invariably distorts the 'meaning' of a story. . . . Too often we forget that as Westerners, we learn these stories through books that underscore their imaginative and imaginary qualities [sic]. Equal emphasis should be placed on their effect on and importance to human interaction. (Abrahams 1983: 18)

It is this value gap that leads to Moore and MacCann's rejection of John Goldthwaite's support of Harris as preserver of the Negro folk tales (Goldthwaite 1985):

Contrary to the claim that without Harris the tales would have been lost, it can be argued that his minstrel-evoking dialect made them objects of mockery and hence more difficult to collect after 1880. . . . For more than a century the 'flow of story' had not been interrupted; the original conditions that generated and fostered storytelling were still in evidence in post-Civil War America: isolating racial oppression, multi-generational family structures, the historical verbal emphasis. . . . In 1880, violence against blacks was on the increase. The cunning schemes and victories of Brer Rabbit were as pertinent as ever. In fact, storytelling did not seriously falter until modern gadgetry – radio, movies, TV – began to usurp the functions of the story ritual. (Moore and McCann 1986: 98)

It is in this complex context that Rhonda Bunbury (an Australian) and Reinbert Tabbert (who teaches in Germany), undertook their empirical work. A rare example of international co-operation (by correspondence over four years), the work considered 'reader response to a popular Australian children's book that had been translated into German, Randolph Stow's *Midnite*. The main themes for investigation were: how do child readers in Australia and Germany respond to the ironic humour of this rather sophisticated book? Also, what effect might translation have on reader response?' Significantly enough, this research, first presented at the IRSCL Congress in Cologne in 1977, first appeared in article form in the *International Review of Children's Literature and Librarianship* in Summer 1988, and was reprinted, with revisions, in *Children's Literature in Education* (20 (1) 1989: 25–35).

Rhonda Bunbury is a lecturer at Deakin University, and has worked extensively with Aboriginal communities in the Northern Territory of Australia; Reinbert Tabbert teaches English at the College of Higher Education in Schwaebisch Gmuend and children's literature at the College of Librarianship in Stuttgart.

A Bicultural Study of Identification: Readers' Responses to the Ironic Treatment of a National Hero
Rhonda Bunbury and Reinbert Tabbert

In considering child reader response to Randolph Stow's *Midnite* in Australia and Germany, we explore four main issues. First we revisit the bushranger in Australian history and literature. Second, we explore the national and universal appeal of bushranging in the central character of Randolf Stow's *Midnite*. Third, we draw on the theoretical aspects of a reader's identification with literary heroes through the work of Hans Robert Jauss. Finally, we explore responses of specific readers, both child and adult, to the ironic presentation of *Midnite*. The second and final parts of the paper are based on taped interviews we conducted in both Germany and Australia. We each used the same questions as starters for the empirical research.

Bushrangers in history and literature

Bushranging was a regular occurrence in Australia during the early days of the colony: those who took up this way of life were known to steal horses and cattle or rob the wealthy squatters in other ways. (These same squatters were wealthy graziers who had helped themselves to – or stolen, some would say – vast tracts of land during the early colonial days.) The bushrangers, who have been popularized through literature and the arts, are those whom history has recorded as 'the wild colonial boys', and who were seen to be most active during the gold rushes of the 1850s. These young men, who shared a contempt for – rather than fear of – authority, were all 'freemen' born in Australia, as distinct from those of an earlier era who were already convicted felons. These freemen, for one reason or another, chose bushranging as a 'career'. History books speak of them as being 'proud and untamed rather than desperate or downtrodden' (Prior et al. 1966: 4). Some turned to the bushranging life for adventure, while others were driven to the life of an outlaw by corrupt police who were known to work outside the law themselves, especially since many other troopers had left their jobs in search of quick riches at the gold diggings. The outcome was the same for the bushrangers whether they turned to bushranging for adventure or out of desperation: death by hanging, or being shot 'on the run'. Were they rogues and criminals or were they heroes worthy of being eulogized? People are still divided today when discussing bushrangers.

Most often, however, bushranger stories underplay the harrowing aspects of a bushranger's life. Instead, the short but adventurous life of the bushranger is romanticized, as in the ballad of 'The Wild Colonial Boy':

Then, come all my hearties, we'll range the mountain side;
Together we will plunder, together we will ride.
We'll scour along the valleys and gallop o'er the plains,
We scorn to live in slavery bowed down by iron chains.

(Edwards 1976: 405)[1]

One of the most famous of the bushrangers was Ned Kelly (1855–80). He was hanged at the age of twenty-five. When captured during his 'last stand', Kelly was asked why he had kept shooting at the police rather than escape. He replied, 'A man would be a nice sort of a dingo to walk out on his mates'. In a land where 'mateship' is so highly valued, Kelly has become a hero for his loyalty and his courage. The stealing of horses and cattle and the shooting of several policemen are details which seem to be overlooked. Instead he is perceived as a man whose family and friends were unjustifiably persecuted by police. And in idiomatic Australian English it is still a compliment to be called 'as game as Ned Kelly'. Many are the songs, poems, plays and novels about him. *Sister Kate* by Jean Bedford (1982) is a novel which tells the Kelly story, a story of victimization by the law, written with sympathetic insight and compassion; it portrays the suffering endured by the women of the Kelly family.

Some nonfiction books published for children try to set the record straight. Michael Dugan, for instance, writes: 'Bushrangers like Ned Kelly have become folk heroes like Jesse James and Billy the Kid. None of them really did anything to deserve their fame' (Dugan 1978). Garry Disher (1984) outlines the means by which bushrangers met their end: death in the bush, execution, shot dead, betrayed, flogging, prison, or simply falling behind the times (thanks to telegraph communication). He then asks, 'Were the bushrangers good guys or bad guys?' And in case the answer is not what he has been working towards, he nominates four vile deeds which the songs, poems and stories forget. Such prose, however, is not heard, in comparison with the more dominant voice of such writers as Rita Spencer:

> The Kelly legend is built on the undeniable fact that a deep sense of injustice drove Ned Kelly to fight authority, this is what made him a great Australian hero. He rebelled against the system that so harshly convicted his father to exile and sent his mother to gaol, that permitted

corrupt police to trap innocent people in a web of lies, that gave the best land to wealthy squatters and left the poor to survive as best they could. He rebelled against a system that meant that Australians did not run their own country. (Spencer 1985: 29)

Such is the literary and historical backdrop for many readers of Randolph Stow's *Midnite* (1967), published for children.[2] The story ridicules a national myth of heroism. Captain Midnite appears to be the most notorious bushranger in Australia more than a hundred years ago. In reality within the story he is a stupid, but strong and good-natured boy of seventeen who, after his father's death, was urged by his clever Siamese cat to turn to bushranging. Besides the cat, the master mind behind it all, other members of his 'gang' are a horse, a cow, a dog and a cockatoo. And there is also an antagonist: Trooper O'Grady, who as a policeman, catches Midnite and at the same time picks his pockets and confesses to be his best friend. Midnite is put into prison three times, but his animals can always be trusted to set him free. When he discovers gold in the Australian desert, Queen Victoria, who outlawed the bushranger, turns to honouring a man who has become a millionaire. Miss Laura, Midnite's sweetheart, who was enthusiastic about the notorious hero, but deeply disappointed when she recognized an uncouth boy under his mask, falls for him again. As his wife she makes him 'promise always to do what I tell you, and to have your hair cut when I say, and visit the dentist, and change your shirt', etc. etc. (ibid.: 121). Not only is Stow's book a parody on a myth of heroism, but it also abounds with criticisms and literary allusions.

National and universal appeal of *Midnite*

How dependent is the understanding of *Midnite* on the background knowledge of bushranging and Australian life in general? The Australian children, aged ten to twelve, who were children of long-standing friends of the Australian writer of this paper, were interviewed in their home. They identified many aspects of Australian life which they thought German children could learn something about through *Midnite*. They listed: bushranging, gold mining, early explorers, squatters in history, Cob and Co. coaches, sheep-dog trials, white cockatoos, Aborigines and the landscape. Adults added: the monarchy's admiration of wealth, however acquired; the invitation from royalty sought by colonists; snobbish attitudes about colonial accents; ballads such as the 'Wild Colonial Boy', which are historical records in their way; the tradition of bushrangers being courteous and civil people, generous to the poor and kind to women and children.

Adults also recognized Australian contempt for authority such as the police and the courts and the expectation of their being corrupt, seen in Trooper O'Grady. Also nominated were the eulogy to 'love and mateship' and even Ned Kelly's dying words 'Such is life'; in fact, as one adult reader put it, 'everything except bush fires'. The same adult recalled Captain Starlight in Boldrewood's *Robbery Under Arms* (1888), a well known adventure novel about bushrangers, called a caricature of bushranging by Clune (1948: ix). Captain Starlight was bold, handsome, a 'gentleman' by birth, charming with the ladies and loyal to his mates. Captain Midnite is possibly a parody of Captain Starlight. Where Captain Starlight is quick witted and a smart operator, Midnite is a fool – and knows it.

Australian readers felt that details about Australia are fundamental to an understanding of the book. On the other hand, readers in Germany (both child and adult, who were reading the story in translation) thought the issue to be unimportant, being attracted by the universal qualities of the story line and its fantastic elements. They responded to Midnite, not as a bushranger in particular, but in more general terms as a robber. An eight-year-old enthused about 'a robber who couldn't robber' (he was speaking in German and the translation is literal).

Concepts of identification

Given the popularity of some of the ballads and books focusing on bushrangers, it seems appropriate to consider the Australian variety of the 'noble bandit' as an apt object for identification. But what exactly is *identification*? It is defined by *Webster's Third New International Dictionary* as 'a mental mechanism wherein the individual gains gratification, emotional support, or relief from anxiety by attributing to himself consciously or unconsciously the characteristics of another person or group'.

As far as literature is concerned, Hans Robert Jauss has

pointed out that in the history of European drama, five types of heroes may be distinguished, which suggest five modalities of identification. We believe that two of those modalities are of special interest for the realm of children's literature: 'admiring' identification and 'sympathetic' identification. You may admire Pippi Longstocking just as any demi-god in traditional drama, and you may sympathize with Peter Rabbit just as with any pitiable creature in a naturalistic play. There is, however, something not quite satisfying about Jauss's definition of a sympathetic hero as 'a middling hero whom the spectator can regard as his own sort' (Jauss 1973–4: 307). We tend to think that just as the status or ability of an admired hero is somewhere above that of the reader, the status or ability of a hero we feel pity for is somewhere below. A hero we feel 'sympathy with' is somewhere in between, but the distinction between 'pity for' and 'sympathy with' seems to have become blurred somewhere in the process of translation.

Literary bushrangers may suggest both admiring and sympathetic identification, which can be realized by children and adults alike. Thus Captain Starlight in Boldrewood's *Robbery Under Arms* is too rebellious and too courageous not to be admired, and Ned Kelly and his family in Bedford's adult novel *Sister Kate* have to suffer under the injustice of the authorities to such a degree that they make us feel pity for them. As for bushranger ballads, one type of implied response is often superseded by the other. Thus we may admire the Wild Colonial Boy, who is called 'a daring youth', and sympathize with him when, in the end, he receives 'a mortal wound'.

Different from these classical presentations of the bushranger and the two types of identification which Jauss suggests is Randolf Stow's *Midnite*, which is in a class of its own. In fact, it seems to suggest a third type of identification in Jauss's terms, which he calls *ironic* identification. Referring to the theatre-goer, Jauss has defined it as follows:

The fact that the spectator can succumb to the magical power of illusion and lose himself [sic] in a merely enjoyable identification has led again and again to deliberately breaking the spell of the imaginary and to undermining the aesthetic attitude of the spectator. Such procedures can be classified as ironic identification. In the spectrum of possibilities for aesthetic identification with the hero, this is the norm-breaking function *par excellence*. (Jauss 1973–4: 297)

In a way, what Jauss is talking about is a dual response: identification and nonidentification at the same time. He says: 'Precisely the non-identification with what is presented is meant to produce a thinking observer' (ibid.: 314). This is a good description of what Brecht wanted to achieve by means of the 'alienation effect'. However, his Mother Courage, who loses all her children by attempting to profit from the war, may more often have been responded to with pity than with critical reflection.

Randolf Stow's story of a wild colonial boy makes use of 'romantic irony' rather than of the Brechtian alienation effect. As the *Dictionary of Literary Terms* says,

> the romantic ironist detaches himself from his own artistic creation, treating it playfully or objectively, thus presumably showing his complete freedom . . . The use of contradictory elements or moods within the work . . . allies romantic irony to the modern critical use of the term paradox. (Barnet et al. 1960: 52)

This definition of romantic irony may help to emphasize that an author's attitude which leads to a suggestion of ironic identification affects not only the central character of a book, but also aspects of the fictional world he or she lives in. Correspondingly our investigations have confirmed that the way a reader responds to the central character has its equivalents in the way he responds to various aspects of the fictional world.

Responses of real readers

We now come to the interesting question: how do real readers respond to the suggestion of ironic identification? Is it a type of identification which can be experienced by children at all? Hans Heino Ewers tends to deny this. 'Unlike adult literature,' he says, 'children's literature does not seem to allow its authors to reclothe its old heroes . . . to parody, to satirize, to treat them ironically, or to make them look foolish. . . . Such reinventions are simply confusing to naive readers' (Ewers 1985: 70, 74). Is this really true? On the basis of what our interviewees told us about their responses to *Midnite*, we have at least strong reservations about this. As mentioned above, Australian children definitely recognized Captain Midnite as a variation of the traditional image of the bushranger. German children were capable of responding to him as a funny divergence either from what a robber or what a hero is supposed to be like. Of course, this does not necessarily mean that they acknowledge him in the proper terms of a parody, recognizing all the elements of caricature.

There is one eleven-year-old boy among our interviewees whose response to *Midnite* even seemed to be in accordance with Jauss's definition of ironic identification. Maybe Thomas's response is an exception. He is the bilingual son of a French mother and a German father, both of them academics. Thomas was enthusiastic about the book, because 'it's beautifully written'. What is particularly striking in his answers is an overruling sense of the ambiguities and paradoxes of the book: 'Midnite really doesn't behave like a bushranger. . . . He is always in between. . . . This reminds me of *Tartarin de Tarascon*. Quite peaceful or quite furious. He assaulted them and was very polite. Funny. . . .' And with reference to the Trooper: 'On the one hand he is Midnite's best friend. On the other hand, he shamelessly takes advantage of him'. And so to the genre of the books: 'As it is *told* it is rather a story [which for him means that "the things could have happened"]. But the way it is *written* it is a little like a fairy tale, somehow.'

Thomas seems to have the introspective ability to sense a similar ambiguity in his own response: 'I think the author writes the book so that you are the invisible observer.' His reason for this observation is that the author is not using the first person. Thomas is capable of quite a different response. When he was reading Astrid Lindgren's *Mio, my Mio*, he said, 'I was completely inside the story.' The interviewer asked: 'And you wouldn't say that about this book? There you are the observer, you said.' 'Yes, but you are also part of it. I see myself as one of the gang – but one who is not mentioned. It's quite curious.' This is perhaps as close as a child can get to a description of ironic identification, where the child reader sustains both the intense involvement which comes with 'identification' as well as the (less frequent?) and more distanced stance of the spectator.

If Thomas is an exception in expressing a sort of dual

response to the main character, almost all the children seemed to notice some elements of paradox or contradiction in Stow's book. Usually such observations are embedded in a series of simpler responses, as in the conversation of three Australian children, aged ten, eleven and twelve years, who in recalling their pleasure in reading the book, nominated such situations as the following:

> Mathew: I liked how all the ladies liked Midnite then Miss Wellborn didn't like him when she saw his face.
>
> Andrew: I liked it after Midnite had been bushranging. Trooper O'Grady came and bushranged him (in return).
>
> Rebecca: I liked it when Gyp (the dog) stopped and looked puzzled in the middle of rounding up the sheep – as though he had forgotten how to do sheep dog trials.

Each of these situations the children found funny, and they were content to recall them. Trying to explain *why* these events were funny was not a fruitful activity.

When the researchers gently probed for fuller responses from the children, it was evident that the children were able to articulate their responses. The different levels of children's responses to literature have been more fully explored elsewhere by one of us (Bunbury 1980), interviewing children aged seven, nine and eleven years, who responded to short stories, folk tales and poems. Here we analyse responses within a Piagetian framework. An extract from their conversation about *Midnite* reveals the children's different capacities for understanding complexities of the book. Ten-year-old Rebecca sees Trooper O'Grady in simple terms as 'breaking a promise'. Twelve-year-old Mathew interprets these same activities as 'corrupt'; which is much more akin to an adult interpretation, though it falls short of the explicit recognition of parody:

> Rebecca: Midnite was silly, but he was a nice person. He does what everyone tells him to do, except for Trooper O'Grady.
>
> Andrew: Trooper O'Grady wanted to be his friend all the time.

Researcher:	Was it a good thing that Midnite wanted to be friends with Trooper O'Grady?
Rebecca:	· In a way, but Trooper O'Grady took things off people. The Trooper was silly.
Researcher:	You used the same word 'silly' to describe both Midnite and Trooper O'Grady, what do you mean by silly?
Rebecca:	Midnite doesn't know anything.
Andrew:	Trooper O'Grady seems smart. He took the carriage off Midnite and pick-pocketed people.
Rebecca:	He broke a promise.
Mathew:	He was corrupt.
Andrew:	He said he was Midnite's friend but Trooper O'Grady put Midnite in gaol.
Researcher:	You also told me Dora the cow was stupid.
Andrew:	She let people think so but she brought all the other cows in when bushranging.
Rebecca:	She's not silly really, just older than she thinks she is.

Here the children are generally experiencing what Jauss would call sympathetic identification where the hero, Midnite, is actually recognized as silly or foolish – yet friendly and likeable enough. The children are very much involved with the story. As J. R. R. Tolkien once wrote, 'Children are capable of literary belief . . . when the storymaker's art is good enough to produce it. . . . That state of mind has been called willing suspension of disbelief' (Tolkien 1966: 36). In fact, what Tolkien is referring to is an important prerequisite not only of admiring and sympathetic identification, but also of ironic identification. Two of the adults we interviewed were not willing to suspend their disbelief. '*Midnite* is about bushranging, and bushranging isn't funny' and 'I just couldn't get interested in the story. I only read it because my children were reading it for you.'

Jill, a twenty-nine-year-old mother of two young children, responded with ease to *Midnite*: 'Maybe to a certain degree . . . you sympathize with him when Miss Laura is so beastly to him', and 'He is the sort of character that I would like to get hold of and shake about.' Perhaps some motherly feelings are involved in this reaction, as they explicitly are in her moral objections to violence in the book: 'Maybe we think too much as adults, but . . . the whole philosophy behind bushranging, that for me would be very questionable'. Jill enjoyed the book, but not in terms of ironic identification as Thomas did. 'It's a book which makes you smile. What appealed to me most was the witticisms.' A story which on the one hand is full of literary references and on the other hand is published as a children's book makes an adult like Jill aware both of her professional training as a teacher and her role as a parent, thus preventing a purely naive abandon to 'literary belief'.

It might seem as if children are better prepared for practising ironic identification than adults. But this is not really true. One of the Australian adults, Joan, a sheep grazier's wife and a seventy-year-old grandmother, became joyfully engaged with the characters. She laughed at the typically Australian way of seeing the trooper and the judge as 'the bad ones'. She took pleasure in the situational humour of the gang of animal friends terrorizing the countryside because, 'They all get their comeuppence in the end.' She appreciated the humour of the language and quoted: 'O'Grady was promoted so he could be an appropriator.'

'Now that isn't for children,' she concluded. Yet she was able to distance herself sufficiently from the story to be able to talk about *Midnite* as a parody of Australian values: the contemptuous response to authority figures of law and order; the mythologizing of bushrangers; the valuing of mateship. For her, these were the most entertaining aspects of the book even though she had been fully engaged with the story and had shared this experience with her children and grand-children. Joan's response was therefore a dual one. In Jauss's terms, she was simultaneously engaged in identification and nonidentification, hence 'the thinking observer'.

Having considered the national and international appeal of *Midnite*, the bushranger, and how this affected child and adult readers, we would like to leave open the issue of how capable children are of practising ironic identification. We have con-sidered a range of responses, from naive child readers, to responsive child readers, to adults who could not identify with the book at all and those who thoroughly enjoyed the process. The best we can say is that the capacity to experience ironic identification extends along a spectrum of reading encounters which vary in intensity. We would argue that those who are capable of fully understanding and responding to the ironic layers of meaning are the richer for it. We hope that further research on this topic will be stimulated.

Notes

1 The reference is to Alphonse Daudet's *Les Aventures prodigienses de Tartarin de Tarascon* (1872). *The Encyclopaedia Britannica*, Macropaedia, Vol. 5 (1976), p. 514, mentions 'its adventurous hero . . . as a caricature of naiveté and boastfulness' and 'the antiromantic irony' of the book.
2 Page citations for *Midnite* in the text are from the Puffin edition (1982). In the German part of the study we used the edition *Kaept'n Mitternacht*, translated by Sybil Graefin Schoenfeldt, published by DTV, Munich, 1975.

4

Poetry, response and education

An important body of contemporary research on children's literature explores the relationships between the characteristics of texts, the readers' response to the texts, and the relationship of these to education, notably reading skills. Both the theory and the practice has centred around the reading and teaching of poetry, an aspect of children's literature frequently neglected. One reason for this may well be the rift between the concept of poetry inside and outside the classroom. As Alan Tucker, himself a poet, has noted:

> When we come to express emotion, to write down even the simplest thing, we quickly find that language is pitiless. Children should not be led into the front line of a language-governed society believing that if only they feel strongly enough the words will come to them. . . . Contemporary academic poetry (which is most modern poetry) deliberately eschews the content-laden poetry (and idea of poetry) prevalent in school teaching. (Tucker 1989: 108)

Generally, though, a great deal of poetry in one form or another is published for children, and the ostensible attitude of the educational world might be summed up in the words of an expert on reading, Jill Bennett: 'Poetry offers a way of seeing and hearing that no other kind of literature can. Its musical quality draws children, appealing to their senses and their emotions' (Bennett 1984: 1).

The difficulties and challenges involved in bringing poem, child and theory together can be demonstrated in the following extracts from the work of Michael Benton. The first article, 'Poetry for children: a neglected art' appeared in *Children's Literature in Education* in 1978.

Poetry has had bad luck. It has suffered a double misfortune: neglect where it most needs attention and concern where it is best left alone. The neglect can be sensed in various ways. Understanding our praxis in dealing with poems is a useful point of entry. The notion of praxis is not an easy one to live with but, if we are to *change* our teaching behaviour as well as to talk, write and read about doing so, then we had best start here. If Raymond Williams ever wants to extend his *Keywords* in a revised edition, 'praxis' has claims for inclusion, for its evolution of meaning from 'accepted practice' to 'a collection of examples to serve for practice in grammar' to 'a means of practice in a subject' to its current coinage, which includes both practical action and self-awareness, is a measure of the way language shapes and responds to our continuing struggle to relate thought and action.

Handling poetry is the area of the primary/middle school curriculum and the secondary English curriculum where teachers feel most uncertain of their knowledge, most uncomfortable about their methods, and most guilty about both. Nor is the neglect of poetry confined to the individual's reading and teaching habits. In the 1970s we have institutionalized it. There are over 600 pages in the Bullock Report: three and a half pages are given to poetry. How is it possible to entitle this monolith *A Language for Life* and to all but ignore the art in which language is at its most alive? Sadly, the neglect comes closer to home. A skim through the six or seven books on children's literature that have formed a mini-publishing boom in this area during recent years demonstrates the scant attention that has been paid to poetry for children. It is significant that in one of the very few pieces on the subject, Ian Serraillier should begin by expressing his surprise that the 471 pages of *Only Connect* (Egoff et al. 1969) contain nothing about verse for children. . . . Why is it that when we speak of children's literature, we mean fiction and exclude poetry?

The neglect shows both in our knowledge and our pedagogy: the body of this article focuses attention on these areas. Yet it would be foolish to proceed without acknowledging the misplaced concern that commonly fills the vacuum left by our lack of interest in and enthusiasm for poems. The concern I mean is that which leads to 'doing' poetry as a duty, feeling that it should form part of the English curriculum and finding a place for it in utilitarian terms. Having found the time for work on poetry, it is all too easy for the conscientious teacher to approach it with strategies more appropriate to the cognitive areas of the curriculum. Concern as a feeling of disquiet thus has the effect of elevating a series of pragmatic concerns into a teaching method: the anxiety to pin the meaning down, to explain words, to take the class on a guided tour through a poem, enlivening it with metaphor hunts and simile chases, inexorably takes over. Worry about rightness, both of a poem's meaning and of our teaching methods, predominates, and the worry is conveyed to the children so that the classroom ambience of poetry becomes one of anxiety at a difficult problem with hidden rules rather than one of enjoyment of a well-wrought object. 'Poetry begins in delight. . . .' With young children, above all, our rightful concern is with this delight. Concern over understanding in the narrow literal sense that requires explanation, annotation and analysis is misplaced. . . .

There are many reasons for our comparative lack of interest in poetry. Two obvious ones are worth underlining. The Bullock Report expresses the first in terms calculated to perpetuate the malaise:

> It has to be acknowledged that poetry starts at a disadvantage. In the public view it is something rather odd, certainly outside the current of normal life; it is either numinous, and therefore rarely to be invoked, or an object of comic derision.

Keep telling the public that, and they will soon believe it. The cultural commonplace that poetry is a minority art is a useful cover phrase when we wish to avoid the question of who makes up this minority. I suspect that only a small proportion of English teachers are paid-up members. Along with the rest of society, most English teachers find reading fiction, watching film and television or going to the theatre more entertaining pursuits than reading verse. Poetry survives in the gaps, if at all. . . . The other truism about poetry is that generally it requires more effort from the reader. It is harder work to remake a poem in the imagination simply because poetry is the most condensed form of language that we have. By the same token, a child's knowledge of what language is and does will become deeper and more subtle through poetry than through any other form of literature. To deprive children of poems is to deny them the society of clear, single voices and an irreplaceable range of feeling. We neglect poetry at our own peril. We need to know more about what is available and what to do with it (Benton 1978: 111, 112–113, 114).

Benton developed these ideas in a paper submitted as evidence to the Cox Committee on English in the National Curriculum for British schools in the late 1980s: 'The importance of poetry in children's learning'. The paper was subsequently quoted in *English for Ages 5–16* (Cox Report) 1989.

There is a two-fold problem in realizing the power of poetry in children's learning: first, we must understand where that power lies and what poetry does better than any other form of language use; and, secondly, we must reappraise our methods of working with poems in school and, in particular, align them with what we have come to know about the nature of literary response and the relationship between literature and learning.

Writing a few years before I. A. Richards's celebrated work, George Sampson reminds the English teacher that: 'If literature in schools is not a delight, if it is not, in all senses, a "re-creation", an experience in creative reception, it is a failure' (Sampson 1970: 101). Sadly, in subsequent years, the combined forces of the criticism industry and the examination system effectively snuffed out much of this delight. 'Practical criticism' became the method with sixth-formers and undergraduates; comprehension exercises became the lot of school children. In the past decade, however, we have begun to learn how to honour George Sampson's principle and to give poetry back to its readers. Reader-response theory and the particular influence of Louise Rosenblatt's transactional theory have altered the climate of poetry teaching. The development of a methodology that is based upon informed concepts of *reading* and *response*, rather than upon conventional, narrowly conceived ideas of *comprehension* and *criticism*, is now the priority. At the heart of contemporary thinking about classroom method is the uniqueness of the reading event. Comprehension can only develop and criticism can only be well founded if they are rooted in the processes of reading and responding.

Certain operational principles follow from this premise:
(i) Reading a poem is different from reading a story or any

other text. Most poems children encounter are short; the words can be taken in within seconds. Re-readings of lines or verses, changes in pace or tone, sorting out complex syntax, savouring an image or a rhyme – all happen within a small compass and dictate a reading process that is more varied and unpredictable than any other. The meanings lie, as it were, in the spaces around the verses and between the words, as well as within the words themselves. These spaces are ones we inhabit mentally as we 'look at' the text from various viewpoints; rather as, when looking at a piece of sculpture, we often feel impelled to move around the object, thus tacitly acknowledging that the vantage points we adopt and the space in which the object is placed affect our perception and understanding. Granted we initially have to read a poem forwards; nonetheless, our ways-in to its meaning will be many and varied. Exposing children to a lot of poetry, so that they hear, read, write, speak, dramatize and illustrate poems as a regular part of their English lessons, is the essential means to give children a sense of themselves as readers of poems; it is the best way, too, to build reading confidence and create the taste for poetry which many young people seem to lack as they go through secondary school.

(ii) Poems are read with both ear and eye. The distinction here is not simply the functional one between speaking a poem aloud or reading it silently. There are aural and visual dimensions in all poetry reading. If we read well, we cannot stop ourselves sounding the words in the head. With younger children, the fun of rhyming sounds and strongly marked rhythms is easy enough to encourage; as children get older, there is a danger that the visual dominates, that the poems stay print-bound on the page. Performances that lift the words off the page – shared readings, choral speaking, taped radio programmes, etc. – are both exacting disciplines in themselves and ways of keeping children alert to the 'auditory imagination' from which poems are created.

(iii) Giving children access to a wide variety of poetry experiences is essential. It has long been accepted practice that children's own writing should be interleaved with their reading of poetry.

(iv) When it is appropriate to dwell on a poem for discussion or study, the key is to provide time and opportunity for individual reflection. Articulating and reflecting upon personal responses are fundamental to the reader's early apprehension of a poem. Jotting around a text or in a journal helps the reader in attending to his or her own responses. Many poems invite these procedures (Benton 1990: 27, 31–2).

The question of how to adequately theorize the reading of a poem, and how to apply this in practical terms, was confronted in *Young Readers Responding to Poems* (Benton et al. 1988). Benton's opening chapter, 'Exploring response' (extracts from which follow) considers the importance of understanding how meanings are made by poets and evoked by readers as the basis for constructing a methodology for communicating these meanings.

Following Rosenblatt (1970, 1978, 1985), this section attempts to capture the aesthetic phenomenon of evoking and responding to poems. It is an elusive goal best approached not by sequential argument but by 'keeping the aesthetic transaction of poem-reading, as it were, central', and describing it from a number of vantage points. The ten statements developed below are responses to this phenomenon with all the potential for expansion, overlap and contradiction that this implies. . . .

1. The reader is invited to 'look at' a poem yet to 'dwell within' it . . .

Poetry-reading is different from story-reading. For, even though novels invite regular circling back and round, the infinite variety displayed by poem texts signals that the initial responses when compared with those provoked by the predictable, linear ways stories are presented, are likely to be more diverse. . . . The sense of artifice is more immediate. We are aware of looking at something which is drawing attention to itself by the way it is presented. The conscious effort of construction that this sort of 'onlooking' (to use D. W. Harding's word) entails accounts for the heightened spatial awareness we experience when reading most poems. . . .

Yet the poem only yields a meaning if we also 'dwell within' it imaginatively. . . . The indwelling value of the poem becomes available to the reader only if his act of reading includes those features that are integral to the nature of the art form. . . .

2. The reader's stance is both 'efferent' and 'aesthetic'
. . . What actually happens when we take a mental walk around a poem . . . is that we adopt a 'shifting stance'; images,

ideas, associations and feelings dart and flicker in the mind as we move to and fro between the 'efferent' and the 'aesthetic'. For, even when we are free from critical or pedagogic pressure to show a definite 'yield' from our reading of a poem . . . the linguistically condensed nature of poetry is such that the reading process has to be 'efferent' enough for us to carry away a meaning as well as 'aesthetic' enough to give us pleasure.

3. *The reader . . . produces the poem from the text yet reacts to what he produces*

Reading is active and reactive together. With a poem the reader experiences this 'double-take' with peculiar power. . . . The . . . reader engages both in the swift interpreting of the words and the reflective interpreting of his responses to the words. The way words are deployed in poems demands this effort to 'attend twice at once' in Ryle's phrase which, because of its impossibility, typically leaves the reader in limbo, somewhere between the deconstruction of a verbal artifice and the development of a personal response. This is an uncomfortable position for the inexperienced reader. . . . A double demand is being made – to read the words and to read his own sensibilities. . . .

4. *The reader's social relationship may be not only with an implied author but also with the real poet*

. . . The social contract between reader and author is different from that of the novel. . . . In fact, in most poetry, Wordsworth's description of this social relationship as 'a man speaking to men' can be taken at face value. With lyric poems especially, the reader's construct of the implied poet may lead to a growing awareness of the real one. This ambiguous social relationship is itself often implied in the way thinking and feeling are expressed in the voice that addresses the reader.

5. *The reader exercises both an intelligence of thinking and an intelligence of feeling* . . .

Poems are places where thinking and feeling remain unified. Thought may subdue feeling; feeling may overwhelm thought . . . unless the reader receives intelligences from both antennae . . . then the poem will not be evoked.

6. *The reader reads with both ear and eye*

There is . . . a tune on the page to be played and a design in the mind to be explicated. . . . Reading [poems] with the ear, words are performed and celebrated in pursuit of the *experience* of meaning; reading them with the eye, words become windows through which we see *extractable* meanings. . . .

7. *Capturing the 'poem' means playing with words within the discipline of form*

The central paradox of all creative activity is that it grows from both freedom and constraint, the play of the imagination operating, in this case, in the rule-governed medium of language. Creative reading of poems means reading like a writer . . . realising how far the constraints of language and form produce expressive freedom.

8. *Reading a poem is an event in time and an artefact in space*

For a poem to be evoked through the interaction of the reader and the text, it must come into existence in two dimensions. 'A poem should not mean/But be' concluded MacLeish (1963: 50–1), insisting that a poem is not a record of experience but the experience *itself*. Its infinitive is to be, not merely to communicate. Of course, a poem *does* communicate but it achieves a 'double discourse'. . . . It . . . comes into being through time [and] through its spatial relationships.

9. *A reader reads both the parts and the whole together*

[T]he reader's pleasure in a poem derives from his awareness of a qualitative and necessary unity. It is qualitative because the reader's valuing of a poem will depend upon how well its constituent parts cohere. . . . We read through and then re-read; we move to and fro about the poem, savouring some lines, asking questions about others; we look for development in feeling, idea or image, but, above all (or, better, unifying all) we read with the assumption that the composition has been well wrought. . . .

10. *The reader uses both the 'auditory imagination' and the 'narrative imagination'*

Just as Eliot's phrase 'auditory imagination' incorporates the elements of sound and rhythm, so the notion of the 'narrative imagination' includes the elements of imagery and story (Benton et al. 1988: 17–24).

For the complex task of charting how these characteristics of reading poems – perhaps especially the ways in which we 'move to and fro about the poem, savouring some lines, asking questions about others' – Benton and his colleagues have developed an ethnographic approach, stressing the importance of reflexivity, context, and flexibility leading to a theorizing of the process of response (Benton et al. 1988: 27–9; see also Benton 1984). However, he is careful to stress the most exciting, as well as daunting aspect of his project – that aspect that might bring him directly into conflict with literary and educational traditionalists.

The mediation of language is an inadequate and cumbersome way of representing the speed and variety of psychic life. . . . However, these evident difficulties are not different in kind from those that beset other modes of enquiry which depend on inference. Much research tends to value the tidily explained above the dimly apprehended. Yet, in order to study the processes of reader response, we must inevitably work with uncertain data. Fleeting images, half-formed notions, inadequately articulated meanings are the yield of introspective recall. It is important to explore these data with all their imperfections, to resist approaches which, by design, exclude material of potential interest and significance (Benton et al. 1988: 26).

Some of the fascinating and fruitful results of the research by Benton and his colleagues are to be found in *Young Readers Responding to Poems*, together with practical suggestions for the classroom, and Benton has developed his ideas in *Secondary Worlds: Literature Teaching and the Visual Arts* (Benton 1992). (Direct advice for teachers on this subject can be found in *Teaching Literature Nine to Fourteen* (Benton and Fox 1985: 28–32), and in *The Reading Environment* (Chambers 1991).)

Benton has not been alone in exploring these areas. Patrick Dias (1986) has pursued the matter in the classroom, developing 'reading-aloud protocols' and distinguishing four types of reader: paraphrasers, thematizers, allegorizers, and problem-solvers. Another framework for analysis was offered by Barrie Wade for working with poetry. His examination of directed and undirected pupils used the taxonomy of judging, interpreting, retelling, associating and explicating (he also has a miscellaneous category) (Wade 1981: 41–2). His conclusion, though, was scarcely optimistic: 'Hopefully this system of analysing informally what goes on in poetry lessons will bring some increase in awareness, insight and confidence. At the horizon is a light no brighter than a spark' (ibid.: 47).

Far more optimistic is Aidan Chambers, whose work with a group of teachers, although somewhat less systematic than Benton's, parallels his attitudes and ideas. Chambers based his procedure on the four successive post-reading processes of 'saying for yourself, saying for others, saying together, and saying the new' (Chambers 1985: 141–4) and a simple basic principle when working with children:

We learned the benefit of banning from our speech, but not from the children's, the question *why*? Even when a child says something as simple as 'I liked this . . .' or 'I hated that . . .' the teacherly instinct is to ask why. The answer, more often than not, is a shaken head, shrugged shoulders, a loss of enthusiasm, a blank stare that hides a sudden sense of failure. . . . The question why so baldly asked is too big to answer. All the talk is itself an attempt, by answering more specific and manageable questions, finally to discover the answer to the ur-questions *why*? . . . By asking why the teacher confronts the child with the impossible. The magnitude of the task is so daunting the child gives up.

But how to avoid asking why? Our solution, when at last we hit upon it, was not only very simple, but proved a turning point in the reconsideration of our teaching methods, for it gave us a new style . . .

The phrase we hit upon was: *Tell me* (Chambers 1985: 155).

There has also been increasing interest in this area, notably from academics who would not normally have much to do with real children in real classrooms. As Roderick McGillis put it 'Not working directly with children, I must take their responses to literature where I can get them' (McGillis 1985: 5) and it is interesting that McGillis quotes with approval one of the great British educationalists, James Britton.

Speaking of children's responses to stories, Arthur Applebee remarks that many of the details they will give special notice to are 'irrelevant from the adult's point of view – as when *Peter Rabbit* is deemed a sad story because poor Mr McGregor has no lettuce' (Applebee 1978: 100). We could call this response to *Peter Rabbit* naive, and then ask with James Britton: is the 'naive response different in kind from that we desire for literature, or merely different in intensity of feeling or complexity or comprehensiveness or verisimilitude? In other words, are such responses . . . the bad currency we seek to drive out, or are they the tender shoots that must be fostered if there is to be a flower at all? Our aim . . . should be to refine and develop responses the children are already making – to fairy stories, folk songs, television serials, their own game-rhymes, and so on. Development can best be described as an increasing sense of form'. As Britton goes on to say, 'The voice of the critic must not be allowed to seem the voice of authority; more harm has probably been done to the cause of literature by this means than by any other. It is all too easy for the immature student, feeling that his own responses are unaccept-able, to disown them and profess instead the opinions of respected critics' (Britton 1982: 32, 33). We must understand that if our students are to acquire literary competence, they must also have confidence. Let us give our students the confi-dence to express what they already know (McGillis 1985: 4, 6).

Finally, two Australian voices in the debate. The first is Jack Thompson, whose *Understanding Teenagers' Reading* (1987) was one of the most distinctive literary/educational explorations of the 1980s. In an article extending that work, and reporting on an extensive research project, Thompson shifts the emphasis rather more towards the operations of the text.

The most active and reflective teenage readers not only see texts as constructs offering an author's evaluation of human behaviour, but they are also interested in considering the ideo-logical implications of this constructedness, and in reflexively exploring their own identities and reading processes. This reflective and reflexive thinking about the ways texts work as structures of cultural transmission, and about the way they themselves work on texts to interpret them, confers consider-able power on readers. They can direct and control their own thinking when they are conscious of it. Control over their own thinking and over the rhetoric of texts gives them more power to operate effectively in their society.

The importance of readers becoming conscious of their own constructive reading strategies (what I call 'reflexiveness', and is generally called 'metacognition' in the United States) cannot be over-emphasized. It applies to all learning processes, includ-ing reading and writing. One of the most productive and unanticipated findings of the research interviews is that this reflexiveness can be taught at each stage of reading develop-ment.

After reading the opening paragraph of a short story or novel to a group of non-readers, I asked them two questions:
1. What happened in your head while you were listening?
2. What do you think might happen in the story?
All of these students were surprised at the notion that they should be doing anything mentally active. They thought that text operated on readers rather than that readers had to operate on text. They assumed that the minds of good readers automatically processed print into understanding; the fact that their minds didn't seem to do this very well indicated that they were 'bad' readers because they were unintelligent. Asking students what questions they were asking of the text read to them led them to ask productive questions, and the enabling security of the interview situation led them to think aloud while doing so (Thompson 1990: 195).

Thompson is concerned with teenagers; Geoffrey Williams works with younger children, and his work on response and reading development returns us to the text. 'Our culture,' he has observed, 'has taken a peculiar turn when it is necessary to argue for the central place of stories in reading and social education' (Williams 1985: 61) – and not only that, but that such fiction is a subtle contributor to the wealth of readings. Criticism must not only take on board multiple readings, but it must give more respect to the text for children, which is, inevitably, far more complex than is generally acknowledged.

Children's fiction so often *invites* interpretative work because texts are open to subtle interpretations of narrative form and patterns of value, even when the language seems plain enough.

Educational discourse about children's fiction, however, rarely acknowledges either the subtlety, openness or complexity of text. Despite vigorous general discussion of the appropriateness of some titles for children, in primary education we have been rather better at listening to children's interpretations in order to guess about their ability to comprehend than at investigating the complexity of the texts themselves. Yet the *form* of texts from which children are invited to learn to read is crucial to an account of what it is to comprehend them. A theory of how written texts mean which neglects form would be so seriously reductive as to be worthless.

Criticism of children's texts could contribute very usefully to debate over contemporary definitions of literacy and literary competence and to debate about what counts as reading development. For example, with more interpretative explorations of multiple senses in children's texts available it would be possible to address the complex problems of comprehension in new ways. 'To interpret a text,' Barthes remarks in *S/Z*, 'is not to give it a (more or less justified, more or less free) meaning, but on the contrary to appreciate what *plural* constitutes it' (Barthes 1976: 5). Critical discussion of the multiple senses of fiction for children is discourse on which teachers might draw to help children expect multiple senses in all narrative, and to learn to discover some that are latent for themselves. The point is not to teach literary critical concepts such as irony to primary children but to deny the *possibility* that a narrative text could have a single meaning and to change pedagogy appropriately. Power relationships between teacher, text, author and young reader, not to mention standardized test constructor, would be changed considerably if criticism of children's texts were to be more readily available.

The issue has general significance in primary education because the interpretation of narrative is more than an aspect of literary competence. Interestingly it is Kermode, the professor of English literature, who remarks in his discussion of narrative 'secrecy' that problems of interpreting: 'seem to be problems of importance for, broadly conceived, the power to make interpretations is an indispensable instrument for survival in the world, and it works there as it works on literary texts' (Kermode 1979: xi). Dominant models of comprehension, as they are constructed by reading schemes, would certainly be forced to change if interpretative debate about texts were more a part of discourse about reading development. The 'power to make interpretations' is not readily developed when only one interpretative possibility is allowed for the texts children encounter.

Neglect of the significance of interpretative criticism, and of *form* in particular, arises largely from an assumption that primary-aged children read only for plot and that therefore the sensibility of the literary critic in investigating form is unnecessary, even irrelevant, to texts for them. Children are intensely interested in plot but whether that is all that is important in their reading of narrative is very questionable. The analogy of children's oral language development, an analogy which has proved so fruitful for reconceptualizing reading processes, is also useful in considering the role of text criticism in primary education (Williams 1988: 3–4).

5

Connections

Given the range of subjects encompassed by 'children's literature' it is clear that many fascinating networks could be explored. Jack Zipes, for example, has opened up new areas of thought about the fairy tale, and suggests possible directions:

> To talk about fairy tales today, especially feminist fairy tales, one must, in my opinion, talk about power, violence, alienation, social conditions, child-rearing and sex roles. It is no longer possible to ignore the connection between the aesthetic components of the fairy tales, whether they be old or new, and their historical function within a socialisation process which forms taste, mores, values, and habits. And it is too simple or simplistic to maintain that children need fairy tales more than any other form of literature to work through psychic disturbances as many pseudo-Freudians like Bruno Bettelheim have done without challenging the premise of the oedipal paradigm. It is also too ethereal and idealistic to argue that the fairy tales contain archetypal patterns which point the way to happiness as many Jungians have done without questioning the historical validity of the archetypes. What is needed is a socio-psychological theory based on the recent findings of feminist investigations and critical reinterpretations of Freud that will help us grasp how fairy tales function historically in a mediatory role within the American and British socialisation processes. (Zipes 1986: 2)

The three articles in this section survey and discuss three areas: the links between children's literature (taken here to include, in American terminology, 'young adult' literature), folklore and science fiction; the limitations and possibilities of psychological criticism; and the burgeoning of cultural studies.

Between them, they provide a partial but challenging picture of the connections that children's literature criticism can make.

Real-izing the Unreal: Folklore in Young Adult Science Fiction and Fantasy
C. W. Sullivan III

As a bibliographic essay would show, there has been a great deal of speculation and commentary concerning the presence and, to a lesser extent, the function of folklore in fiction. Most of that commentary, however, has focused on the classics of literature or on fiction generally considered to have been written for adult readers. Although, as I have shown elsewhere (Sullivan 1990), children's literary experiences begin with folk materials and their literary expectations are in large part shaped by those experiences with folk materials, relatively little folklore-in-literature scholarship has dealt with children's literature and even less with Young Adult (YA) science fiction and fantasy. To be sure, a part of that neglect is due to the problems children's literature (and science fiction and fantasy) has encountered as it has become an academic discipline and a worthy intellectual pursuit; but another part of that neglect is due to the problems inherent in discussing folklore in literature.

In a special issue of the *Journal of American Folklore* on folklore in literature, published in 1957, Richard Dorson suggests that, in spite of the impressive studies of folklore in literature published up to that time, there still remain some major faults with the scholarship. The first, he maintains, is that some scholars do not know what folklore is and proceed, for example, to discuss a writer portraying a regional, ethnic, or even non-urban group as describing ' "folkways", or "folk culture", or "folklore" '. He might also have mentioned here that some critics have only a limited awareness of the materials which constitute folklore, so that while they might recognize bits of a traditional ballad or a folktale embedded in a piece of fiction, they might miss the same author's symbolic or thematic use of a proverb or of traditional food. Secondly, Dorson comments that many critics content themselves with merely listing the traditional items they find in a literary work without making any attempt to analyse those materials. And thirdly,

Dorson asserts that the boundaries between folk culture and popular culture have been so confused that some critics, unable to distinguish between the two, have dealt with materials of popular culture as if they were folk (Dorson 1957: 1–8).

Although it seems most folklorists would rather describe folklore than define it (Dundes 1965a: 1–3; Toelken 1979: 23–47), it is probably necessary here to give some definition. In his *The Study of American Folklore*, Jan Brunvand lists five qualities most folklorists ascribe to folklore:

> (1) its content is oral (usually verbal), or custom-related material; (2) it is traditional in form and transmission; (3) it exists in different versions; (4) it is usually anonymous; (5) it tends to become formularized. (Brunvand 1986: 5)

Brunvand then goes on to define folklore as *'those materials in culture that circulate traditionally among members of any group in different versions, whether in oral form or by means of customary example, as well as the processes of traditional performance and communication'* (ibid.: 7; italics in the original). But perhaps the clearest picture of the range of folklore is provided by Brunvand's chapter headings: 'Folk speech and naming', 'Proverbs and proverbial lore', 'Riddles and other verbal puzzles', 'Rhymes and folk poetry', 'Myths and motifs', 'Legends and anecdotes', 'Folktales', 'Folksongs', 'Ballads', 'Folk music', 'Supersititions, customs and festivals', 'Folk dances and dramas', 'Folk gestures', 'Folk games', 'Folklife', 'Folk architecture', 'Folk crafts and art', 'Folk costumes', and 'Folk foods'. As long as items within these categories are passed on traditionally (orally or by customary example) and exist in variations, they can be considered folklore.

Progress in folklore-in-literature scholarship has certainly been made since Dorson's 1957 comments. In 'The study of folklore in literature and culture' Alan Dundes argues that there are

> only two basic steps in the study of folklore in literature and in culture. The first is objective and empirical; the second is subjective and speculative. The first might be termed identification and the second interpretation. Identification essentially consists of a search for similarities; interpretation depends upon the delineation of differences. (Dundes 1965b: 136)

Identification requires the literary critic to determine whether or not the item thought to be folklore has variants which exist independently of the piece of fiction under scrutiny. Having ascertained the presence of folklore, the critic must then interpret that use. Barre Toelken suggests that

> the questions asked about the use of folklore in literature are almost exactly the same ones asked about imagery and symbol: What is the relation between what is said and how it is said? Are the images and symbols related to the content? In the case of folklore, has the author used materials to deepen and extend his meaning or only for window dressing? (Toelken 1979: 334)

The folklorist, therefore, must know something about literary criticism, and the literary critic must be able to identify folklore.

At about the same time that Dorson was criticizing the state of folklore-in-literature scholarship, Ray Frantz was writing an article on Twain's *Huckleberry Finn* which exemplified the kind of scholarship Dorson, and later Dundes, Toelken and others, would encourage. Admitting that 'in most cases [Twain used folklore] only as a kind of window dressing', Frantz argues that in *Huckleberry Finn* Twain 'employed folklore with such care to influence structure, support thematic development, provide plot motivation, and depict character that folklore emerges as organically important to the novel as a whole and fundamental to an appreciation of his accomplishment in this work' (Frantz, 1957: 314). Frantz's article was a harbinger, and folklore-in-literature scholarship since has improved dramatically in those areas that Dorson criticized.

Frantz's methodology in interpreting the folk materials in *Huckleberry Finn* could be applied to any novel or short story in which folklore is actively and aesthetically employed. However, some literary uses of folklore may be more specialized. A. Leslie Harris's 'Myth as structure in Toni Morrison's *Song of Solomon*' goes beyond the implications of the title and asserts that Morrison uses myth not only to provide the structure of events in the novel, but also to make the concepts in the novel more comprehensible. Morrison's use of mythology, Harris contends, makes 'contemporary, localized events and characters speak to those [readers] who cannot share her characters' background or experiences' (Harris 1980: 69). In other words, Morrison is employing the universality of myth to make the readers of one culture understand literary characters and concepts from a culture unfamiliar to them.

It seems to me, following Harris's interpretation of Morrison and applying it to YA science fiction and fantasy, that a major function of the folk materials in YA science fiction and fantasy is to make the reader more readily able to understand the unusual people and places about which he or she is reading. That is, the strange worlds and cultures of science fiction's future, fantasy's middle earth or faerie, or the altered present occasionally found in both can be made more real to the young reader by the inclusion of familiar items, actions, characters and plots which come directly from traditional sources or have their analogues and variants in contemporary folk materials.

It is important to note here, especially in regard to the study of science fiction and fantasy, that some folk materials which appear in fiction may be authentic, traditional materials while others may be intentionally created to appear to resemble or recall traditional materials. In 'A schema for the study of the sources and literary simulations of folkloric phenomena' Neil Grobman suggests that a major problem in folklore-in-literature scholarship is 'the lack of coordination and effort of scholars of folklore and literature in establishing a unified procedure for assessing how authors use folklore in their writing' (Grobman 1979: 17). Grobman suggests twelve different literary modes in his article, four categories with three variables in each category, in which folklore might be used. The three variables determine how the author acquired the folk material used: (1) as a native participant in the tradition; (2) from observing the folk whose materials were borrowed; or (3) by studying reference works and/or other literary sources. Each of those three variables can be applied to four categories which describe how the author uses the folk materials in his or her fiction: (1) included 'to give verisimilitude and local color'; (2) adapted 'usually to make a point or make the traditions more universally and popularly understood'; (3) used 'as models for production of folklore-like material'; and (4) used 'as a source for metaphorical language or structural symbolism' (Grobman 1979: 28–30). Grobman describes these variables and categories in considerably more detail, with examples, and provides a chart as well.

Adapting Grobman's schema to the study of folk materials in YA science fiction and fantasy is relatively easy. The three variables remain the same because authors can use their own traditions, traditions they have observed in other groups, or traditional materials they have studied to create the future worlds of science fiction or other worlds of fantasy. The terminology in the four categories requires only some readjustment. The traditional materials can still provide 'verisimilitude and local color', but (in combination with the third category of use) it is often the verisimilitude and local colour of an imagined world, the creation Tolkien has called a logically cohesive Secondary World ('On fairy-stories'). The second category is especially important. Science fiction or fantasy authors make their Secondary Worlds more real to the reader by showing that the beings there have some or many of the same traditional practices as the people the reader knows; this is especially true in fantasy as the Secondary World depicted may be much more different from the world of the reader than the science fiction world of the future might be. The third category is also important in science fiction and fantasy as authors use the folklore of this modern or historical world as a model to create the folklore indigenous to the Secondary World; this created folklore must be recognized as folklore even though it does not exist in the reader's culture (although it can exist in the novel alongside folklore taken directly from the reader's culture). And the fourth category is similar to the third as authors use narrative structures and symbols from traditional stories as models for the narrative structures and symbols in the science fiction or fantasy story.

J.R.R. Tolkien's *The Hobbit* is certainly a classic in fantasy for young readers (and for young listeners), and one of the reasons for its appeal, and the appeal of its sequel, *The Lord of the Rings*, is the vast amount of traditional materials that Tolkien includes in his narratives. It is likely that Tolkien acquired all of that traditional material in only two of the three variable ways Grobman delineates. Some of the material came from Tolkien's own culture, Grobman's first variable, and has its documentable variants and analogues in British and American folklore; the rest of his traditional inclusions, the larger share and the most obvious inclusions, came from his extensive study of northern European literatures, languages and cultures, Grobman's third variable. And all of that traditional material is embedded in a narrative that contains other rhetorical structures and devices to make the reader comfortable with the Secondary World Tolkien depicts.

The simplest traditional materials in *The Hobbit* are the superstitions and proverbs that any reader might recognize as common to his or her culture as well as the culture of Tolkien's Middle Earth (Taylor 1962). Early in the novel, when Thorin Oakenshield expresses doubts about Bilbo's fitness for the upcoming quest, Gandalf remarks, ' "You asked me to find the fourteenth man for your expedition, and I chose Mr. Baggins. Just let anyone say I chose the wrong man or the wrong house, and you can stop at thirteen and have all the bad luck you like, or go back to digging coal" ' (Tolkien 1982: 18–19). Even though Gandalf makes the connection for the reader, Tolkien expects the reader to know, as he does, that thirteen is an unlucky number in general (and not something particular to this novel). This is an obvious example of Tolkien's including traditional materials familiar to the reader for verisimilitude; he is using a familiar superstition to make a fantasy character and situation more real.

Many of the proverbs in *The Hobbit* are also from Tolkien's own cultural background and function in a similar way to the belief in the lucky number. Proverbs such as 'Out of the frying-pan and into the fire' (ibid.: 90, 98), 'Third time pays for all' (ibid.: 210, 233), and 'Where there's life there's hope' (ibid.: 233) are all proverbs with which even the youngest reader could be familiar. But in addition to using them for verisimilitude, as he uses the superstition, Tolkien uses familiar proverbs to prepare the reader for invented ones. Bilbo's 'Escaping goblins to be caught by wolves' became, Tolkien tells us, 'a proverb, though we now say "out of the frying-pan into the fire" in the same sort of uncomfortable situations' (ibid.: 98). In this case, Tolkien makes it clear to the reader that Middle Earth has its own proverbs, just as our world does; later on, he allows the native proverbs to stand on their own. Bilbo repeats his father's saying, 'Every worm has his weak spot', and acknowledges that, like many such sayings, this one probably did not come from his father's 'personal experience' (ibid.: 219); and still later, after a nearly disastrous teasing of the dragon, Smaug, when he is singed by the dragon's fiery breath, Bilbo remarks, 'Never laugh at live dragons', and Tolkien continues 'it became a favourite saying of his, and later passed into a proverb' (ibid.: 225).

On a somewhat more complex level, and still perhaps from his own personal and cultural experiences, Tolkien includes traditional riddles and riddling talk in his narrative. All of the riddles Bilbo exchanges with Gollum far under the mountains are traditional British and American true riddles (Taylor 1951), and Tolkien could have heard any or all of them as he grew up. The riddling contest, with the survival of Bilbo as its prize, dates back to the Bible and to Oedipus' contest with the Sphinx, and Tolkien's acknowledgement of that tradition – Bilbo 'knew, of course, that the riddle-game was sacred and of immense antiquity, and even wicked creatures were afraid to cheat when they played at it' (Tolkien 1982: 79) – probably came from study rather than experience. In addition to its immediate function in the narrative at that point, the riddle-game prepares the reader for the riddling conversation between Bilbo and Smaug, wherein Bilbo, when asked, identifies himself as, among other things, 'Ringwinner', 'Luckwearer', and 'Barrel-rider', which, Tolkien tells the reader, 'is the proper way to talk to dragons' (ibid.: 221).

Tolkien's inclusion of teasing rhymes might also come from his own experience (Brunvand 1986: 119–20). Bilbo's teasing of the spiders in Mirkwood may sound like so much nonsense to the adult reader with its 'Lazy Lobs' and 'Attercops', but children are very adept at this sort of verbal teasing. Children use the nonsense syllables 'na-na/na-*na*-na' frequently in this five-beat sequence and with the proper intonation (which the printed word cannot capture) as a teasing rhyme. Sometimes there are more beats, and later names and attributes might give the rhyme more power, but the meaningless syllables are sufficient. Moreover, Tolkien's 'Lazy Lob and crazy Cob / are weaving webs to bind me; / I am far more sweet than other meat, / but still they cannot find me' (ibid.: 159) has the rhythm of the traditional nursery rhyme which has been changed on the playground to a variety of teasing rhymes, such as, 'Johnny's mad, and I'm glad / And I know what'll please him. / A bottle of ink to make him stink / And _____ to squeeze him' (Brunvand 1986: 119). These recognizable folk materials – superstitions, proverbs, riddles and teasing rhymes – have the effect of making the faerie world of Middle Earth more immediate and more real to the young reader who recognizes them as items heard within the family or peer group.

More obvious, and certainly more intensively studied, are

the traditional materials Tolkien adapted from his studies, both those which fascinated him in his childhood and led him to write his first dragon story at the age of seven, and those of his professional career, through which he became Merton Professor of English Language and Literature at Oxford (Carpenter 1977: 23). These materials come largely from the same Scandinavian and Teutonic myths and legends that gave the young Tolkien the story of Sigurd and Fafnir (ibid.: 22) which seems to underlie so much of his later writing, from critical pieces like 'Beowulf: the monsters and the critics' to the great fantasies, *The Hobbit* and *The Lord of the Rings*.

Tolkien's Scandinavian borrowings begin with Gandalf and the Dwarfs, both their characters, which can be traced, generally, to Scandinavian concepts about wizards and dwarfs, and their names, which appear in Sturluson's *Prose Edda* (Young 1966: 41–2). The trolls, elves, goblins, shape-changers, ancestral swords, faithful black arrows and dragons (with vulnerable underbellies) are among the specific items in *The Hobbit* which have referents in Scandinavian myth and legend. More generally, various ideas or concepts from the Scandinavian myths and legends appear in *The Hobbit*. The good king as one who is generous with his treasure, a generous ring-giver, is echoed in Tolkien's comment that Dain 'dealt his treasure well' (Tolkien 1982: 291). The death in battle which provides the warrior entrance to Valhalla is echoed in Thorin's last heroic stand; and the comitatus spirit and family loyalty which structure the final battle in *Beowulf* are not lacking in Fili and Kili who die 'defending [Thorin] with shield and body, for he was their mother's elder brother' (ibid.: 291). And the emphasis on the power of tales, songs and music throughout the novel most certainly echoes the northern European societies in which the bard, scop or skald was a revered member. Not many readers will pick up on all of these borrowings, but every borrowing they do pick up on will increase their interaction and familiarity with the book, making it, again, more real.

On the most complex level, Tolkien is telling what C.S. Lewis would have called a Good Story (Lewis 1966: 3). It is also a good traditional story, following the *Märchen* or magic tale pattern almost point for point.

The Märchen is, in fact, an adventure story with a single hero. . . . The hero's (or heroine's) career starts, as everyone else's, in the dull and miserable world of reality. Then, all of a sudden, the supernatural world involves him and challenges the mortal, who undertakes his long voyage to happiness. He enters the magic forest, guided by supernatural helpers, and defeats evil powers beyond the boundaries of man's universe. Crossing several borders of the Beyond, performing impossible tasks, the hero is slandered, banished, tortured, trapped, betrayed. He suffers death by extreme cruelty but is always brought to life again. Suffering turns him into a real hero: as often as he is devoured, cut up, swallowed, or turned into a beast, so does he become stronger and handsomer and more worthy of the prize he seeks. His ascent from rags to riches ends with the beautiful heroine's hand, a kingdom, and marriage. The final act of the Märchen brings the hero back to the human world; he metes out justice, punishes the evil, rewards the good. (Dégh 1972: 63)

Some of the events in *The Hobbit* are metaphorical rather than literal – Bilbo's death-and-rebirth episode with Gollum, for example – but the novel does follow the *Märchen* pattern. Bilbo, of course, does not get married; the story of the Ring is not yet finished. That story – enhanced and made more real with the same sort of traditional materials found in *The Hobbit* – continues in *The Lord of the Rings* which does, in fact, end with marriages contracted and justice dispensed (and, according to Appendix B, children born and generations continued).

Tolkien's use of the *Märchen* structure makes the story more real as well. From the 'one morning long ago in the quiet of the world' (Tolkien 1982: 3), Tolkien's equivalent of 'Once upon a time', to Bilbo's 'laughing' and handing Galdalf 'the tobacco jar' (ibid.: 303), Tolkien's 'and they lived happily ever after', *The Hobbit* follows the structure and fulfils the requirements of the traditional tale and in doing so rewards the reader who has, from previous experiences with fairy tales and legends, some expectations of what a good story should contain. Even though the reader may not be consciously aware of or able to articulate those expectations, they are there and are rewarded by a narrative like *The Hobbit* which fulfils them. The *Märchen* structure makes the story more real, therefore, precisely because it enables Tolkien to present a tale with the weight of tradition behind it.

149

All of this traditional material, whether from Tolkien's own cultural heritage or borrowed from the Scandinavians and others, fits into the comfortable rhetorical style of *The Hobbit*. At the beginning of the novel Tolkien virtually stops the narrative flow to present a homy portrait of a creature who has a comfortable home and likes his comforts. Regardless of the thematic or symbolic importance of this first picture of Bilbo, it does serve to make the reader see him as a real and likeable person. The much-maligned authorial intrusions are also a part of this rhetorical strategy; they, too, serve to make the reader comfortable and, instead of interrupting the story actually serve to emphasize the essential story-ness of the narrative, just as do the author intrusions in *Beowulf* and *Sir Gawain and the Green Knight*, two works from which Tolkien learned much. And finally, because he was writing a traditional oral tale and not a modern novel, as I have argued elsewhere (Sullivan 1984) the combination of the traditional materials and the traditional rhetorical story make *The Hobbit* (and, by extension, *The Lord of the Rings*), a real story.

Robert A. Heinlein, like J.R.R. Tolkien, published his fiction for young readers some time ago and, like Tolkien, set standards which subsequent writers are having a hard time meeting (Sullivan 1985). Unlike Tolkien's fantasies, however, Heinlein's twelve juvenile science fiction novels have received less attention than they deserve, and Heinlein's use of traditional materials has largely gone unnoticed. On the one hand, traditional materials and novels about the future seem mutually exclusive, especially as science fiction writers are expected to use science and technology to make their worlds real to the reader. On the other hand, however, the world of the future can be just as strange, even with its logically extrapolated science and technology, as the world of fantasy. Heinlein eliminates some of that strangeness by placing his main characters in familiar situations: school in *Red Planet* and *Space Cadet*, homesteading and a Boy Scout troop in *Farmer in the Sky*, and pet ownership in *Red Planet* and *The Star Beast*, to name just a few. Heinlein also uses folk materials to bridge the gap between the reader's world and the world of the future.

An examination of Heinlein's uses of folklore can also begin with familiar proverbs. Like Tolkien, Heinlein uses traditional proverbs and other familiar sayings as chapter titles as well as in the texts of his novels. In *Rocket Ship Galileo*, one boy admits that he has been jealous of another's success and says, 'I can straighten out and fly right' (Heinlein 1977b: 53). Later in the novel, in a debate over what they might see on the dark side of the moon, one character says to another, 'Don't let him pull your leg' (ibid.: 102); and in *Between Planets*, one character admits, 'Grandmother Isobel was just pulling your leg' (Heinlein 1978a: 106). Other traditional sayings include the proverbial comparisons 'pretty as a picture' and 'deader than a doornail' (Heinlein 1977b: 8, 44) as well as other traditional metaphors: 'I'll fix his clock' (ibid.: 87), 'Soup's on' and 'I'm going to catch forty winks' (Heinlein 1978b: 66, 90), 'Mother knows best' (Heinlein 1954: 131), 'Fish or cut bait' (Heinlein 1955: 121), and 'Half a Loaf is Better than None' (Heinlein 1978c: 43). These last three are also chapter titles in their respective books, and the title of *The Rolling Stones* (1952) stands for the whole proverb and provides a key to a major theme in the novel. Heinlein, like Tolkien, includes familiar proverbs to make the characters more real.

He also uses familiar proverbs as a model for and to prepare the reader for his created ones. In *Rocket Ship Galileo*, someone needing to be calmed down is told, 'Don't burn out your jets before you take off' (1977b: 30), and a similar remark, 'Don't blow your tubes' appears in *Space Cadet* (1978b: 36). It is also in *Space Cadet* that Heinlein invents the first of his alien cultures, the Venerians, and he provides them with a couple of their own proverbs. At one point, the leader of the Venerians, creatures who look somewhat like seals and inhabit the watery parts of Venus, tells one of the humans to instruct another human 'that her nose need not twitch'. The human who understands Venerian speech translates that as, 'She says not to get in an uproar' (1978b: 187). Later in the same novel, the proverb, 'Tell thy impatient daughter to chase her fish and I will chase mine' (ibid.: 196) receives no translation/explanation for the reader's benefit. Heinlein is using easily identifiable folklore models here to create folklore-like material, in this case, to make a futuristic setting and alien culture more real to the reader.

While not a formally trained philologist like Tolkien, Heinlein nevertheless understood much about the nature of language and, in his novels, displayed his understanding of the power of names in certain teasing rituals. Sometimes the nicknames are innocent, as they are when Betty and John Thomas call each other 'Knothead' and 'Slugger' in *The Star Beast* (Heinlein 1954: 23). In *Red Planet*, however, when one of the humans now living on Mars does something foolish, something that a newcomer to the planet might do, he is called a 'tourist' (Heinlein 1977a: 8) in much the same way as an inexperienced easterner in the American west of the late 1800s would have been called a 'tenderfoot'. Similarly, the humans who have settled on cloud-covered Venus and consider the planet home are called 'fog-eaters' which, as Heinlein explains, 'was merely ragging, no worse than "Limey" or "Yank" – unless the tone of voice and context made it, as now, a deliberate insult' (1978a: 13). Heinlein not only relates the created nickname to traditional ones, but also provides a lesson in language use that Lewis Carroll would have appreciated: words can take their meaning from context. Don Harvey, in *Between Planets*, does not react to the insult, but in other novels such insults have more severe consequences. In *Citizen of the Galaxy*, a former slave now in the Guard throws a bowl of mashed potatoes at the person who has teased him once too often about his former status (Heinlein 1957: 185–6). And in *Time for the Stars*, the telepaths who provide ship-to-ship and ship-to-earth communications are called 'freaks' by the regular crew. When one of the telepaths objects and the matter reaches the Captain, he orders such name-calling stopped and explains, 'I once saw a crewman try to knife another one, just because the other persisted in calling him "skinhead" ' (Heinlein 1978c: 75). Heinlein's use of name-calling, like Tolkien's use of insult rhymes, is solidly based in folklore and would be immediately recognizable to and considered realistic by his young readers.

Heinlein, like Tolkien, borrowed materials for his fiction from his professional studies, but where Tolkien looked to the myths and legends of the Scandinavians and Celts, Heinlein looked to American folklore and history. In *Farmer in the Sky*, a title surely intended to echo the traditional nursery rhyme, 'The Farmer in the Dell', Heinlein entitles one chapter 'Johnny Appleseed'. The novel describes the settling and terraforming of Ganymede, one of Jupiter's moons, and Heinlein uses the 'Johnny Appleseed' reference to describe one of the settlers, Johann Schultz, who not only tries to grow apple trees but passes out seeds to other new settlers, and to link the settlement of Ganymede with the European-American settlement of the American west. In *Tunnel in the Sky*, the men who guide settlement parties to new planets are described as follows: 'The captain of the party sported a little goatee, mustaches, and rather long hair' (Heinlein 1955: 23); at the end of the novel, in case the reader missed the earlier hint, Heinlein describes another captain: 'He was dressed in fringed buckskin, in imitation of a very old style; he wore a Bill Cody beard and rather long hair' (ibid.: 252). And in *Space Cadet* Heinlein has one of his main characters continually refer to his uncle Bodie, a traditional liar/tall-tale teller (Brunvand 1986: 201–3; Toelken 1979: 112) who, according to his nephew, has outrun race horses (Heinlein 1978b: 23), 'rassled' a grizzly (ibid.: 34), eaten Mexican jumping beans to escape from prison (ibid.: 183), and accomplished any number of other traditional feats.

The references to such characters of American legend as Johnny Appleseed and Buffalo Bill are but two of many throughout the series as Heinlein seeks to model characters and forces in his Future History series on similar characters and forces in American folklore and history. In *Rocket Ship Galileo*, one young man's father forbids him to take part in what may well be a very risky space venture, but the boy's mother wins permission by appealing to a family history within American national history, asserting '[T]his country was not built by people who were afraid to go. Ross's great-great-grandfather crossed the mountains in a Conestoga wagon and homesteaded this place. He was nineteen, his bride was seventeen. It's a matter of family record that their parents opposed the move. . . . I would hate to think that I had let the blood run thin' (Heinlein 1977b: 42). There are various references to the settlement of the American west in Heinlein's novels, and to much of the rest of American history – and some world history – as well, references which make the future more real by anchoring it in models from a legendary and historical past familiar to his readers.

Heinlein's most complex use of folklore is in his creation of alien cultures with worldviews different from the reader's traditional European-American worldview (Attebery 1979: 328; Toelken 1979: 225–61). Heinlein prepares the reader for new cultural worldviews early in *Space Cadet*, the second novel in the series. One new cadet, Tex Jarman, has been reprimanded for eating pie with his fingers and explains the reprimand later to a friend, Matt Dodson, 'A patrol officer is supposed to be able to move in all society – if your hostess eats with her knife, then you eat with your knife. . . . He said pie wasn't important, but it was part of a larger pattern – for instance that you must never mention death on Mars or to a Martian' (Heinlein 1978b: 62–3). Later in the novel, Heinlein presents the native Venerian society, a matrilinear culture of seal-like creatures whose dominant pronoun is 'she', not 'he', and who are ruled by a 'mother' and, from farther away, 'a great mother of many' (ibid.: 167–217). It is in this society, where eating is a private affair accomplished alone in a curtained chamber, that Tex, who was reprimanded before, fully understands the importance of being able to 'eat pie with a fork' (ibid.: 188).

It is also in *Space Cadet* that Heinlein first makes it clear that the 'new' cultural worldview of space travel will be significantly different from the 'old' worldviews of earthbound cultures. When Matt returns home on leave he discovers that his worldview has grown beyond the nationalistic and divisive political attitudes of his parents (1978b: 113–24). In fact, quite a few of the adults in Heinlein's books are much less open-minded and less ready to meet the future than their children. Rod Walker's parents and aunt cannot understand his survival test on another planet in *Tunnel in the Sky*, John Thomas Stuart's mother is willing to sell his 'pet' in *The Star Beast*, and Max Jones has to escape his 'down on the farm' stepmother before he can go into space in *Starman Jones*. But there are also adults who know what is going on. Early in the series the adult is often an uncle or uncle-figure, like Donald Cargraves in *Rocketship Galileo*. Although there are some sharp parents early on, parents as a group seem to get smarter as the series progresses. The parents in *The Rolling Stones* and *Have Space Suit – Will Travel* both have professional degrees (science, medicine, and the like) and a broad knowledge of the humanities; instead of impediments to the future, they help to usher in the new culture and worldview.

Heinlein's understanding of cultural worldview, and his knowledge of the ways in which folklore and history have contributed to the development of the twentieth-century Euro-American cultural worldview allow him to create something larger than the traditional *Bildungsroman* with which he is generally credited (Williamson 1978: 19). First, he is able to select from folklore and history those elements which will be recognizable to the reader and which will define for the reader such concepts as the 'pioneer spirit' and the 'prepared/capable individual' which Heinlein sees as important and identifying characteristics of that worldview. Secondly, having identified those characteristics for the reader, Heinlein then builds his future human cultures on them so that the prepared individual with pioneer spirit is the successful person in the future setting Heinlein creates. In addition, Heinlein uses those characteristics (and others) as a backdrop against which to create believable alien cultures – believable because they are based on recognizable cultural principles and because the reader has been educated, by Heinlein at least, to be ready 'to eat pie with a fork' when the situation demands. Heinlein's human futures and his alien futures, with their separate cultural worldviews, are more real for the grounding he gives them in folklore and history.

Much YA fantasy and science fiction could be explored along these critical lines, and it might be that those authors who have created the most engaging, most complete and most believable Secondary Worlds in their fiction are also the ones who have tapped most directly into traditional materials and then used those traditional materials for their own sake and as models by which to create folklore indigenous to those fictional worlds. Folklore has always been a force for cultural stabilization, providing those materials to which the members of the culture return again and again in the form of ritual behaviour and providing guidance in the culture's ways and expectations through the traditional wisdom of proverbs and the traditional examples in myths, legends and folktales – just to name the obvious (Bascom 1965). Thus the reader who finds traditional materials – from a single proverb to a complete folktale structure – in the fiction he or she is reading also finds points at which the lives and world of the characters touch his or her life and world. The presence of those traditional materials in science fiction and fantasy for young readers makes those strange new worlds less strange, more real.

Good Friends, or Just Acquaintances? The Relationship between Child Psychology and Children's Literature
Nicholas Tucker

The time lag between psychological theory and any popular take-up outside the profession varies from the almost immediate to the still pending, watch this space. Some psychoanalytic ideas, for example, made themselves felt fairly soon in terms either of passionate endorsement or else indignant denial. Cognitive psychology, dealing with the less emotionally charged issue of how we learn, has had to wait longer before making any general impact. Much depends therefore on how dramatic the psychological findings are and on the salience of their chief advocates. There is also the matter of how close the psychological theory is to the general mood of the time. Psychoanalysis, with its perpetual looking back into every past aspect of the individual, was particularly suited to a culture where fascination with the self had often come to replace more typical nineteenth-century interests in social, religious or community issues. Behaviourism, by contrast, always found fewer resonances in this same self-absorbed culture, and what literary references there are to its particular techniques are generally hostile.

Turning specifically to children's literature, the number of nods within it aimed in the direction of any specific school of psychology have always been sparse. This is not surprising. Authors with ready access to childhood themselves in terms of either personal memory or private fantasy generally have no need for any psychological key before feelings and memories about the past can begin to flow. Indeed, the ability to write about childhood can itself act as a process of therapy and understanding where past experience is concerned. Children's authors can therefore become their own psychologists when reconstructing their own childhoods and that of the imaginary characters they invent. Any child psychologists writing with similar authority about childhood matters can in this sense seem rivals to children's authors rather than colleagues. So what psychologists actually have to say about childhood often stands a good chance of either being ignored or else mocked by authors happy with the maps of childhood that they create in their books. Any child psychology they need can be made up as they go along in accordance with the demands of the plot and the personalities of the characters they have created.

Yet to the extent that children's authors are inevitably influenced by the culture within which they live, some of those psychological theories of childhood which have become widely taken up will eventually begin to work their way into their writing. This is particularly likely to happen in those stories where questions of motivation and personality figure most prominently. How should unpleasant or badly behaved child characters be portrayed, for example; as born nasty or as the result of poor parenting? What are the really important influences upon children when young? In both framing and attempting to answer such questions, individual authors usually prove laws only to themselves. But while some will have nothing to do with psychological explanation at all, others may indeed follow up some current psychological theory concerning childhood every now and again.

The exact contribution made by psychology to the writing of children's fiction can therefore never be described as a consistent, across-the-board phenomenon. Even so, the broad psychological movements I shall now briefly outline have all had some important effects on children's literature both past and present. Discussing these movements in rough chronological order does not imply that succeeding psychological theories necessarily always replaced those that went before. More commonly, various aspects of all these theories may be used at times by children's writers when it comes to trying to explain different types of human behaviour in their novels. The end results often amount to something of a psychological mishmash, with many children's writers following a tradition of partial psychological explanation and partial moral assessment so common in the fictional treatment of child characters past and present.

In the novels of Charles Dickens, for example, the explanations put forward to account for the different way various child characters behave change from child to child at the whim of the novelist himself. In *Oliver Twist* (1837–8), the Artful Dodger is shown clearly as a creature of his environment while Oliver is portrayed as driven by purely inner forces of goodness and nobility consistent with the exalted social origins whose existence he only discovers at the end of the book. In

David Copperfield (1849–50) Steerforth's poor character is shown as the result of unwise parenting; David himself is always guided by a good inner spirit, while Uriah Heep seems born evil. But while psychologists must try to be consistent when searching for a developmental theory to explain human behaviour, novelists are perfectly free to pick and choose between theories of behaviour ranging from the environmental to the demonic, often in the same novel. So if various important psychological theories have been sampled by different novelists at times, few have ever been followed to the letter except perhaps for the theories of Jean-Jacques Rousseau (1712–78), the first quasi-psychologist to have a major effect on the fictional treatment of children in literature.

Rousseau actually condemned book-reading in his famous study of a perfect childhood, *Emile* (1762). As he puts it himself, 'Men may be taught by fables; children require the naked truth' (Rousseau 1969: 1). So apart from *Robinson Crusoe* (1719), which Rousseau did approve of, children were expected to turn to nature rather than to books for knowledge both about life and about themselves. A rather similar message was later suggested by Wordsworth, particularly in *The Prelude* (1850), once again with childhood in mind. The results of such influences have been endemic in much children's literature ever since, with the great bulk of stories written for them set in the countryside rather than in the town and often featuring children shown learning the hard way how to sail a boat, build a fire or catch a fish.

Just as characters in today's television soap operas are never seen watching or talking about other soap operas, children in such literature are rarely shown doing any reading. They are too occupied instead learning at first hand from Mother Nature, with real mothers usually as well out of the way as they were in *Emile* itself. The paradox of trying to advocate such do-it-yourself adventures through the agency of private reading, an activity involving little more physical effort from a child than merely sitting in a chair, can be a hard one for an author to outface. In the novels of Richard Jefferies and Arthur Ransome, for example, the determination of the author to get across the physical skills they write about with such enthusiasm shows itself in periodic, densely written descriptions of this or that activity. But as technical details multiply and paragraphs get longer, the final result is often obscure.

What begins as a description of physical skill may finish as a highly abstract discussion well beyond the reach of all but the best-informed young readers, who – should they already possess and therefore understand such skills themselves – might anyhow be just as likely to be exercising them at that moment as to be reading a story about them.

A possible element of compensatory fantasy must also be borne in mind here, both on the part of the reader and the writer. Authors, often from quite bookish childhoods themselves, may get an extra kick from writing about real or imagined unbookish childhood activities. Writing in a reasonably lively way about the influence of reading, on the other hand, is a much harder task, even though it may well be that books themselves have often proved the most important influence in many an author's early years. Child readers, meanwhile, indulging in solitary reading may also get an agreeable thrill from imagining themselves coping heroically within an active environment. But for whatever reasons, the image of the child always learning best from or in the presence of nature remains an important literary ideal right up to our own times, despite evidence from contemporary surveys revealing the loneliness and privation of many children living in the British countryside now. Dissident stories hinting that all may not always be well for modern country children written by keen-eyed authors like Jan Mark (*Handles*, 1983) or Jill Paton Walsh (*Gaffer Sampson's Luck*, 1987) continue to chip away at this image in their own fashion.

Some parents after reading *Emile* actually tried to raise their own children on such principles, almost invariably with little success (Darton 1982: 146–7). A number of children's writers also accepted Rousseau's message in its entirety, as in Mrs Inchbald's witty fable *Nature and Art* (1796). But in general, Rousseau's ideals were part of a general cult of sensibility holding that it was more important for children to follow their instincts at their own pace than for them to become acquainted through books and teaching with the culture in which they were born. Almost the opposite was true of the earlier and never quite so influential theories of another great quasi-psychologist, John Locke. In his ideal education, children were to be allowed plenty of books so long as these were reasonably informative rather than full of 'useless trumpery' (Darton 1982: 18). For Locke believed that the child, born with no knowledge, could only learn from appropriate experience, with well-designed children's books a particularly good way of providing such learning.

This idea, shared of course by many who had never heard of Locke himself, has also remained as a pervasive influence in children's literature. Children's books today may not slip in the odd educational lesson as obtrusively as did nineteenth-century writers like R.M. Ballantyne, who rarely missed an opportunity to dwell on the flora and fauna found in the foreign parts he chose as settings for his adventure stories. Yet there is still a strong tendency to instruct both morally and about diverse matters of random knowledge in much modern children's literature. By the same token, children's books now that deal with matters thought undesirable, whether sexually, morally or politically, are still often attacked for the 'bad' message they convey to readers. Those making this type of criticism are consciously or unconsciously holding to the theory of learning by association outlined by Locke. This stated that children are affected by all experience, positively in the case of good experiences and negatively when the reverse is true. Each child, therefore, is the sum of all such experiences, and where literature is concerned, Locke believed that it behoves us to see that children's stories always aim at being wholesome, educational and generally useful. Such a message can still be heard on many an educational platform today.

The last quasi-psychologist I would pick out as particularly influential on children's literature is the German educationalist Friedrich Froebel. His insistence on the importance of story-telling, folk songs and traditional games in the education of young children gave the cause of literature a large boost both within schools and without. Locke might well have suspected more 'useless trumpery' at work as Froebel's kindergarten children sang their nursery songs or listened to fairy tales. But the concept of play as the best type of early learning helped put an end to the idea that books should always act as a form of instruction for young readers. Henceforth nonsense often stood as good a chance as solemn commonsense in the nursery, with importance now given to the intrinsic appeal of language itself as well as to its particular content.

Championing myth and legend as a form of wisdom rather than as undesirable relics of peasant superstition also allowed more children access to that special type of magical thinking that has always been so meaningful to them, either in literature or in oral tale-telling. Taking up the cause of very small children meant too that their particular needs were treated more seriously, including their literary needs. This belief would eventually lead to increased nursery education, more children's libraries and of course to many more books. With picture books in particular getting both cheaper and brighter with the advance of new printing techniques towards the end of the nineteenth century, the stage was set for the massive growth in children's literature for all.

The biggest upset facing conventional ideas about children and their favourite literature was still to come, in the shape of Freud. In a sense his essential message remains as subversive today as it was when psychoanalytic concepts began to become better known. Something of a literary man himself, Freud often used ideas from fiction and myth to illustrate his theories. Thus, 'It begins to dawn on us that the many fairy tales which begin "Once upon a time there was a king and queen" only mean to say that there was once a father and mother' (Freud 1973: 192). Or: 'The poet enables us to enjoy our own day-dreams without shame or guilt' (Freud 1925: 5). In dreams, and no doubt in children's stories too, Freud believed that large animals were often symbolic representations of parents while small animals either stood for siblings or for child-readers themselves (Peller 1959).

It was the reasoning behind these bold pronouncements which was to have such an effect. For while traditional associationist psychology believed that children were the sum of their external experience, Freud reversed this equation. For him, it was a child's inner life that really mattered. Particularly important here were the fantasies and feelings that were either inherited as part of the human condition or else were the inevitable outcome of the tensions inseparable from all family life, happy or unhappy. Such fantasies could often be extremely aggressive not to say sadistic, frequently revolving around strong sexual interest.

Many myths and fairy tales contain vivid reflections of those fantasies mentioned by Freud as illustrating a child's pent-up aggressive feelings towards its parents at moments when tempers are lost and imaginary revenge is sought. *Snow White*, for example, explores the idea of the murderous mother-figure who must be killed to safeguard the life of her own child. *Jack and the Beanstalk* describes how a boy kills off a father-figure with the compliance of his mother. Many authors have incorporated elements of these themes in their own stories. A version of *Cinderella* can be found in Jane Austen's *Mansfield Park* (1814), for example, and aspects of *Beauty and the Beast* are suggested in Dickens's *Great Expectations* (1860–1). The continuing popularity of such fairy-tale themes suggests that Freud was right in believing that the inner tensions these fantasies reveal have always been present throughout history and have always found some reflection in favourite stories.

Most prevalent of all in fairy stories is the Oedipal myth, central to all Freudian psychology and reflecting a child's principal need to kill off in fantasy their main parental rival of the same sex, so allowing them unlimited access to the desired parent of the opposite sex (Freud 1973: 118). While any direct wish to kill a parent even in fantasy would generally arouse too much guilt, Freud argued that it was a different matter to enjoy reading stories about the extermination of parental symbols suitably disguised as traditional-style villains. As it is, giants, ogres, dragons and other monsters can stand very well for the resented, powerful father in the child's imagination. Witches meanwhile symbolize the resented side of motherhood, together with those wicked stepmothers, coiled, silky-voiced serpents and tempting mermaids who get their evil way by sexual allure rather than through traditional spells. And who other to outwit or slay these monsters than the young fairy-tale hero or heroine, setting out from home little more than a child, yet a couple of pages later often ready to take on marriage and a respected adult place in society? Although such fairy tales were once enjoyed by all ages, Freudian critics constantly stressed how much there is in them for those younger members of an audience, always particularly appreciative of any story in which they can at last walk tall and act big.

Hunting the symbol in this way quickly became something of a literary-psychoanalytic game, helping make children's literature more interesting to some adults who might otherwise have cared little for it. But any implications here for new ways of critically assessing contemporary children's literature remained vague. Books once considered good for children mainly because they were about good child characters setting good examples now indeed sometimes looked more questionable. Just as Freud defined the 'good' as merely dreaming about what the 'bad' actually get up to, so too could extra-pious literature be seen as another form of repression through which child-readers are denied any insight into the less respectable side of their own fantasy lives.

On the other hand, neither Freud nor his followers, almost all of whom led conventional middle-class existences, would ever have countenanced a modern children's literature giving direct expression to the unsocialized, aggressive and acquisitive forces existing within every individual which Freud believed always had to be kept at bay if civilization is to continue. As it was, American-style horror comics in the 1950s were quite as condemned by psychoanalytic spokesmen as they were by representatives from education and the church (Barker 1984). Yet their pseudo-Gothic, sadistic imaginings did in fact often resemble the descriptions of unconscious aggressive fantasies found for example in the work of Melanie Klein, another influential psychoanalyst.

One answer psychoanalytically inclined commentators found to the critical dilemma of what exactly should be included in modern children's books was to ignore such literature altogether. Instead, they concentrated on those traditional fairy stories and myths that most clearly lend themselves to Freudian interpretation. Various stories in the Grimm collection were especially relevant here, dealing as they do with taboo matters such as cannibalism, incest, torture, murder and bestiality. Because these stories were traditional they could get away with using such strong material in a way that would not be true of modern writing for children. A psychoanalyst like Bruno Bettelheim in his study *The Uses of Enchantment* (1976) not only totally endorsed the genius of fairy tales for the way they discuss those feelings that mean most to children, but also dismissed all modern children's literature as vapid by comparison. Indeed, his opinion of it was so low that he did not even attempt to sample it properly, citing only two examples of such modern decadence in the whole of his book (Tucker 1984: 33–41).

This ignorance of modern children's literature among most psychologists is typical, although some psychoanalytic critics did eventually get round to discussing classics from the more immediate past. *Alice's Adventures in Wonderland* (1865), *Peter Pan* (1904), *Treasure Island* (1883) and various other books have in time received psychoanalytic scrutiny, with more modern writers now also beginning to be considered in studies like Margaret and Michael Rustin's *Narratives of Love and Loss* (1987). In fact, modern children's literature by authors like Robert Westall, Anne Fine, Katherine Paterson and many others now offer all readers, including interested psychologists, a particularly rich mixture of human emotions for attention and analysis. But while it could once be assumed that almost every educated adult would be acquainted with children's classic novels read during their own childhood, common knowledge today about any modern classic for children can no longer be taken for granted. In our televisual age, every plot of every modern children's book must first be painfully spelled out in detail before any further type of analysis can begin. This helps make any reasonable discussion of contemporary children's fiction, psychological or otherwise, very difficult for a general audience.

The upshot of this is that while children's books themselves have changed enormously in the last fifty years, many adults remain ignorant or unconvinced of the reality of such changes. Those adults answering to this description would be genuinely surprised, for example, to know that there is now much more emphasis upon sexual feeling in children's books. The greater frankness following on from the psychoanalytic revolution has also played an important role in helping lead to this change. Sibling rivalry too – something particularly stressed by Adler, one of Freud's psychoanalytic contemporaries – can also now be mentioned as a normal family phenomenon. Family rivalry in former children's books was only alluded to in order to condemn it for its possibly appalling consequences, as in Mrs Sherwood's *The Fairchild Family* (1818) or Annie Keary's remarkable novel *The Rival Kings* (1857). Late twentieth-century children's writers by contrast have so absorbed the idea of the inevitability and occasional ferocity of sibling rivalry that if anything it is now over-stressed in many stories, leaving those families that get on fairly well somewhat unrepresented in contemporary fiction.

Other crumbs from the psychoanalytic table seized on by literary critics include the endorsement of fantasy not simply as a context for winning imaginary victories in the unconscious but as a valid metaphor for the passage of human life itself. For Carl Jung, fairy tales are often symbolic of the individual's struggle from the primitive, animal level to the world of higher consciousness and personal fulfilment. Forests, monsters, castles, valued helpers and all the various trials encountered on the way are aspects of the positive and negative side to the reader's own self. Although J.R.R. Tolkien and C.S. Lewis wrote their own literary fantasies from a Christian rather than a psychoanalytic background, the seriousness with which Tolkien himself has since been treated owes something to the way that Jung and others have helped turn the idea of myth into a psychological treasure-house for those setting out on their own quest for personal understanding.

Melanie Klein's particular psychoanalytic vision of children's capacity for sadistic reverie has not so far had much effect on children's literature. For her, infancy was a time for intense aggression aimed at the mother, arising from an infant's over-riding wish to keep this parent all to themselves. When balked of this fierce desire, Klein believed that the infant took revenge by indulging in fantasies of destroying the mother in various painful ways. But at the same time, such violent fantasies can also come back to haunt the child, terrified (once their bad mood has passed) that all their aggression might actually have killed off the mother. Klein also believed that infants projected their own aggression on to persecutory parental figures in their imagination, who would then come back in nightmares or fantasies to threaten the infant with the same violence that the infant had originally wished upon them.

Klein's one essay about children's literature, where she writes about Colette's fable *L'enfant et les sortilèges*, is neither well known nor easy to read (Mitchell 1986). Yet some of her main ideas have to an extent been absorbed, often by those who have never heard of her. There is, for example, greater tolerance today of depictions of violence and death in books for smaller children. Those rougher, tougher nursery rhymes once shunned by inter-war anthologists now grace the pages of Raymond Briggs's influential collection *The Mother Goose Treasury*, first put together in 1966. Picture books since, like the *Frances* series by Russell and Lillian Hoban (1960–), Maurice Sendak's *Where the Wild Things Are* (1963), and John Burningham's *Come Away from the Water, Shirley* (1978) and many others have all explored childish fantasies revolving around resentment of parents, jealousy towards siblings or the occasional wish for murderous revenge.

Psychoanalytic influences apart, much else in psychology this century has had its own effect upon children's literature. Jean Piaget, for example, did a great deal to change attitudes towards small children. Like his fellow-countryman Rousseau, Piaget was not a great advocate of books for the young. Instead he always believed that children learn best when confronted by experience itself rather than by pre-digested, bookish instruction. Because of his teaching, backed up by educationists like Susan Isaacs and Maria Montessori, a new child-centred theory of teaching was established, based on advocating a better understanding of how small children think during their early years. Such thinking, Piaget argued, was not simply the result of arbitrary misunderstandings of adult thought. Instead, it had its own rules and structures. Those wishing to communicate with children effectively had better learn such rules for themselves first.

One result of this change of emphasis was the decline of the bad old textbook written in a style well above most children's heads. These were gradually replaced by books placing more emphasis on illustration and less on verbal explanation. Such illustrations were now often drawn without too much fussy detail, making it easier for pupils to understand and learn from them. Piaget's constant stress here was on the active nature of learning, with pupils in his estimation always eager to make their own sense of the material that most interested them. Books that still tried to anticipate this process by telling young readers exactly how they should be thinking about any topic would now more often be seen as merely counterproductive.

Instead, children were increasingly presented with clearly illustrated books written in plain language at an intellectual level they could be expected to follow. Whether the topic was sexual instruction, religious knowledge, history or geography, the main aim was always to get information across at a child-centred level. The effect of this approach was always clearer in non-fiction than in fiction, with *Comment la souris reçoit une pierre sur la tête et découvre le monde* (1971) – the one children's picture book Piaget ever worked on as a special adviser – little more than a lifeless compendium of childlike guesses about the general workings of the daily weather. But Piaget's particular genius was always more concerned with the development of children's logical thought than with the development of their imagination.

Once presented with interesting stories written at their own level, many children often proved to be more advanced than Piaget ever estimated in terms of their understanding of ordinary human thoughts, feelings and behaviour. Ideas of empathy, individual psychology or comparative justice, for example, could all make sense even to a very young audience once described in the context of a lively story involving characters around the same age and stage as their readers. As various post-Piagetian psychologists were to discover, even children under six were capable of making intelligent comments on their favourite stories, at times showing evidence of quite complex reasoning ability (see Donaldson 1978). The same children, faced by Piaget's more abstract questions, might indeed have seemed bewildered simply because they could not understand or identify with the way things were being put to them.

One serious limitation of Piaget's theories was their neglect of children's feeling for narrative as opposed to logic. He himself always saw children principally as lone explorers of the inanimate world. Post-Piagetian psychologists, by contrast, believe that children in fact often find social situations a good deal easier to comprehend, and indeed at times can manifest a certain social sophistication in their understanding much in advance of their comprehension of the non-social world. This school of thought was enormously enhanced by the rediscovery during the 1960s of the work of the great Russian psychologist Vygotsky, whose principal argument was that the true significance of language as the essential tool for learning had hitherto been overlooked.

For Vygotsky, play and language represented the most fundamental of human attempts to transcend the here and now in order to construct symbolic models for the better understanding of the nature of the world we live in. Because of a child's highly developed social sense, the different cultural associations surrounding the use of language will often mean as much to him or her as will the actual meaning of individual words. One child, for example, will quickly learn that language in all its variety is something to be relished and encouraged; another will, equally quickly, soon understand the reverse if this happens to be true. It is parents then later on schools that principally hand down linguistic tools to children. Those that provide them with plenty of positive verbal stimulation are also providing them with the abundant mental scaffolding necessary to help them in time to construct their own rich models of the world.

For children brought up in this type of linguistic atmosphere, language will be seen as a vital and empowering process, invaluable for asking questions or conversing about mutual interests. Such children can also borrow potentially useful 'scripts' from their parents, for example in learning how to imitate the way a parent answers the phone or constructs a shopping list. But parents and schools who are niggardly in their attitudes towards play and language will be passing on a much more limited set of tools for children trying to make sense of the present and also plan in the imagination for the future.

The implications here for children's literature are considerable. Fiction has always been a medium wherein the child's here and now can be transcended, enabling the child to move into foreign worlds and different social roles. The ability to indulge in this type of imaginative play constitutes what Vygotsky saw as the ultimate difference between humans and animals, since only humans can use their brains to envisage a different way of doing things at another period of time. Such ideas can be tested out first in language, play or through the imagination. For Jerome Bruner, an American psychologist working along the same lines, part of the appeal of myth is that it offers readers a range of metaphysical identities against which the individual can compare his or her own spread of multiple identities (Bruner 1979). By reducing the complexities of everyday life to a series of symbolic forms and choices, myth can also help readers find a pattern in their own concepts of themselves and the reality within which they live.

Myth, and mythopoeic literature in general, first frames then offers some answers to many of the immemorial problems of existence. At other levels, fiction provides a more mundane commentary on human affairs. It describes, for example, what people say or do in which situations, so suggesting a link between a reader's own sense of self and their understanding of how others may operate in the same social situation. It also describes feelings that readers recognize from their own experience, or emotions foreign to particular readers but still important when it comes to trying to understand the thoughts and behaviour of others.

In this way fiction maintains a continuous form of dialogue with those readers who find themselves comparing their own personalities, reactions, emotions, thoughts and modes of speech with those of the author and the characters in his or her book. Such comparisons can suggest new possibilities to readers in the conduct of their own lives. Whether readers then take up any of these possibilities is another matter. But giving them a type of choice that is both wide and informed is something else that literature at its best has to offer.

Vygotsky's emphasis on the important cultural overtones of language also helped focus more attention on the meaning behind words in fiction. The issue of racist or sexist uses of language in children's books was once dismissed as a comparatively unimportant matter. But when it was argued that particular words or phrases carried a whole network of implications for young readers, some of which might prove to be extremely negative, then such matters came to be seen as more significant. Vygotsky's belief that children usually learn more from each other also had important implications for the treatment of fiction in the classroom. Much of the recent work on reader response now focuses on the interaction between individual readings of a story and the way such readings once expressed in public so often grow, modify and deepen (Hayhoe and Parker 1990).

This realization that others' opinion on anything may be different from one's own is an essential step in Vygotsky's outline of how young brains best develop. As he saw it, the more different hypotheses an individual is aware of, the more able that individual then becomes at understanding complex situations that demand to be looked at from a number of points of view. The fact that children often learn this type of developmental step better from each other relates to their ability to follow childlike reasoning, their own and other's, more easily than they usually follow most adult reasoning. To the extent that children's fiction provides a highly appropriate forum for discussion and speculation about motivation, character, or even simply what comes next at a stage half-way through a story, successful classroom discussion of different reader responses lends itself well to Vygotsky's main purposes.

So it is no accident that arguments for the importance of

providing fiction in schools now often stress not simply the literary merits of books but also the opportunity they give pupils for the better understanding both of themselves and of others through discussion, comparison and introspection. At the same time, modern children's authors like Alan Garner, William Mayne, Jan Mark and Margaret Mahy no longer write fiction that can always be understood easily at first glance. Instead, they often leave gaps in their stories for interested readers to fill in for themselves, either privately in the imagination or out loud in classroom discussion.

The most recent psychological developments have tended to concentrate more on the nature of fiction, and the covert as well as overt nature of its message, and also on the personal nature of each individual reader's response to it. Modern linguistic critics such as Saussure insist that meaning in a text is something necessarily imposed on readers by the arbitrary nature of language itself. Other critics like Norman Holland (1974) go along with Barthes and others in the various structuralist schools of criticism. The main belief here is that each individual can make sense of a text only by creating their own version of it in their imagination in accordance with their own particular needs and experiences.

Such arguments have yet to have any serious impact on the writing of children's fiction, and later developments in psychoanalytic thinking, particularly in the work of Lacan, may well remain too obscure for all but a tiny coterie. However, the effect of all these recent critical theories upon the current discussion of children's literature has been marked. On the question of the personal nature of all literary responses, some have argued that no critic can ever attempt to justify their own reaction to a text as in any way valid for everyone else. If that critic is also trying to answer for child-readers, there is more doubt now whether he or she can be sure that their own reconstruction of what a child wants can ever have any meaning for all children, or even for one. This particular point of view has alarmingly nihilist implications for all critics of children's literature. It is not an argument that will simply go away, and must eventually be met one way or another.

The general obscurity of much recent critical discussion of literature has led to a chasm opening up between the academic treatment of children's literature and criticism of it at a more popular level. Many children's authors must now be puzzled

by the latest, more recondite developments in critical theorizing about their books; so too will most teachers, parents and
of course child-readers as well. This is not a healthy situation,
and the days when authors like C.S. Lewis and J.R.R. Tolkien
could address their audience equally clearly both as writers
and as critics already seem remote. Yet the present gulf
between literary practice and literary theory could widen even
further as more ingenious academic critics give it their full
attention.

But while discussion of reader response often exists at present at a dauntingly jargon-infested level, other psychological
approaches continue to have a more accessible type of influence on public opinion. The patient observations of child
behaviour earlier on this century made by psychologists like
Arnold Gesell have provided a much clearer picture of the
different stages of child development. More is known now
about how children play, what they believe and what they like
doing best. Baby-care books have taken up many of these
findings, and picture books increasingly reflect a closer knowledge of developmental stages in the early years. If and when
small children go through a phase of mild anxiety or disturbance, for example, it is now less easy to put the blame on the
influence of undesirable books. On the contrary, research
almost always concludes that such specific influence to the
bad is highly unlikely to come from one source alone, given
everything else going on in a child's life at the time. The
modern author or illustrator therefore has much greater freedom now, with the public pillorying of fiction as a prime
suspect for leading a child astray now a thing of the past.

On the other hand, most leading children's authors and
illustrators are also much less well known now than would
once have been the case, and must consequently fight harder
for any sort of public recognition. The fact that television and
video are blamed more than books for sometimes having a
bad influence upon the young simply reflects the greater
importance today of visual over literary stimulation in the lives
of most children. Whether this occasional scapegoating of television is as unfair and unfounded as was so much criticism of
former children's literature remains a controversial area, in
need of more research.

Social scientists have an obvious future role to play here,
just as they have already done this century when it comes to

adding to the public grasp of important social issues. The complex nature of deviancy, handicap or poverty, for example, is much better understood today, and this increased understanding has manifested itself in some children's literature tackling such issues. Villains in children's books were once regularly drawn from various social minorities, the physically odd or the mentally unstable. Today, we have been taught that the mere fact of coming from a different race, class or physique to the majority is no longer enough to label any fictional character as suspect even before anything else becomes clear about them.

Greater knowledge and awareness of gender issues has also helped the slow process of seeing off those out-of-date sexual sterotypes once such a feature of children's publishing. More too is known about the actual readership of children's books. What few nineteenth-century surveys of reading there were existed at a very amateur level, producing unlikely candidates such as *Alice's Adventures in Wonderland* or the novels of Charles Dickens as children's favourite reading. But better-organized research using social science techniques has helped force publishers and writers into realizing that the standard audience for children's books is not simply a middle-class two-child family living quietly with mother in the suburbs while father goes out to work. Today's greater awareness of changing family patterns, new ethnic minorities and the needs of previously marginalized readers such as the handicapped has helped lead to more adventurous writing and publishing for all types of children.

At an individual level, the old moral-medical model for explaining individual deviancy has also wilted in the face of psychological research. Maladjusted children are less often seen now as diseased or merely missing out on some essential moral fibre. The new stress on individual disturbance as something that is often compounded by severe social problems has led to stories that show far more understanding of those bullies, tell-tales or juvenile thieves whom it was once so satisfying to dislike and then condemn out of hand in the former, morally polarized world of so much children's fiction. This more complex view of the causes of individual behaviour has resulted in a number of stories that may appear fairly static on the surface but where the main adventures are more taken up with inner journeys of psychological understanding where some of the chief characters are concerned. Those adventures where physical danger and ultimate survival are the chief concern are still with us in the world of children's books. But even they more commonly discuss the psychological dimension to heroism as well, in contrast to the former stress on courage and endurance alone.

As to the future, there is no guarantee that today's commonly accepted psychological theories at either a popular or an academic level will last with the years. Psychology is a far more normative study than those who argue for its purely scientific status are prepared to admit. Both it and children's literature will go on evolving, setting new norms in time and continuing to have a two-way influence upon each other. For while psychologists are now quite good at painting the wider picture of different developmental processes, individual psychological portraits have always been best created by novelists. What possible effects such literature may in turn have had upon psychological thinking over the years remains an even more mysterious and still relatively unexplored topic.

Cultural Studies, New Historicism and Children's Literature
Tony Watkins

1

In *Keywords*, Raymond Williams describes culture as 'one of the two or three most complicated words in the English language' (Williams 1976: 76). Culture is an ambiguous term: a problem shared, perhaps, by all concepts which are concerned with totality: ideology, history, society, myth.

'Cultural studies' is equally ambiguous; the field, as Brantlinger argues, has 'emerged from the current crises and contradictions of the humanities and social science disciplines not as a tightly coherent, unified movement with a fixed agenda, but as a loosely coherent group of tendencies, issues and questions' (Brantlinger 1990: ix). Another commentator refers to it thus: 'Cultural studies is a whirling and quiescent and swaying mobile which continuously repositions any participating subject.' Essentially interdisciplinary, it 'bears both the traces and, often, the firm outlines of history, sociology, literature, psychology, linguistics, philosophy, anthropology and some elements of economics' (Dunn 1986: 71).

However, most commentators would agree with the following as a workable definition: 'Cultural studies is concerned with the generation and circulation of meanings in industrial societies' (Fiske 1987: 254).

In children's literature studies, the work of Fred Inglis, Jacqueline Rose and Jack Zipes, although in many ways very different, may be thought of as arising within a cultural studies framework (Inglis 1975 esp. Chs 6 and 7; Inglis 1981; Rose 1984; Zipes 1979).

In this essay I would like to give a simplified sketch of the field, and summarize a recent framework that could be applied to children's literature. I then consider two approaches that share something of the same preoccupations as cultural studies – New Historicism and New Cultural History, and offer an example of the way the cultural studies approach works with children's literature.

2

The pioneering work of F. R. Leavis and Denys Thompson (*Culture and Environment*, 1933) carried with it the heavy legacy of Arnold's ideas in *Culture and Anarchy*. Raymond Williams's work in the late 1950s suggested a clear historical location for the idea of culture and accounted for the responses of such critics as Arnold and Leavis:

> The organising principle of this book is the discovery that the idea of culture, and the word itself in its general modern use, came into English thinking in the period which we commonly describe as that of the Industrial Revolution. . . . It thus becomes an account and an interpretation of our responses in thought and feeling to the changes in English society since the late eighteenth century. Only in such a context can our use of the word 'culture', and the issues to which the word refers be adequately understood. (Williams 1958: vii)

More recently, the important work of Hoggart, Hall and Johnson (see Dunn 1986 and Widdowson 1982) at the Centre for Contemporary Cultural Studies at the University of Birmingham has seen a Marxist-structuralist approach overcoming the Leavisite (Dunn 1986: 79), while Marxism has sometimes had a structuralist inflection, and sometimes an ethnographic one.

> Some basic Marxist assumptions underlie all the British work in cultural studies. They start from the belief that meanings and the making of them (which together constitute culture) are indivisibly linked to social structure and can only be explained in terms of that structure and its history. Correlatively, the social structure is held in place by, among other forces, the meanings that culture produces. . . . These meanings are not only meanings of social experience, but also meanings of self, that is, constructions of social identity for people living in industrial capitalist societies that enable them to make sense of themselves and of their social relations. (Fiske 1987: 254–5)

What, then, are the most important features of cultural studies if we are to understand its relevance to the study of children's literature? At the risk of gross oversimplification, five characteristics can be drawn from recent accounts of the field.

First is a belief that reality can only be made sense of through language or other cultural systems which are embedded within history: 'Thus the idea of an objective, empirical "truth" is untenable. Truth must always be understood in terms of how it is made, for whom and at what time is it "true". Consciousness is never the product of truth or reality, but rather of culture, society and history' (ibid.: 256).

Secondly, cultural studies is Marxist in the conceptualization of society as characterized by the struggle for social power. In cultural terms, the struggle is for meaning: dominant groups attempt to render as 'natural' meanings which serve their interests, whereas subordinate groups resist this process in various ways, trying to make meanings that serve *their* interests (ibid.: 255). An obvious example is the cultural struggle between patriarchy and feminism; but, of course, divisions into groups in society can be along lines of race, class, age, and so on, as well as gender.

Thirdly, cultural studies has tried to theorize subjectivity as a sociocultural construction. Brantlinger argues that cultural studies is 'anti-individualist and anti-subjectivist because it locates the sources of meaning not in individual reason or subjectivity, but in social relations, communication, cultural politics. The stress on culture implies the social construction of meanings *but it also implies* the existence of forms of political or communal reason transcending subjectivity' (Brantlinger 1990: 16). Some theorists, under the influence of Althusserian or poststructuralist thinking, replace the idea of the individual by the idea of the 'subject'. The 'subject' and his/her 'subjectivity' is a social construction and it is thus always open to change. All cultural systems, including language, literature and the products of mass communication, play a part in the construction and reconstruction of the subject. It is in this way, according to the Althusserian wing of cultural studies, that ideology is constantly reproduced in people.

The fourth characteristic of cultural studies is the way it views acts of communication, including the 'reading process'. Communication in language is a social practice which offers a social position for the addressee to take up. During the 1970s, attention moved from the primacy of the text to a position where

> The text can no longer be seen as a self-sufficient entity that bears its own meaning and exerts a similar influence on all its readers . . . the text does not determine its meaning so much as delimit the arena of the struggle for that meaning by marking the terrain within which its variety of readings can be negotiated. (Fiske 1987: 269)

Under the influence of concepts such as hegemony, reading is seen as a process of negotiation. Stuart Hall, in an important paper (Hall 1980), postulated three reading strategies produced by three general social positions that people may occupy in relation to dominant ideologies: the dominant, the negotiated and the oppositional. However, Morley, trying to account for the variety of readings he found in his research into the *Nationwide* audience (Morley 1980) replaced Hall's three categories of reading by a more flexible model in which

> Reading becomes a negotiation between the social sense inscribed in the program and the meanings of social experience made by its wide variety of viewers: this negotiation is a discursive one. . . . Exploring the strategies by which subordinate subcultures make their own mean-

ings in resistance to the dominant is currently one of the most productive strands in cultural studies. (Fiske 1987: 268–70)

The relevance of this notion to children's literature is not difficult to perceive. The increasing emphasis on ethnography in cultural studies, when applied to the field of children's literature, would lead us to study the meanings children and adults actually make or appear to make of the texts they read and view.

The fifth characteristic of cultural studies is its use of ideology as a central concept. The view derived from the writings of Marx and Engels that ideology is illusion, or 'false consciousness', has now been considerably modified. But, as I mentioned earlier, Althusser's reinterpretation of Marx's concept of ideology did influence cultural studies, and Althusser's definition of ideology carried with it something of the notion of a 'false consciousness' masking individuals' realization of the 'real' conditions of their existence.

John B. Thompson, in two important studies (Thompson 1984, 1990), distinguishes two very different senses with which the concept is used in studies of ideology: on the one hand there is what he calls 'the neutral conception of ideology'. Writers who adopt this definition assume that 'ideology operates like a sort of social cement, binding the members of a society together by providing them with collectively shared values and norms . . . one speaks of "systems of thought", of "systems of belief" of "symbolic practices" which pertain to social action or political projects' (Thompson 1984: 4–5). The other sense of ideology

> is essentially linked to the process of sustaining asymmetrical relations of power – that is, to the process of maintaining domination. The use of the term expresses what may be called a *critical conception* of ideology. It preserves the negative connotation which has been conveyed by the term throughout most of its history and binds the analysis of ideology to the question of critique. (ibid.: 4)

Thompson's own position is close to the latter use of the term. He defines ideology thus: 'Ideology, broadly speaking, is *meaning in the service of power*' (Thompson 1990: 7), and argues that to study ideology, 'is to study the ways in which meaning (or signification) serves to sustain relations of domination' (Thompson 1984: 4).

3

Thompson's most recent book, *Ideology and Modern Culture* (1990), sets out a brilliant programme for the cultural analysis of texts, especially the texts of mass communication, and it is worth summarizing something of his approach as it could represent a coherent programme of research in children's literature. His approach to culture involves

> *the social uses of symbolic forms*. We are concerned with whether, to what extent and how (if at all) symbolic forms serve to establish and sustain relations of domination in the social contexts within which they are produced, transmitted and received. This approach may lead us to regard a symbolic form or system as ideological in one context and as radical, subversive, contestatory in another; it may lead us to regard a discourse on human rights, for instance, as supportive of the status quo in one context and as subversive in another. The analysis of symbolic forms as ideological requires us to analyse these forms in relation to the specific social-historical contexts within which they are employed and take hold. (ibid.: 8)

Following the work of the anthropologist, Clifford Geertz, and the philosopher, Paul Ricoeur, Thompson proposes what he calls 'a depth hermeneutics framework for cultural analysis'. The framework comprises three principal phases or procedures. 'The first phase, which may be described as "social-historical analysis", is concerned with the social and historical conditions of the production, circulation and reception of symbolic forms' (ibid.: 22). In this phase, Thompson reasserts the importance of history in cultural analysis.

'The second phase of the depth-hermeneutical framework may be described as "formal or discursive analysis" . . . an analytical phase which is concerned primarily with the internal organization of symbolic forms, with their structural features, patterns and relations' (ibid.: 22). But Thompson warns that this type of analysis can easily become 'misleading' and 'an abstract exercise', if 'disconnected from social-historical conditions and oblivious to what is being expressed by the symbolic forms whose structure it seeks to unveil'.

The third phase of the depth-hermeneutical framework, called 'interpretation', is

> concerned with the creative explication of what is said or represented by a symbolic form. . . . It uses social-historical analysis and formal or discursive analysis to shed light on the social conditions and structural features of a symbolic form, and it seeks to interpret a symbolic form in this light, to explicate and elaborate what it says, what it represents, what it is about. (ibid.: 22)

The framework can, of course, be used to interpret ideology. With ideology, the interpretation draws on the phases of social-historical analysis and formal or discursive analysis, 'but it gives them a critical emphasis: it employs them with the aim of disclosing meaning in the service of power. The interpretation of ideology is depth hermeneutics with a critical intent' (ibid.: 22).

Interestingly, in his earlier book, *Studies in the Theory of Ideology*, Thompson states that one of the kinds of discursive analysis which is particularly useful for the investigation of ideology is

> the analysis of *narratives*. For ideology, in so far as it seeks to sustain relations of domination by representing them as 'legitimate', tends to assume a narrative form. Stories are told which justify the exercise of power by those who possess it, situating these individuals within a tissue of tales that recapitulate the past and anticipate the future. (Thompson 1984: 11)

Thompson also underlines the importance in the cultural analysis of ideology of the process of 'reading' or 'appropriation'. It is clear that a message constructed in certain ways may be understood very differently by different readers or 'recipients'. Further, the act of 'reading' is part of the process of self-formation and self-understanding:

> The process of appropriation is an active and potentially critical process in which individuals are involved in a continuous *effort to understand*, an effort to make sense of

179

the messages they receive, to relate to them and to share them with others. . . . They are not passively absorbing what is presented to them, but are actively, sometimes critically, engaged in a continuing process of self-formation and self-understanding. (Thompson 1990: 25)

Thompson's depth-hermeneutical framework offers exciting possibilities for the analysis of children's literature and other forms of media texts for children. It combines a sensitive social-historical understanding of texts with a critique of their possible ideological uses within certain contexts.

4

There are two other developments that, in many ways, attempt something of the interdisciplinary and totalizing approach of cultural studies and, as with cultural studies, they are likely to play an increasing role in the study of children's literature.

New Historicism is somewhat of an umbrella term, covering a range of related theoretical approaches, as the collection of essays entitled *The New Historicism* testifies. New Historicism, like cultural studies, attempts to cross disciplinary boundaries, in this case 'the boundaries separating history, anthropology, art, politics, literature and economics' (Veeser 1989: ix). Some of the work seems to draw upon Marxism within a poststructuralist context, but Veeser points out that 'New Historicism is as much a reaction against Marxism as a continuation of it' (ibid.: xi).

New Historicism draws equally upon the cultural anthropology of Clifford Geertz and Victor Turner to describe culture in action. (Some of the contributors to Veeser's collection favour the term 'cultural poetics' rather than New Historicism.) New Historicism comes close to cultural studies with its 'concern with the historical, social and political conditions and consequences of literary production and reproduction: The writing and reading of texts, as well as the processes by which they are circulated and categorized, analysed and taught, are being reconstrued as historically determined and determining modes of cultural work' (Montrose 1989: 15).

New Historicism, like cultural studies, resists the polarization of the linguistic and the social. Rather, 'the prevailing tendency . . . is to emphasize their reciprocity and mutual constitution. On the one hand, the social is understood to be discursively constructed; and on the other, language-use is understood to be always and necessarily dialogical, to be socially and materially determined and constrained' (ibid.: 15). At the same time, some New Historicists 'delight in anecdote, narrative and what Clifford Geertz calls "thick description" as a will to construe *all* of culture as the domain of literary criticism – a text to be perpetually interpreted, an inexhaustible collection of stories from which curiosities may be culled and cleverly retold' (ibid.: 19).

New Historicism renders problematic the old critical distinction between literary text and history as foreground and background, renegotiating the relationships between texts and other cultural practices within history. Montrose, in a ringing phrase, argues for what he calls, 'The Historicity of Texts and the Textuality of History'. Such a concept implies 'a dynamic, temporal model of culture and ideology', in which the meaning of a text cannot be stabilized. New Historicism is distinguished from the older historicist approach to literature by displaying a self-consciousness of what is involved in the project of historical criticism, namely 'a realization and acknowledgement that our analyses and our understandings necessarily proceed from our own historically, socially and institutionally shaped vantage points' (ibid.: 23).

As a result of this acknowledgement, class, gender and ethnicity have been foregrounded in historical literary and cultural analyses, a point which Brantlinger echoes in his discussion of cultural studies: ' "difference" – the threat or promise of "the Other" – will continue to be the central organizing category for postmodernist cultural and literary theory' (Brantlinger 1990: 163).

In the USA the humanities have been criticized for maintaining the status quo, whereas in Britain, cultural materialist critics (developing the ideas associated with the work of Raymond Williams) have emphasized the 'historical uses to which an historical *present* puts its versions of the English past' (Montrose 1989: 27). In the area of children's literature studies, Mitzi Myers has suggested what a radical New Historicism of children's literature would do; and her agenda of work resembles one that might be found within the area of cultural studies:

A New Historicism of children's literature would integrate text and socio-historic context, demonstrating on the one hand how extraliterary cultural formations shape literary discourse and on the other how literary practices are actions that make things happen – by shaping the psychic and moral consciousness of young readers but also by performing many more diverse kinds of cultural work, from satisfying authorial fantasies to legitimating or subverting dominant class and gender ideologies. . . . It would want to know how and why a tale or poem came to say what it does, what the environing circumstances were (including the uses a particular sort of children's literature served for its author, its child and adult readers, and its culture), and what kinds of cultural statements and questions the work was responding to. (Myers 1988: 42; see also 'Introduction', pp. 11–12)

Amongst historians, a somewhat similar new approach is developing, called 'The New Cultural History'. In the collection of the same name, Lynn Hunt argues that in the new cultural history

in place of sociology, the influential disciplines are anthropology and literary theory. . . . At the moment, the anthropological model reigns supreme in cultural approaches. . . . The deciphering of meaning, then, rather than the inference of causal laws of explanation, is taken to be the central task of cultural history, just as it was posed by Geertz to be the central task of cultural anthropology. (Hunt 1989: 10–12)

But there is the same debate over the Geertzian approach to culture to be found in cultural studies and New Historicism. Some historians question 'the validity of a search for meaning in the Geertzian interpretive mode because it tends to efface differences in the appropriation or uses of cultural forms. The urge to see order and meaning obscures the existence of conflict and struggle' (ibid.: 12). Hunt sees two main models in the new cultural history: the anthropological and the literary. However, 'Although there are many differences within and between anthropological and literary models, one central tendency in both seems currently to fascinate historians of culture: the use of language as metaphor' (ibid.: 16).

Hunt concludes her introduction to the collection with a plea to historians and those who practise cultural studies: 'the more cultural historical studies become and the more historical cultural studies become, the better for both' (ibid.: 22).

I have tried to elucidate the main characteristics of a growing body of work concerned with culture and history and have suggested something of its value for the student of children's literature. Finally, I offer, tentatively, an example of the kind of work that might be carried out in the field of children's literature, using some of the ideas and frameworks outlined above.

5

Social reality is a vast network of narratives that we use to make sense of experience, to understand the present, the past and the future. Narratives give us the shape of our identity as individuals and as members of a socially symbolic reality. As Barbara Hardy puts it 'we dream in narrative, daydream in narrative. . . . In order really to live, we make up stories about ourselves and others, about the personal as well as the social past and future' (Hardy 1977: 13). Narratives help us turn the constant flow of events into intelligible experience. We relate narratives to one another in many forms: from gossip to literature there stretches a continuum of stories. This way of seeing things enables us to give children's literature its proper place: as Fred Inglis puts it, novels can be thought of as 'the disciplined and public versions of the fictions we must have if we are to think at all' (Inglis 1981: 310).

Stories contribute to the formation and re-formation in our children of the cultural imagination, a network (as the American anthropologist Clifford Geertz and, more recently, the French philosopher Paul Ricoeur have argued) of patterns and templates through which we articulate our experience (Geertz 1973; Ricoeur 1986). So the stories we tell our children, the narratives we give them to make sense of cultural experience, constitute a kind of mapping, maps of meaning that enable our children to make sense of the world. They contribute to children's sense of identity, an identity that is simultaneously personal and social: narratives, we might say, shape the way children find a 'home' in the world.

But the concept of 'home' can have resonances that go well

beyond the idea of a physical space in which children live. For example, we can distinguish three different, but related senses of 'home' as it operates at the level of the cultural imagination. First, 'home' can refer, as Patrick Wright puts it, to 'the interior space in which some recognition can be given to the endowments and potentials which have no opportunity for realisation in the world as it is' (Wright 1985: 110).

A second meaning of 'home', and one that has a powerful effect in shaping our children's identity through the cultural imagination, is constructed through the images we supply and the stories we tell of the land in which we live: our 'homeland'. Raymond Williams demonstrated the importance of the images of 'the country and the city' (Williams 1975) for an understanding of English culture, and children's writers, especially writers of fantasy, are a rich source of such images of landscape and townscape. Such works of fantasy construct images of an imaginary homeland that help sustain myths of national identity, community and common heritage.

Ernst Bloch, in discussing the principle of *hope* which lies at the heart of utopia, suggests a third and even more profound meaning in the concept 'home' in the cultural imagination: 'What is envisioned as home [*Heimat*] in childhood is in actuality the goal of the upright gait toward which human beings strive as they seek to overcome exploitation, humiliation, oppression and disillusionment. The individual alone cannot attain such a goal, which is only possible as a collective enterprise' (Bloch 1988: xxvii).

We use a wide range of narratives to imagine how the world is and how it might be: from easily recognizable folk tales, short stories and novels to what we could call vast overarching mythic proto-narratives that do not appear in themselves as written texts but nevertheless underpin our beliefs about the world. These mythic proto-narratives, like all narratives, shape our social and cultural imagination, contributing to the mapping of our experience of social reality. Although these proto-narratives are socially constructed fictions, they are not 'untrue'. Because we live by forms of fiction, they are a necessary part of the meaning-making process in our lives. However, such fictions are open to revision: the high-level proto-narratives may change as events and collective forces dismantle the old narratives and construct new ones.

One example of such an overarching proto-narrative is the

mythology of a nation, or the myth of national identity. Richard Slotkin reminds us that the transmission of such cultural myths can have very powerful effects on adults and children because the myths act both psychologically and socially:

> The mythology of a nation is the intelligible mask of that enigma called the 'national character'. Through myths the psychology and world view of our cultural ancestors are transmitted to modern descendants, in such a way and with such power that our perception of contemporary reality and our ability to function in the world are directly, often tragically affected. (quoted in Yanarella and Sigelman 1988: 3)

Thus, national myths work largely unconsciously but nevertheless powerfully, to shape a part of adults' and children's cultural imagination. As two political commentators have argued recently, such myths 'take on the character of collective representations that reconcile and unite many contradictory aspects of the past' and thus 'form parts of a national identity and a common heritage' (Yanarella and Sigelman 1988: 4). These national myths, like other kinds of cultural myth, are woven into the literature we give our children.

In the rest of this essay I intend to take narratives from different symbolic levels and show how they may relate to one another. I want to suggest how one might reveal the myths of national identity in two well-known works of children's literature, one from American culture and one from English culture: *The Wizard of Oz* and *The Wind in the Willows*. In other words, I want to explore the 'Americanness' of *The Wizard of Oz* and the 'Englishness' of *The Wind in the Willows*.

In comparing the two novels, what struck me immediately was that they are both structured upon the oppositions of 'home' and 'adventure'. Such an opposition is, of course, a recurrent motif in children's literature, but the form in which this opposition is explored is different in the two novels. *The Wizard of Oz* is what Baum calls 'a modernized fairy tale in which the wonderment and joy are retained and the heartaches and nightmares are left out' (Baum 1979: 1). *The Wind in the Willows*, on the other hand, is an animal fantasy in which adventure offers excitement but also disruption and danger to animals who learn to recognize that true wisdom lies in accepting their 'home', that is, their place in society.

The novels were published within a few years of one another (*The Wizard of Oz* was published in America in 1900; *The Wind in the Willows* was published in Britain in 1908), and they represent very different responses to the social changes common to both countries at that time: in particular, the development of industrialization and technology and the associated changes in the relations between social classes. Yet it is perhaps because the novels may be regarded as responses to specific historical circumstances that the myths of national identity are so strongly woven into them. Although both novels depict utopian solutions to problems associated with the changes, *The Wizard of Oz* presents a utopia that, in many ways, is progressive and oriented to the future, whereas *The Wind in the Willows* presents an essentially nostalgic utopia.

The Wizard of Oz was the first in a series of fourteen 'Oz' books that were published between 1900 and 1920. Baum had been born into an upper-class family, the son of an oil executive, but a series of disasters resulted in his downward social mobility. Before he wrote *The Wizard of Oz* Baum had experienced life as a salesman, storekeeper and journalist. In the South Dakota of the 1890s, as editor of a small-town newspaper, he witnessed the plight and poverty of the farmers. His sympathies, says Martin Gardner, 'seem always to have been on the side of the labouring classes' (Gardner and Nye 1959: 29). It was against this background that Baum wrote *The Wizard of Oz* and interestingly, it was against the background of the Great Depression of 1930s America that MGM's famous film of *The Wizard of Oz*, starring Judy Garland, was made in 1939.

The novel opens with an image of home and landscape: Dorothy's small wooden house situated in the middle of the Kansas prairies. But it is a grey, arid landscape supporting a way of life that has taken all joy and laughter from Dorothy's Aunt Em and Uncle Henry (Baum 1979: 2). From here Dorothy is whirled away by a cyclone to a country that seems to be the very opposite of Kansas: Oz is small, colourful and fertile:

The cyclone had set the house down, very gently – for a cyclone – in the midst of a country of marvelous beauty. There were lovely patches of greensward all about, with stately trees bearing rich and luscious fruits. Banks of gorgeous flowers were on every hand, and birds with rare and brilliant plumage sang and fluttered in the trees and bushes. A little way off was a small brook, rushing and sparkling along between green banks, and murmuring in a voice very grateful to a little girl who had lived so long on the dry gray prairies. (Baum 1979: 9)

Oz is wealthy where Kansas was poor. As Brian Attebury points out. 'Oz is not plagued with droughts and crop failures, nor with bankers and mortgages, as Kansas most assuredly was' (Attebury 1983: 281). But symbolically, Dorothy has not left America. She has entered a symbolic landscape that, as Attebury argues, '[forms] America's image of the western frontier: it is the Garden of the World set in the midst of the Great American Desert' (ibid.: 281). It is an American utopia incorporating elements that draw upon and contribute to the myths of national identity. For example, in *The Wizard of Oz* and the later Oz books, the tension between the pastoral ('the kingdom of love') and technology ('the kingdom of power') is resolved (Bewley 1983: 204).

The magic in Oz is scientific in character but the magical technology is strictly controlled by the central government. As Marius Bewley puts it 'By this prohibition, which placed government restrictions on promiscuous and uncontrolled "technological" experimentation, Oz [retained] her pastoral landscape and guaranteed her people's happiness' (ibid.: 205). Bewley goes on to argue that the transformation of magic 'into a glamorized version of technology and applied science' is part of what makes Oz an unmistakably American fairyland.

In the politics of this American utopia, the great and powerful Wizard turns out to be a common man from Omaha. Dorothy, the ordinary girl from Kansas, works to return home in the company of a scarecrow, a tin woodman and a cowardly lion. They all find they have powers that they had not realized they possessed. The 'American myth' of individualism and self-reliance is praised but, as Timothy Cook argues, only within the context of a community that takes advantage of the individual's special and particular talents (Cook 1988: 43).

It is clear that *The Wizard of Oz* and Baum's subsequent novels for children can be seen as contributing to the myth of American national identity. It has been claimed by various critics and commentators that 'in Oz, Baum actually added another state to the Union'; that it is 'the first American fairyland' whose characters have become 'part of our language and folklore' (Thompson 1983: 178, 176); the virtues of Oz, it has been argued, 'are the homely American virtues of family love, friendliness for the stranger, sympathy for the underdog, practicality and commonsense in facing life, reliance on one's self for solutions to one's problems' (Nye 1983: 174).

It is interesting and important how the position of women in the novels has been ambiguously conceptualized by critics. On the one hand, that Dorothy has been seen as heir to the 'essential American character', that of 'the explorer, the wanderer, who penetrates ever wilder regions of the world or the mind and comes back relatively unscathed'; in short, Dorothy is that 'peculiarly American' character, 'the pioneer woman' (Attebury 1983: 294). On the other hand, another critic describes Oz as 'a little girl's dream-home' whose atmosphere is 'feminine not masculine': 'Oz is a family-style Utopia. . . . It is simply the perfect home, built on love, permeated by happiness, filled with a big loving family. . . . Oz is a fairyland small-town or surburban home tailored to the pattern of a little girl's dream' (Nye 1983: 171–2). Myths of American national identity are thus woven into Baum's novels, although they can be interpreted in different ways.

It could be argued that there are many features of *The Wizard of Oz* that are oriented towards a 'more progressive' future: it presents images of hope in which the tension between the pastoral dream and technology is resolved; the common man from Omaha, the ordinary girl from Kansas, and those who lack confidence in themselves all find they have powers they had not realized. A girl is given a central role and allowed, in part, to act as an intrepid pioneer adventurer before returning 'home'.

Do we detect the same elements in Kenneth Grahame's *The Wind in the Willows*? Like Baum, Grahame wrote his novel in the midst of turbulent social conditions. Jan Marsh tells us that the collapse of agriculture in the 1870s and 'the grave decline in rural population which resulted . . . prompted a sudden rush of nostalgia for rural life . . . with the traditional countryside of England apparently disappearing for ever, pastoral attitudes were reasserted with intensity' (Marsh 1982: 3–4).

The pastoral attitudes were embraced most readily by the professional middle classes, the only ones who, 'cushioned financially by the proceeds of the hated industrial system', could afford to move to the country or to holiday there in weekend cottages or gypsy-style caravans. Grahame rose eventually to the professional middle class by being appointed to one of the Bank of England's top three positions.

For the society of late Victorian England, the attraction of the countryside was partly religious and partly political. Jan Marsh explains that faith in a conventional creator was being undermined by Darwinism, 'and Nature offered a viable alternative – the earth as the source of all goodness in place of God, a mystical deity without the archaic mythology' (Marsh 1982: 5). Thus, she argues, 'Drawing on Romanticism and classical ideas of pantheism, love of Nature helped to fill the gap, enabling many late Victorians to dispense with God gradually, as it were, without losing their sense of immanent divinity' (ibid.: 35). This feature of the historical context is expressed most clearly, of course, in the chapter entitled 'The Piper at the Gates of Dawn'.

Politically, riots in the cities produced among the middle classes: 'terror of revolution and mob violence, the supposed dangers latent in an anarchic, industrialized, no longer rural-subservient proletariat' (Green 1982: 1299), and we shall see how that aspect of the political context was woven into the novel.

Like *The Wizard of Oz*, Grahame's novel is constructed upon the opposition of 'home' and 'adventure', and it too begins with an image of 'home'. But instead of the grey Kansas prairie, we have a comfortable, secure place underground, disturbed only by a 'spirit of divine discontent and longing' for adventure (Grahame 1967: 7). The themes of 'home' and 'homesickness' run right through the novel. There are the powerful images of home: above all the famous description of Badger's kitchen (ibid.: 67). Then there is the essence of nostalgia itself as Mole suddenly smells his old home. The word 'nostalgia' is derived from two Greek words meaning, literally, homesickness, and Mole displays just these symptoms:

> The call was clear, the summons was plain. He must obey it instantly, and go. 'Ratty!' he called, full of joyful excitement, 'hold on! Come back! I want you, quick!'
>
> 'O, come along, Mole, do!' replied the Rat cheerfully, still plodding along.
>
> 'Please stop, Ratty!' pleaded the poor Mole in anguish

of heart. 'You don't understand! It's my home, my old home! I've just come across the smell of it, and it's close by here, really quite close. And I must go to it, I must, I must! O, come back, Ratty! Please, please come back!' (Grahame 1967: 89)

But 'home', in the novel, means more than a literal place. 'Home' is bound up with one's place in society, one's position in the class structure. The novel presents a world in which problems are caused by the failure of the animals to accept their limitations; instead, they try to be independent, to venture away from the safety of their homes. For example, Mole's solitary walk results in his becoming a victim of 'the terror of the Wild Wood'. He eventually comes to recognize his limitations and to accept his place in the order of things:

> Mole saw clearly that he was an animal of tilled field and hedgerow, linked to the ploughed furrow, the frequented pasture, the lane of evening lingerings, the cultivated garden-plot. . . . he must be wise, must keep to the pleasant places in which his lines were laid and which held adventure enough, in their way, to last for a lifetime. (Grahame 1967: 83)

As for Toad, he 'lets the side down' – through his addiction to the new attractions of the motor car. Modern technology, in the form of the motor car, is presented in a highly ambivalent manner. Toad sees the motor car as: ' "The poetry of motion! The real way to travel! The only way to travel!" ' (ibid.: 41) But the motor car is also the source of noise and terror and danger in the countryside and it becomes the cause of Toad's downfall. Toad abandons the values of his 'home' in society through his betrayal of the leisured middle-class existence of the River-Bankers. He squanders the money left him by his father, gives the other animals a bad name, and is responsible for letting the insurgents take over Toad Hall. As Badger explains severely: ' "Independence is all very well, but we animals never allow our friends to make fools of themselves beyond a certain limit; and that limit you've reached" ' (ibid.: 112). However, when Toad eventually expresses true contrition, the River-Bankers rally round to help him regain his ancestral home, Toad Hall. The house is described as a 'handsome, dignified old house of mellowed red brick', 'a self-contained gentleman's residence dating in part from the 14th century', with 'handsome Tudor' windows and banqueting hall, 'but replete with every modern convenience': a description that reads a little like the estate agents' advertisements that appeared week after week in the magazine *Country Life* of the time. The stoats, weasels and ferrets of the Wild Wood are driven back through the collective efforts of what Jules Zanger describes as 'thinly described types' from the ordered world of nineteenth-century England (Zanger 1977: 159).

The heritage of the River-Bankers is saved, a newly purged aristocrat, now acting like an upper middle-class gentleman squire, is restored to his traditional home, and hierarchy and order are restored to society. The aristocratic, heroic values are, of course, simultaneously mocked and praised. But, above all, what is restored at the end of the novel is a vision of the good life: order, tranquility, harmony: the virtues that men like Ruskin believed were being destroyed by industrial progress. But it is the utopia of a particular social group, the River-Bankers; it is a way of life that Peter Green has described as 'the rentier's rural dream', with the countryside not as a place of work but redefined as an Arcadia of rural leisure. Just as the Land of Oz may be seen as a 'great good place', a utopia, so too can *The Wind in the Willows* be seen as utopian. But this great good place is what has been called 'a full rich portrait of the earthly paradise' of the English countryside: the River Thames near Cookham; and, as the middle classes of Grahame's time were in terror of revolution by the so-called urban proletariat, so the rural utopia of *The Wind in the Willows* is threatened by the stoats, weasels and ferrets from the Wild Wood.

Moreover, it is a predominantly male paradise: women are relegated to subsidiary roles: as the gaoler's daughter ('a pleasant wench and good-hearted, who assisted her father in the lighter duties of his post') and the barge-woman.

Grahame's novel encapsulates an image of England which developed at the end of the nineteenth century. According to this myth, the 'real' England is a rural Arcadia and, as Martin Wiener argues, it was 'a picture of an unchanging England . . . to set against social unrest and foreign threats' (Wiener 1981: 55). This myth of 'the real England' is powerful and long lasting: it still strongly shapes the sense of British identity and it forms an important line of imagery in British children's literature. The image of the English landscape that developed in late Victorian Britain was essentially one of southern England, rather than northern England or Wales or Scotland. One historian describes the image of the landscape in this way:

> It is rolling and dotted with woodlands. Its hills are smooth and bare, but never rocky or craggy (the male/female word associations are fascinating) in fact hardly 'great hills' at all. Above all it is cultivated and it is post-enclosure countryside. . . . This 'south country' was the product of an urban world, and an urban world at a particular point in time – the late 1870s through to the early 1900s. (Howkins 1986: 64)

It is also a mythic image that arises out of conflicts of social values. As Martin Wiener puts it, 'progress versus nostalgia, material growth versus moral stability were expressed in the two widespread contrasting cultural symbols Workshop and Garden (or Shire). Was England to be the Workshop of the World or a Green and Pleasant Land?' (Wiener 1981: 6). As this quotation suggests, it was not just a way of seeing the countryside. Bound up in the image of 'Englishness' were cultural values relating to work, to architecture, to gender, and a model of society itself: 'an organic and natural society of ranks, and of inequality in an economic and social sense, but one based on trust, obligation and even love' (Howkins 1986: 80).

This complex idea of 'Englishness' runs through the line of 'country-bred' fantasy from Grahame to Tolkien and Richard Adams. They all construct nostalgic images of an imaginary homeland that help sustain myths of national identity, community and common heritage. In *The Wind in the Willows*, *The Lord of the Rings* and *Watership Down*, nostalgia manifests itself as an anti-industrial stance (although there is considerable ambivalence in Grahame's depiction of the motor car) combined with a deep respect for a hierarchical feudal system in which 'individuals gain identity and obtain security within the organic society established according to tradition and natural qualification' (Cook 1988: 55). But it is important to realize that it is also a society in which females are either absent or, if they do appear, are conceived along very traditional lines as idealized goddess figures or romantic heroines; or else they are kept firmly in place as homemakers. The strongest emotion in the novels is that of male comradeship: a feeling engendered in the nineteenth-century public school and sustained through two world wars. The books are male versions of nostalgia, articulated upon deep structural oppositions of 'adventure' and 'home'. These nostalgic longings, with all their ideological implications, are blended with mythic images of the English landscape, an intense hatred of industrialization and a strong belief in hierarchy.

I have argued that such books tell stories that contribute to children's unconscious sense of the 'homeland'. But if we ask, 'What meanings of the homeland do children or, indeed, adults take away from such books?', we run into profound difficulties. At the risk of oversimplification, the situation appears to be something like this: on the one hand we have the 'preferred meanings' established by the 'interpretive community' of academics like me and others in the field of children's literature; on the other hand we have the meanings which are revealed as adults and children actualize these narratives and mobilize their meanings to make sense of their lives. I do not mean to imply that the two sets of meanings are necessarily distinct and different, but I am trying to suggest something of the complexity of the situation. For as Tony Bennett argues, the literary text 'is historically redetermined during the process of its reception, figuring not as the source of an effect but the site on which plural and even contradictory effects may be produced during the course of its history as a received text' (Bennett 1981: 56). In other words, we cannot be certain what meanings groups of readers will take from the literature they read. The meanings which children or adults take from a text will be different for different groups at different points in history. As John Thompson argues, in the passage I quoted earlier, we must be concerned with 'the social uses of symbolic forms' (Thompson 1990: 8). What happens when such conservative texts 'enter history' in the process of their reception? It is then that the complexity of their cultural meanings is revealed.

The stories told in *The Wizard of Oz* and *The Wind in the Willows* can be appropriated to serve the interests of the leisure industries, as, for example, with the 'Disneyfication' of *The Wizard of Oz* in the USA. Again, texts can be conscripted into the service of the 'National Heritage' that serves to reinforce an idealized picture of the national home. The national heritage is sustained through what Hewison calls 'the Heritage Industry' (Hewison 1987). In Britain, it is an industry aided by organizations like the National Trust, the English Tourist Board and English Heritage. Part of the national heritage is a national geography which lies 'hidden away' just beyond the reaches of an industrialized Britain, promising another world existing alongside the everyday which can provide what Patrick Wright calls, 'that momentary experience of utopian gratification in which the grey torpor of everyday life in contemporary Britain lifts and the simpler, more radiant measures of Albion declare themselves again' (Wright 1985: 76).

The sites of this national geography can be reached by courtesy of the English Tourist Board, according to a series of advertisements the Board ran in 1983, which featured the characters from *The Wind in the Willows*. In these advertisements Toad, Mole and Rat drive in a vintage car to explore 'the real England' of ancient monuments and small villages with pastoral and comic-pastoral names: 'Sheepwash', 'Butterwick', 'Buttocks Booth'. The copywriters promised the following: 'Hidden just beyond the noise of the motorway you'll find secret places that have barely changed for hundreds of years.' Such advertising can be seen as 'commodity fetishism', simply turning nostalgia into a commodity, exploiting it as a touristic resource, and thus serving the ideological interests of the capitalistic industry of national heritage. There is something to be said for such a view. And yet, as Patrick Wright reminds us, 'national heritage involves positive energies which certainly can't be written off as ideology. It engages hopes, dissatisfactions, feelings of tradition and freedom' (Wright 1985: 78).

I have argued that narratives shape our reality. The stories we offer our children can help them shape their sense of identity, help them find a home in the world. But the meanings of a text depend upon the history of its reception and the way meanings are mobilized in human experience and history. Texts of nostalgic rural fantasy may be appropriated to serve ideological interests. But such texts of nostalgia may also be appropriated by adults and children in the service of what Bloch calls 'concrete utopias' (Bloch 1988: xxvii) opposed to the present narrow conceptions of what it means to be human: we might say that, instead of 'back to the future', it will be a case of 'forward to the past'. The 'meanings' of such works lie in their use by children and adults, making sense of the

world within the constraints of history. Even apparently ideological texts may act as forms of critical utopia, measuring the
gap between what is and what might be, and so may be used
to present new ways of what it means to be human. Images
of idyllic pastoralism may offer our children, in the words of
Jack Zipes,

> 'wish-images and wish-landscapes [that] measure the dis-
> tance we have yet to go to achieve real happiness. . . .
> they are the traces of utopia that constitute the cultural
> heritage [and they] point to the ultimate realization of a
> promised land that has yet to find its appropriate form.'
> (Bloch 1988: xxxix)

That promised land is the land of 'hope' and a far, far better
'home' than we have ever known.

References

INTRODUCTION

Ahlberg, J. and A. (1986) *The Jolly Postman*, London: Heinemann.

Bettelheim, B. (1976) *The Uses of Enchantment: The Meaning and Importance of Fairy Tales*, New York: Knopf.

Burningham, J. (1984) *Granpa*, London: Cape.

Chambers, A. (1982) *Plays for Young People to Read and Perform*, South Woodchester, Glos.: Thimble Press.

— (1985) *Booktalk*, London: Bodley Head.

Crago, H. (1974) 'Children's literature: on the cultural periphery', *Children's Book Review* 4(4): 157–8.

Darton, F. J. H. (1982) *Children's Books in England* (1932) 3rd edition, revised by Brian Alderson, Cambridge: Cambridge University Press.

Derrida, J. (1976) *Of Grammatology*, Trans. Gayatri Chakravorty Spivak, Baltimore and London: Johns Hopkins University Press.

Hearne, B. (1991) 'Research in children's literature in the US and Canada: problems and possibilities', in The International Youth Library (ed.) *Children's Literature Research, International Resources and Exchange*, Munich: K. G. Saur.

Hunt, P. (ed.) (1982) *Children's Literature Research in Britain*, Cardiff: University of Wales Institute of Science and Technology.

— (1991) *Criticism, Theory, and Children's Literature*, Oxford: Blackwell.

Meek, M. (1988) *How Texts Teach What Readers Learn*, South Woodchester, Glos.: Thimble Press.

Myers, M. (1988) 'Missed opportunities and critical malpractice: New Historicism and children's literature', *Children's Literature Association Quarterly* 13(1): 41–3.

Newton, K. M. (1986) *In Defence of Literary Interpretation*, London: Macmillan.

Nodelman, P. (1985) 'Interpretation and the apparent sameness of children's novels', *Studies in the Literary Imagination* 18(2) Fall: 5–20.

— (1990) 'The hidden meaning and the inner tale: deconstruction and the interpretation of fairy tales', *Children's Literature Association Quarterly* 15(3): 143–48.

Pickering, S. (1982) 'The function of criticism in children's literature', *Children's Literature in Education* 13(1): 13–18.

Reynolds, K. (1990) *Girls Only? Gender and Popular Fiction in Britain, 1880–1910*, Hemel Hempstead: Harvester Wheatsheaf.

REFERENCES

Richards, J. (ed.) (1989) *Imperialism and Juvenile Literature*, Manchester: Manchester University Press.

Roscoe, W. (1855) 'Fictions for children', in L. Salway (ed.) *A Peculiar Gift: Nineteenth-Century Writings on Books for Children*, Harmondsworth: Kestrel.

Rose, J. (1984) *The Case of Peter Pan, or, the Impossibility of Children's Fiction*, London: Macmillan.

Sontag, S. (1966) *Against Interpretation*, New York: Dell.

Spender, D. (1989) *The Writing or the Sex? or Why You Don't Have to Read Women's Writing to Know it's No Good*, New York: Pergamon Press.

Thompson, J. (1987) *Understanding Teenagers' Reading*, North Ryde, NSW: Methuen.

Wall, B. (1991) *The Narrator's Voice. The Dilemma of Children's Fiction*, London: Macmillan.

Williams, G. (1986) 'Letter to the editor', *Reading Time*, 101: 11.

1 IDEOLOGY

Dixon, B. (1977) *Catching them Young 1, Sex, Race and Class in Children's Fiction*, London: Pluto Press.

Leeson, R. (1985) *Reading and Righting*, London: Collins.

Moore, D. and MacCann, O. (1986) 'The Uncle Remus travesty', *Children's Literature Association Quarterly* 11(2): 96–100; 11(4): 205–9.

Stephens, J. (1992) *Language and Ideology in Children's Fiction*, London: Longman.

Sutherland, R. D. (1985) 'Hidden persuaders: political ideologies in literature for children', *Children's Literature in Education* 16(3): 143–58.

Watson, J. (1986) 'Challenging assumptions: ideology and teenage fiction in today's global village', *International Review of Children's Literature and Librarianship* 1(3): 65–71.

Hollindale: Ideology and the Children's Book

Bawden, N. (1975) 'The imprisoned child', in E. Blishen (ed.) *The Thorny Paradise*, Harmondsworth: Kestrel.

Crompton, R. (1930) *William the Bad*, London: Newnes.

Dixon, B. (1977) *Catching them Young 1, Sex, Race and Class in Children's Fiction*, London: Pluto Press.

Grunsell, R. (1978) *Born to be Invisible*, London: Macmillan Education.

Inglis, F. (1981) *The Promise of Happiness*, Cambridge: Cambridge University Press.

Leeson, R. (1985) *Reading and Righting*, London: Collins.

Lewis, C. S. (1980) 'On three ways of writing for children', reprinted in S. Egoff, G. T. Stubbs and L. F. Ashley (eds) *Only Connect*, Toronto: Oxford University Press.

Musgrave, P. W. (1985) *From Brown to Bunter: The Life and Death of the School Story*, London: Routledge & Kegan Paul.

Price, S. (1984) *From Where I Stand*, London: Faber & Faber.

Treece, H. (1970) 'Writing for children', in Owens and Marland (eds) *The Practice of English Teaching*, Glasgow: Blackie.

Waller, G. (1986) *English Poetry of the Sixteenth Century*, London: Longman.

2 CRITICISM: THE STATE OF THE ART

Britton, J. (1977) 'The role of fantasy', in M. Meek, A. Warlow and G. Barton (eds) *The Cool Web: The Pattern of Children's Reading*, London: Bodley Head.

Gilead, S. (1988) 'The undoing of idyll in *The Wind in the Willows*', *Children's Literature* 16: 145–58.

Hughes, F. A. (1978) 'Children's literature, theory and practice', *ELH* 45: 542–61.

Hume, K. (1984) *Fantasy and Mimesis: Responses to Reality in Western Literature*, London: Methuen.

Lewis, D. (1990) 'The constructedness of texts: picture books and the metafictive', *Signal* 62: 131–46.

Moss, A. (1985) 'Varieties of children's metafiction', *Studies in the Literary Imagination* 18(2): 79–92.

Paul, L. (1990) 'The new 3Rs: repetition, recollection, and recognition', *Children's Literature Association Quarterly* 15(2): 55–7.

Rabkin, E. S. (1976) *The Fantastic in Literature*, Princeton: Princeton University Press.

Sale, R. (1978) *Fairy Tales and After: from Snow White to E. B. White*, Cambridge, Mass.: Harvard University Press.

Smith, G. (1987) 'Inner reality: the nature of fantasy', in M. Saxby and G. Winch, *Give Them Wings: The Experience of Children's Literature*, South Melbourne: Macmillan.

Stephens, J. (1991) ' "Did I tell you about the time I pushed the Brothers Grimm off Humpty Dumpty's wall?" Metafictional strategies for constituting the audience as agent in the narratives of Janet and Allan Ahlberg', in M. Stone, *Children's Literature and Contemporary Theory*, Wollongong: New Literatures Research Centre.

—— (1992) *Language and Ideology in Children's Fiction*, London: Longman.

Swinfen, A. (1984) *In Defence of Fantasy*, London: Routledge & Kegan Paul.

Waugh, P. (1984) *Metafiction*, London: Methuen.

Wolfe, G. K. (1990) 'History and criticism', in N. Barron (ed.) *Fantasy Literature, A Reader's Guide*, New York: Garland.

Moss: Metafiction, Illustration, and the Poetics of Children's Literature

Ahlberg, J. and A. (1981) *Peepo!*, Harmondsworth: Penguin (Kestrel).

Anno, M. (1988) *Upside Downers*, London: Macmillan.

Bakhtin, M. (1981) *The Dialogic Imagination*, London: University of Texas Press.

REFERENCES

Barthes, R. (1975) *S/Z*, trans. R. Miller, London: Cape.

Belsey, C. (1980) *Critical Practice*, London: Methuen.

Bowles, S. (1987) 'New horizons?', *Books for Keeps* 42: 17.

Brooke-Rose, C. (1981) *A Rhetoric of the Unreal*, Cambridge: Cambridge University Press.

Browne, A. (1976) *Through the Magic Mirror*, London: Hamish Hamilton.

—— (1977) *A Walk in the Park*, London: Hamish Hamilton.

—— (1983) *Gorilla*, London: MacRae.

Burningham, J. (1977) *Come Away from the Water, Shirley*, London: Cape.

—— (1977) *Time to Get Out of the Bath, Shirley*, London: Cape.

Carle, E. (1970) *The Very Hungry Caterpillar*, London: Hamish Hamilton.

Cass, J. (1984) *Literature and the Young Child* (1967), London: Longman.

Chambers, A. (1978) *Breaktime*, London: Bodley Head.

—— (1985) *Booktalk*, London: Bodley Head.

Chatman, S. (1980) 'The rhetoric of difficult fiction', *Poetics Today* 1(4): 23–66.

Crago, H. (1979) 'Cultural categories and the criticism of children's literature', *Signal* 30: 140–50.

Culler, J. (1975) *Structuralist Poetics*, London: Routledge & Kegan Paul.

Dipple, E. (1988) *The Unresolvable Plot*, London: Routledge.

Doonan, J. (1986) 'The object lesson – picture books of Anthony Browne', *Word and Image* 2(2): 159–72.

Eagleton, T. (1986) 'Capitalism, modernism and postmodernism', in *Against the Grain*, London: Verso.

Egoff, S. (1981) *Thursday's Child*, Chicago: American Library Association.

Higonnet, M. (1990) 'The playground of the peritext', *Children's Literature Association Quarterly* 15(2): 47–9.

Hoban, R. (1974) *How Tom Beat Captain Najork and his Hired Sportsmen*, London: Cape.

—— (1975) *A Near Thing for Captain Najork*, London: Cape.

—— (1980) *Riddley Walker*, London: Cape.

—— (1981) *The Great Fruit Gum Robbery*, London: Methuen.

—— (1982) *The Battle of Zormla*, London: Methuen.

Hunt, P. (1985a) *A Step Off the Path*, London: MacRae.

—— (1985b) 'Necessary misreadings: directions in narrative theory for children's literature', *Studies in the Literary Imagination* 18(2): 107–21.

Hutcheon, L. (1984) *Narcissistic Narrative*, London: Methuen.

—— (1988) *A Poetics of Postmodernism*, London: Methuen.

Keeping, C. (1977) *Joseph's Yard* (1969), London: Oxford University Press.

—— (1977) *Intercity*, London: Oxford University Press.

—— (1984) *Sammy Streetsinger*, London: Oxford University Press.

Kermode, F. (1968) *Continuities*, London: Routledge & Kegan Paul.

Kitamura, S. (1984) *Lily Takes a Walk*, Glasgow: Blackie.

Knowles, T. (1980) *The Book Mice*, London: Evans.

Lodge, D. (1977) *The Modes of Modern Writing*, London: Arnold.

— (1981) *Working with Structuralism*, London: Routledge & Kegan Paul.

Maruki, T. (1983) *Hiroshima Story*, London: Black.

Marquez, G. G. (1970) *One Hundred Years of Solitude*, London: Cape.

McAfee, A. (1984) *The Visitors Who Came to Stay*, London: Hamish Hamilton.

McEwan, I. (1985) *Rose Blanche*, London: Cape.

McHale, B. (1987) *Postmodernist Fiction*, London: Methuen.

McKee, D. (1982) *I Hate My Teddy Bear*, London: Andersen Press.

— (1987) *Snow Woman*, London: Andersen Press.

Meek, M. (1983) 'Novels: a selection', *Signal Review of Children's Books* 1: 49–54.

Moebius, W. (1986) 'An introduction to picture-book codes', *Word and Image* 2(2): 141–58.

Nodelman, P. (1985) 'Interpretation and the apparent sameness of children's novels', *Studies in the Literary Imagination* 18(2): 5–20.

Oram, H. (1982) *Angry Arthur*, London: Andersen Press.

— (1984) *In the Attic*, London: Andersen Press.

Pienkowski, J. (1979) *Haunted House*, London: Heinemann.

Rasmussen, B. (1987) 'Irony in picture books: some examples', *Orana* 23(4): 180–6.

Rees, D. (1980) *The Marble in the Water*, Boston: The Horn Book.

Rice, P. and Waugh, P. (eds) (1989) *Modern Literary Theory: A Reader*, London: Arnold.

Rose, J. (1984) *The Case of Peter Pan*, London: Macmillan.

Rushdie, S. (1981) *Midnight's Children*, London: Cape.

Sarland, C. (1983) 'The Secret Seven vs. the Twits: cultural clash or cosy combination?', *Signal* 42: 107–13.

— (1985) 'Piaget, Blyton and story: children's play and the reading process', *Children's Literature in Education* 16(2): 102–9.

Scholes, R. (1975) *Structural Fabulation*, Notre Dame, IN: Notre Dame University Press.

Testa, F. (1981) *The Paper Aeroplane*, London: Faber.

— (1982) *Never Satisfied*, London: Abelard.

Townsend, J. (1971) *A Sounding of Storytellers*, Harmondsworth: Kestrel.

Waugh, P. (1984) *Metafiction*, London: Methuen.

Whalen-Levitt, P. (1984) 'Picture play in children's books – a celebration of visual awareness', in P. Barron and J. Burley (eds) *Jump Over the Moon*, New York: Holt, Rinehart & Winston.

Wollen, P. (1982) *Readings and Writings*, London: Verso.

Paul: Intimations of Imitations: Mimesis, Fractal Geometry and Children's Literature

Abrams, M. H. (1953) *The Mirror and the Lamp*, Oxford: Oxford University Press.

Aristotle (1961) *Poetics*, trans. K. Telford, Gateway Editions.

Auerbach, E. (1968) *Mimesis: The Representation of Reality in Western*

Literature, trans. W. R. Trask, Princeton, NJ: Princeton University Press.

Brooks, P. (1987) 'The storyteller', *The Yale Journal of Criticism* 1: 1.

Calvino, I. (1988) *Six Memos for the Next Millennium*. The Charles Eliot Norton Lectures, Cambridge, Mass.: Harvard University Press.

Cave, T. (1988) 'New representations of old', *Paragraph* 11: 1.

Derrida, J. (1985) 'Living on: border lines', trans. J. Hulbert, in H. Bloom et al. (eds) *Deconstruction and Criticism*, Continuum.

Gleick, J. (1987) *Chaos: Making a New Science*, Harmondsworth: Penguin.

Havelock, E. (1963) *Preface to Plato*, Cambridge, Mass.: Harvard University Press.

—— (1986) *The Muse Learns to Write: Reflections on Orality and Literacy from Antiquity to the Present*, New Haven: Yale University Press.

Hughes, T. (1967) *Poetry in the Making*, London: Faber & Faber.

—— (1984) *What is the Truth: A Farmyard Fable for the Young*, London: Faber & Faber.

Jarrell, R. (1977) *The Bat Poet*, New York: Collier Books.

Mandelbrot, B. (1977) *The Fractal Geometry of Nature*, Salt Lake City: W. H. Freeman.

Ong, W. J. (1982) 'From mimesis to irony: the distancing of voice', in P. Hernandi (ed.) *The Horizon of Literature*, Lincoln, Nebraska: University of Nebraska Press.

Prendergast, C. (1986) *The Order of Mimesis: Balzac, Stendhal, Nerval, Flaubert*, Cambridge: Cambridge University Press.

Rich, A. (1979) *On Lies, Secrets and Silence: Selected Prose 1966–1978*, New York: Norton.

Riffaterre, M. (1983) *Text Production*, New York: Columbia University Press.

Gilead: Magic Abjured: Closure in Children's Fantasy Fiction

Apter, T. E. (1982) *Fantasy Literature: An Approach to Reality*, Bloomington: Indiana University Press.

Auerbach, N. (1987) 'Alice in Wonderland: a curious child', in H. Bloom (ed.) *Lewis Carroll*, New York: Chelsea, pp. 31–44.

Bakhtin, M. M. (1981) *The Dialogic Imagination: Four Essays by M. M. Bakhtin*, ed. Michael Holquist, Austin: University of Texas Press.

Barrie, J. M. (1985) *Peter Pan* (1911) [*Peter Pan and Wendy*], New York: Bantam.

Baum, L. Frank (1958) *The Wizard of Oz* (1900), New York: Scholastic.

Bettelheim, B. (1978) *The Uses of Enchantment: The Meaning and Importance of Fairy Tales*, Harmondsworth: Penguin.

Birkin, A. (1979) *J. M. Barrie and the Lost Boys: The Love Story That Gave Birth to Peter Pan*, New York: Potter.

Briggs, J. (1987) *A Woman of Passion: The Life of E. Nesbit, 1858–1924*, New York: New Amsterdam.

Brown, N. O. (1959) *Life against Death: The Psychoanalytic Meaning of History*, London: Sphere.

Carpenter, H. (1985) *Secret Gardens: A Study of the Golden Age of Children's Literature*, Boston: Houghton, Mifflin.

Carroll, L. (1960) *Alice's Adventures in Wonderland* and *Through the Looking-Class. The Annotated Alice*, ed. Martin Gardner, Harmondsworth: Penguin.

— (1977) *'The Wasp in the Wig.' A 'Suppressed' Episode of 'Through the Looking-Glass and What Alice Found There'*, ed. and introd. Martin Gardner, New York: Potter.

Clausen, C. (1982) 'Home and away in children's fiction', *Children's Literature* 10: 141–52.

Cott, J. (1981) *Pipers at the Gates of Dawn: The Wisdom of Children's Literature*, New York: Random House.

Coveney, P. (1967) *The Image of Childhood. The Individual and Society: A Study of the Theme in English Literature*, Baltimore: Penguin.

Dunbar, J. (1970) *J. M. Barrie: The Man and the Image*, Boston: Houghton, Mifflin.

Empson, W. (1950) '*Alice in Wonderland*: the child as swain', in *Some Versions of Pastoral* (1935), London: Chatto, pp. 251–94.

Geduld, H. M. (1971) *Sir James Barrie*, New York: Twayne.

Gordon, J. B. (1987) 'The *Alice* books and the metaphors of Victorian childhood', in H. Bloom (ed.) *Lewis Carroll*, New York: Chelsea, pp. 17–30.

Jackson, R. (1981) *Fantasy: The Literature of Subversion*, London: Methuen.

Knoepflmacher, U. C. (1983) 'The balancing of child and adult: an approach to Victorian fantasies for children', *Nineteenth-Century Fiction* 37: 497–530.

— (1986) 'Avenging Alice: Christina Rossetti and Lewis Carroll', *Nineteenth-Century Literature* 41: 299–328.

— (1987) 'Of Babylands and Babylons: E. Nesbit and the reclamation of the fairy tale', *Tulsa Studies in Women's Literature* 6: 299–325.

— (1988) 'Roads half-taken: travel, fantasy, and growing up', *Proceedings of the Thirteenth Annual Conference of the Children's Literature Association*, N.p.: Children's Literature Association: 48–59.

Lanes, S. G. (1971) *Down the Rabbit Hole: Adventures and Misadventures in the Realms of Children's Literature*, New York: Atheneum.

Madden, W. A. (1986) 'Framing the *Alices*', *PMLA* 101: 362–73.

Nesbit, E. (1956) *The Enchanted Castle*, Harmondsworth: Puffin.

Rabkin, E. S. (1976) *The Fantastic in Literature*, Princeton, NJ: Princeton University Press.

Rackin, D. (1982) 'Blessed rage: Lewis Carroll and the modern quest for order', in *Lewis Carroll: A Celebration*, ed. E. Guiliano, New York: Potter, pp. 15–25.

— (1987) 'Love and death in Carroll's *Alices*', in H. Bloom (ed.) *Lewis Carroll*, New York: Chelsea, pp. 111–27.

Rose, J. (1984) *The Case of Peter Pan: Or, The Impossibility of Children's Fiction*, London: Macmillan.

Sendak, M. (1973) *In the Night Kitchen*, Harmondsworth: Puffin.

REFERENCES

—— (1963) *Where the Wild Things Are*, New York: Scholastic.
Simon, E. M. (1978) *The Problem Play in British Drama 1890–1914*, ed.
   J. Hogg, Salzburg Studies in English Literature: Poetic Drama and
   Poetic Theory, Salzburg: University of Salzburg Press.
Streatfeild, N. (1958) *Magic and the Magician: E. Nesbit and Her
   Children's Books*, London: Schuman.
Timmerman, J. H. (1983) *The Fantasy Genre*, Bowling Green, KY: Bowl-
   ing Green University Popular Press.
Todorov, T. (1973) *The Fantastic: A Structural Approach to a Literary
   Genre*, trans. Richard Howard, Cleveland: Press of Case Western
   Reserve University.
Tolkien, J. R. R. (1964) 'On fairy stories', in *Tree and Leaf*, London:
   Unwin, pp. 11–70.
Travers, P. L. (1934) *Mary Poppins*, Harmondsworth: Puffin.
Winnicott, D. W. (1971) *Playing and Reality*, Harmondsworth: Penguin.

3 INTERNATIONALISM

Abrahams, R. D. (1983) *African Folktales*, New York: Pantheon.
Alderson, B. (1987) 'Lone voices in the crowd: the limits of multicultu-
   ralism', in S. R. Gannon and R. A. Thompson (eds) *Cross-Cultural-
   ism in Children's Literature*, Pleasantville, NY: Pace University.
Bunbury, R. (1986) *Looking at Literature*, Victoria: Deakin University
   Open Campus Program.
—— (1988) 'Introduction' to *Through Australian Eyes*, Victoria: Deakin
   University.
Dankert, B. (1991) 'Internationalism in children's literature research
   today', in International Youth Library (ed.) *Children's Literature
   Research: International Resources and Exchange*, Munich: K. G. Saur.
Goldthwaite, J. (1985) 'The black rabbit: part one', *Signal* 47: 86–111.
Hazard, P. (1947) *Books, Children and Men*, Boston: The Horn Book.
Kinnell, M. (1987) 'Cross-cultural futures: research and teaching in
   comparative children's literature', *International Review of Children's
   Literature and Librarianship* 2(3): 161–73.
Moore, O., and MacCann, D. (1986) 'The Uncle Remus travesty',
   Children's Literature Association Quarterly 11(2): 96–100; 11(4): 205–9.
Ray, S. (1982) *The Blyton Phenomenon*, London: Deutsch.

Bunbury and Tabbert: A Bicultural Study of Identification: Readers' Responses to the Ironic Treatment of a National Hero

Barnet, S., Berman, M. and Burto, W. (1960) *A Dictionary of Literary
   Terms*, Boston: Little, Brown.
Bedford, J. (1982) *Sister Kate*, Ringwood, Victoria: Penguin.
Boldrewood, Rolf (1974) *Robbery Under Arms* (1888), Sydney: Rigby.
Bunbury, R. (1980) 'Can children read for inference?', in R. M. Bun-
   bury (ed.) *Children's Literature: The Power of Story*, Melbourne:
   Deakin University.

Clune, F. (1948) *Wild Colonial Boys*, Sydney: Angus & Robertson.

Disher, G. (1984) *Bushrangers*, Melbourne: Nelson.

Dugan, M. (1978) *Bushrangers*, Sydney: Macmillan.

Edwards, R. G. (1976) *The Big Book of Australian Folksongs*, Adelaide: Rigby.

Ewers, H. H. (1985) 'Old heroes in new dress', *The Lion and the Unicorn* 9: 70–4.

Jauss, H. R. (1973–4) 'Levels of identification of hero and audience', *New Literary History* 5: 283–317.

Prior, T., Wannen, B. and Nunn, H. (1966) *A Pictorial History of Bushrangers*, London: Hamlyn.

Spencer, R. (1985) *Everyday Life in Australia: Bushrangers*, Sydney: Hodder & Stoughton.

Stow, R. (1982) *Midnite* (1967), Harmondsworth: Penguin.

Tolkien, J. R. R. (1966) 'On fairy stories', in *The Tolkien Reader*, New York: Ballantyne.

4 POETRY, RESPONSE AND EDUCATION

Applebee, A. (1978) *The Child's Concept of Story*, Chicago: University of Chicago Press.

Barthes, R. (1976) *S/Z*, trans. R. Miller, London: Cape.

Bennett, J. (1984) *Poetry for Children*, South Woodchester, Glos.: The Thimble Press.

Benton, M. (1978) 'Poetry for children: a neglected art', *Children's Literature in Education* 9(3): 111–26.

—— (1984) 'The methodology vacuum in teaching literature', *Language Arts* 61(3).

—— (1990) 'The importance of poetry in children's learning', in *CLE Working Papers 1*: Southampton: Centre for Language in Education, University of Southampton, pp. 27–36.

—— (1992) *Secondary Worlds. Literature Teaching and the Visual Arts*, Buckingham: Open University Press.

—— and Fox, G. (1985) *Teaching Literature Nine to Fourteen*, Oxford: Oxford University Press.

—— et al. (1988) *Young Readers Responding to Poems*, London: Routledge.

Britton, J. (1982): *Prospect and Retrospect*, ed. G. Pradl, London: Heinemann Educational.

Chambers, A. (1985) *Booktalk*, London: Bodley Head.

—— (1991) *The Reading Environment*, South Woodchester, Glos.: The Thimble Press.

Dias, P. (1986) 'Making sense of poetry: patterns of response among Canadian and British secondary school pupils', *English in Education* 20(2): 44–53.

Egoff, S., Stubbs, G. T. and Ashley, L. F. (1969) *Only Connect*, Toronto: Oxford University Press.

Kermode, F. (1979) *The Genesis of Secrecy*, London: Harvard University Press.

MacLeish, A. (1963) 'Ars poetica', in *Collected Poems*, Boston: Houghton Mifflin.

McGillis, R. (1985) 'The child as critic: using children's responses in the university classroom', *Children's Literature Association Quarterly* 10(1): 4–6.

Rosenblatt, L. (1970) *Literature as Exploration*, London: Heinemann.

— (1978) *The Reader, The Text, The Poem*, Carbondale: Southern Illinois University Press.

— (1985) 'The transactional theory of the literary work: implications for research', in C. R. Cooper (ed.) *Researching Response to Literature and the Teaching of Literature*, Norwood, NJ: Ablex.

Sampson, G. (1970) *English for the English* (1921), Cambridge: Cambridge University Press.

Thompson, J. (1987) *Understanding Teenagers' Reading*, Sydney: Methuen.

— (1990) 'Adolescents and literary response: the development of readers', *Children's Literature Association Quarterly* 15(4): 189–96.

Tucker, A. (1989) 'Taking time', *Signal* 59: 98–117.

Wade, B. (1981) 'Assessing pupils' contributions in appreciating a poem', *Journal of Education for Teaching* 7(1): 41–9.

Williams, G. (1985) 'Literature and the development of interpersonal understanding', in L. Unsworth, *Reading: an Australian Perspective*, Melbourne: Thomas Nelson.

— (1988) 'Naive and serious questions', in M. Meek and C. Mills (eds) *Language and Literacy in the Primary School*, London: Falmer Press.

5 CONNECTIONS

Zipes, J. (1986) *Don't Bet on the Prince. Contemporary Feminist Fairy Tales in North America and England*, London: Methuen.

Sullivan: Real-izing the Unreal: Folklore in Young Adult Science Fiction and Fantasy

Attebery, L. (1979) 'The fiddle tune: an american artifact', in J. Brunvand (ed.) *Readings in American Folklore*, New York: Norton, pp. 324–33.

Bascom, W. (1965) 'Four functions of folklore', in A. Dundes (ed.) *The Study of Folklore*, Englewood Cliffs, NJ: Prentice-Hall, pp. 279–98.

Brunvand, J. (1986) *The Study of American Folklore*, 3rd edn, New York: Norton.

Carpenter, H. (1977) *Tolkien: Biography*, Boston: Houghton.

Dégh, L. (1972) 'Folk narrative', in R. Dorson (ed.) *Folklore and Folklife*, Chicago: University of Chicago Press, pp. 53–83.

Dorson, R. (1957) 'The identification of folklore in American literature', *Journal of American Folklore* 70: 1–8.

Dundes, A. (1965a) *The Study of Folklore*, Englewood Cliffs, NJ: Prentice-Hall.

—— (1965b) 'The study of folklore in literature and culture: identification and interpretation', *Journal of American Folklore* 78: 136–42.

Frantz, R. W. Jr (1957) 'The role of folklore in *Huckleberry Finn*', *American Literature* 29: 314–27.

Grobman, N. R. (1979) 'A schema for the study of the sources and literary simulations of folkloric phenomena', *Southern Folklore Quarterly* 43: 17–37.

Harris, A. L. (1980) 'Myth as structure in Toni Morrison's *Song of Solomon*', *Melus* 7(3): 69–76.

Heinlein, R. A. (1952) *The Rolling Stones*, New York: Ace.

—— (1954) *The Star Beast*, New York: Ace.

—— (1955) *Tunnel in the Sky*, New York: Ace.

—— (1957) *Citizen of the Galaxy*, New York: Ace.

—— (1958) *Have Space Suit – Will Travel*, New York: Ace.

—— (1975a) *Farmer in the Sky* (1950), New York: Ballantine.

—— (1975b) *Starman Jones* (1953), New York: Ballantine.

—— (1977a) *Red Planet* (1949), New York: Ballantine.

—— (1977b) *Rocket Ship Galileo* (1947), New York: Ballantine.

—— (1978a) *Between Planets* (1951), New York: Ballantine.

—— (1978b) *Space Cadet* (1948), New York: Ballantine.

—— (1978c) *Time for the Stars* (1956), New York: Ballantine.

Lewis, C. S. (1966) 'On stories' (1947) in W. Hooper (ed.) *Of Other Worlds*, New York: Harcourt, pp. 3–21.

Sullivan, C. W. III (1984) 'Name and lineage patterns: Aragorn and Beowulf', *Extrapolation* 25: 239–46.

—— (1985) 'Heinlein's juveniles: still contemporary after all these years', *Children's Literature Association Quarterly* 10: 64–6.

—— (1990) 'Narrative expectations: the folklore connection', *Children's Literature Association Quarterly* 15: 52–5.

Taylor, A. (1951) *English Riddles from Oral Tradition*, Berkeley: University of California Press.

—— (1962) *The Proverb*, Hatboro, PA: Folklore Associates.

Toelken, B. (1979) *The Dynamics of Folklore*, Boston: Houghton.

Tolkien, J. R. R. (1966) 'On fairy-stories' (1947), in *The Tolkien Reader*, New York: Ballantine, pp. 3–84.

—— (1982) *The Hobbit* (1937), New York: Ballantine.

Williamson, J. (1978) 'Youth against space: Heinlein's juveniles revisited', in J. Olander and M. Greenberg (eds) *Robert A. Heinlein*, New York: Taplinger, pp. 15–31.

Young, J. (trans.) (1966) *The Prose Edda*, Berkeley: University of California Press.

Tucker: Good Friends, or Just Acquaintances? The Relationship Between Child Psychology and Children's Literature

Barker, M. (1984) *A Haunt of Fears*, London: Pluto Press.

Bettelheim, B. (1976) *The Uses of Enchantment: The Meaning and Importance of Fairy Tales*, New York: Knopf.

Bruner, J. (1979) *On Knowing*, New York: Belknap.

Darton, F. J. H. (1982) *Children's Books in England*, 3rd edn. Cambridge: Cambridge University Press.

Donaldson, M. C. (1978) *Children's Minds*, London: Collins.

Freud, S. (1925) 'The relation of the poet to the daydreamer' (1908), in *Collected Papers IV*, London: Hogarth Press.

— (1973) *Introductory Lectures on Psychoanalysis*, Harmondsworth: Penguin.

Hayhoe, M. and Parker, S. (1990) *Reading and Response*, Milton Keynes: Open University Press.

Holland, N. (1974) *Five Readers Reading*, New Haven: Yale University Press.

Mitchell, J. (1986) *The Selected Melanie Klein*, Harmondsworth: Penguin.

Peller, L. E. (1959) 'Daydreams and children's favourite books: psychoanalytic comments', *The Psychoanalytic Study of the Child* 14: 414–33.

Rousseau, J. J. (1969) *Emile* (1762), Harmondsworth: Penguin.

Rustin, M. and M. (1987) *Narratives of Love and Loss*, London: Verso.

Tucker, N. (1984) 'Dr Bettelheim and enchantment', *Signal* 43: 33–41.

Watkins: Cultural Studies, New Historicism and Children's Literature

Arnold, M. (1963) *Culture and Anarchy* (1869), Cambridge: Cambridge University Press.

Attebury, B. (1983) 'Oz', in M. P. Hearn (ed.) *The Wizard of Oz*, New York: Schocken Books.

Baum, L. F. (1979) *The Wizard of Oz* (1900), New York: Ballantyne Books.

Bennett, T. (1981) 'Marxism and popular form', *Literature and History* 7(2): 138–65.

Bewley, M. (1983) 'The land of Oz: America's great good place', in M. P. Hearn (ed.) *The Wizard of Oz*, New York: Schocken Books.

Bloch, E. (1988) *The Utopian Function of Art and Literature: Selected Essays*, trans. J. Zipes and F. Mecklenberg, Cambridge, Mass.: MIT Press.

Brantlinger, P. (1990) *Crusoe's Footsteps: Cultural Studies in Britain and America*, New York: Routledge.

Cook, T. E. (1988) 'Democracy and community in American children's literature', in E. J. Yanarella and L. Sigelman (eds) *Political Mythology and Popular Fiction*, New York: Greenwood Press.

Dunn, T. (1986) 'The evolution of cultural studies', in D. Punter (ed.) *Introduction to Contemporary Cultural Studies*, London: Longman.

Fiske, J. (1987) 'British cultural studies and television', in R. C. Allen (ed.) *Channels of Discourse: Television and Contemporary Criticism*, London: Routledge.

Gardner, M. and Nye, R. (1959) *The Wizard of Oz and Who He Was*, East Lansing: Michigan State University Press.

Geertz, C. (1973) *The Interpretation of Cultures*, New York: Basic Books.

Grahame, K. (1967) *The Wind in the Willows* (1908), Harmondsworth: Penguin.

Green, P. (1982) 'The rentier's rural dream', *Times Literary Supplement*, 26 November: 1299–1301.

Hall, S. (1980) 'Encoding/decoding', in CCCS (Centre for Contemporary Cultural Studies), *Culture, Media, Language*, London: Hutchinson.

Hardy, B. (1977) 'Towards a poetics of fiction: an approach through narrative', in M. Meek, A Warlow and G. Barton (eds) *The Cool Web: the Pattern of Children's Reading*, London: Bodley Head.

Hewison, R. (1987) *The Heritage Industry*, London: Methuen.

Howkins, A. (1986) 'The discovery of rural England', in R. Colls and P. Dood, *Englishness: Politics and Culture 1880–1920*, London: Croom Helm.

Hunt, L. (1989) 'Introduction: history, culture and text', in L. Hunt (ed.) *The New Cultural History*, Berkeley: University of California Press.

Inglis, F. (1975) *Ideology and the Imagination*, Cambridge: Cambridge University Press.

—— (1981) *The Promise of Happiness: Value and Meaning in Children's Fiction*, Cambridge: Cambridge University Press.

Leavis, F. R. and Thompson, D. (1933) *Culture & Environment*, London: Chatto & Windus.

Marsh, J. (1982) *Back to the Land: the Pastoral Impulse in England from 1880 to 1914*, London: Quartet Books.

Montrose, L. A. (1989) 'Professing the Renaissance: the poetics and politics of culture', in H. A. Veeser (ed.) *The New Historicism*, London: Routledge.

Morley, D. (1980) *The 'Nationwide' Audience: Structure and Decoding*, London: British Film Institute.

Myers, M. (1988) 'Missed opportunities and critical malpractice: New Historicism and children's literature', *Children's Literature Association Quarterly* 13(1): 41–3.

Nye, R. B. (1983) 'An appreciation', in M. P. Hearn (ed.) *The Wizard of Oz*, New York: Schocken Books.

Ricoeur, P. (1986) *Lectures on Ideology and Utopia*, New York: Columbia University Press.

Rose, J. (1984) *The Case of Peter Pan, or, The Impossibility of Children's Fiction*, London: Macmillan.

Thompson, J. B. (1984) *Studies in the Theory of Ideology*, Cambridge: Polity Press.

—— (1990) *Ideology and Modern Culture: Critical and Social Theory in the Era of Mass Communication*, Cambridge: Polity Press.

Thompson, R. P. (1983) 'Concerning *The Wonderful Wizard of Oz*', in M. P. Hearn (ed.) *The Wizard of Oz*, New York: Schocken Books.

Veeser, H. A. (ed.) (1989) *The New Historicism*, London: Routledge.

Widdowson, P. (ed.) (1982) *Re-reading English*, London: Methuen.

Wiener, M. J. (1981) *English Culture and the Decline of the Industrial Spirit 1850–1980*, Cambridge: Cambridge University Press.

REFERENCES

Williams, R. (1958) *Culture and Society 1780–1950*, London: Chatto & Windus.

—— (1975) *The Country and the City*, St Albans: Paladin.

—— (1976) *Keywords: a Vocabulary of Culture and Society*, London: Fontana.

Wright, P. (1985) *On Living in an Old Country: the National Past in Contemporary Britain*, London: Verso.

Yanarella, E. J. and Sigelman, L. (1988) *Political Mythology and Popular Fiction*, New York: Greenwood Press.

Zanger, J. (1977) 'Goblins, morlocks and weasels: classic fantasy and the industrial revolution', *Children's Literature in Education* 8(4): 154–62.

Zipes, J. (1979) *Breaking the Magic Spell: Radical Theories of Folk and Fairy Tales*, London: Heinemann.